Unity 2021 Shaders and Effects Cookbook

Fourth Edition

Over 50 recipes to help you transform your game into a visually stunning masterpiece

John P. Doran

BIRMINGHAM—MUMBAI

Unity 2021 Shaders and Effects Cookbook
Fourth Edition

Copyright © 2021 Packt Publishing

All rights reserved. No part of this book may be reproduced, stored in a retrieval system, or transmitted in any form or by any means, without the prior written permission of the publisher, except in the case of brief quotations embedded in critical articles or reviews.

Every effort has been made in the preparation of this book to ensure the accuracy of the information presented. However, the information contained in this book is sold without warranty, either express or implied. Neither the author, nor Packt Publishing or its dealers and distributors, will be held liable for any damages caused or alleged to have been caused directly or indirectly by this book.

Packt Publishing has endeavored to provide trademark information about all of the companies and products mentioned in this book by the appropriate use of capitals. However, Packt Publishing cannot guarantee the accuracy of this information.

Publishing Product Manager: Pavan Ramchandani
Senior Editor: Mark Dsouza
Content Development Editor: Divya Vijayan
Technical Editor: Saurabh Kadave
Copy Editor: Safis Editing
Project Coordinator: Manthan Patel
Proofreader: Safis Editing
Indexer: Manju Arasan
Production Designer: Aparna Bhagat

First published: June 2013
Second edition: February 2016
Third edition: June 2018
Fourth edition: October 2021

Production reference: 1141021

Published by Packt Publishing Ltd.
Livery Place
35 Livery Street
Birmingham
B3 2PB, UK.

ISBN 978-1-83921-862-0

www.packt.com

To my daughter, Johanna Mai Doran, and to my wife, Hien, for being my loving partner throughout our joint life journey.

– John P. Doran

Contributors

About the author

John P. Doran is a passionate and seasoned technical game designer, software engineer, and author who is currently based in Songdo, South Korea. His passion for game development began at an early age.

For over a decade, John has gained extensive hands-on expertise in game development, working in various roles ranging from game designer to lead UI programmer in teams consisting of just himself to over 70 people in student, mod, and professional game projects, including working at LucasArts on *Star Wars: 1313*. Additionally, John has worked in game development education teaching in Singapore, South Korea, and the United States at schools including the DigiPen Institute of Technology and Bradley University. To date, he has authored over 10 books on game development.

John is currently an instructor at George Mason University Korea. Prior to his present ventures, he was an award-winning videographer.

> *I want to thank everyone at Packt for their assistance in the book-creation process, especially Pavan Ramchandani, Divij Kotian, Divya Vijayan, and Rohit Rajkumar. I am also grateful for the great advice and suggestions from my technical reviewers, Floris Groen and Kenneth Lammers. I'm incredibly proud of this edition of the book, and I hope everyone else is too.*

About the reviewers

Floris Groen is an experienced software engineer and shader expert from the Netherlands. He taught himself how to use graphics APIs in his late teens and went on to become a graphics programmer. He has worked in the gaming industry, as well as in architectural visualization, where he contributed to several game titles and software products. During that time, he has coded two rendering engines as part of successful commercial software. Floris is currently working on bringing digital humans to life by using a context-sensitive procedural animation system combined with realistic shaders and lighting. In the past, he has volunteered as a coach for an initiative to get more women into the tech industry.

Kenneth Lammers has over 15 years of experience in the gaming industry, working as a character artist, technical artist, technical art director, and programmer. Throughout his career, he has worked on titles such as *Call of Duty 3*, *Crackdown 2*, *Alan Wake*, and *Kinect Star Wars*. He currently owns and operates Ozone Interactive with his business partner, Noah Kaarbo. Together, they have worked with clients such as Amazon, Eline Media, IGT, and Microsoft. Kenny has worked for Microsoft Games Studios, Activision, and Surreal, and has recently gone out on his own, operating CreativeTD and Ozone Interactive. Kenny authored the first edition of *Unity Shaders and Effects Cookbook* by Packt Publishing and was very happy to be a part of the writing, updating, and reviewing of this book.

Table of Contents

Preface

1
Post Processing Stack

Technical requirements	2	Getting ready	23
Installing the Post Processing Stack	2	How to do it...	23
		How it works...	26
Getting ready	2	Setting the mood with color grading	27
How to do it...	4		
Getting a filmic look using grain, vignetting, and depth of field	14	Getting ready	27
		How to do it...	28
		Creating a horror game look with fog	31
Getting ready	14		
How to do it...	14	Getting ready	31
How it works...	22	How to do it...	31
Mimicking real life with bloom and anti-aliasing	23	How it works...	36

2
Creating Your First Shader

Technical requirements	38	How to do it...	42
Creating a basic Standard Shader	38	How it works...	45
		There's more...	46
Getting ready	39		

Adding properties to a shader	48	Using properties in a Surface Shader	54
Getting ready	48	How to do it...	54
How to do it...	49	How it works...	59
How it works...	52	There's more...	60
See also	53	See also	62

3
Working with Surface Shaders

Technical requirements	64	Creating a shader with normal mapping	72
Implementing diffuse shading	65	Getting ready	74
Getting ready	65	How to do it...	76
How to do it...	65	How it works...	80
How it works...	69	There's more...	80
Accessing and modifying packed arrays	70	Creating a Holographic Shader	83
How to do it...	70	Getting ready	83
There's more...	72	How to do it...	84
See also	72	How it works...	87
		There's more...	88
		See also	88

4
Working with Texture Mapping

Technical requirements	89	How it works...	103
Adding a texture to a shader	90	Creating a transparent material	104
Getting ready	91	Getting ready	105
How to do it...	91	How to do it...	107
How it works...	95	How it works...	109
There's more...	96	Packing and blending textures	110
See also	98	Getting ready	111
Scrolling textures by modifying UV values	98	How to do it...	113
Getting ready	98	How it works...	118
How to do it...	99		

Creating a circle around your terrain	119	How to do it...	123
		How it works...	126
Getting ready...	120	There's more...	126

5
Understanding Lighting Models

Technical requirements	130	How to do it...	149
Creating a custom diffuse lighting model	130	How it works...	151
		Creating a Blinn-Phong Specular type	155
Getting ready	131	Getting ready	156
How to do it...	132	How to do it...	156
How it works...	135	How it works...	159
Creating a toon shader	138	See also	160
Getting ready	139	Creating an Anisotropic Specular type	160
How to do it...	141		
How it works...	144	Getting ready	162
There's more...	145	How to do it...	163
Creating a Phong Specular type	147	How it works...	168
Getting ready	148		

6
Physically Based Rendering

Technical requirements	173	Creating mirrors and reflective surfaces	183
Understanding the metallic setup	173		
		Getting ready	184
Getting ready	174	How to do it...	185
How to do it...	175	How it works...	187
How it works...	177	See also	189
See also	177	Baking lights into your scene	189
Adding transparency to PBR	178	Getting ready	189
Getting ready	178	How to do it...	189
How to do it...	179	How it works...	194
See also	183	See also	196

7
Vertex Functions

Technical requirements	198	How it works…	211
Accessing a vertex color in a Surface Shader	198	There's more…	212
		Implementing a snow shader	215
Getting ready	198	Getting ready	215
How to do it…	200	How to do it…	216
How it works…	202	How it works…	218
There's more…	203	See also	220
Animating vertices in a Surface Shader	203	Implementing a volumetric explosion	220
Getting ready	204	Getting ready	221
How to do it…	205	How to do it…	223
How it works…	209	How it works…	226
Extruding your models	209	There's more…	228
Getting ready	210	See also	229
How to do it…	210		

8
Fragment Shaders and Grab Passes

Technical requirements	232	How it works…	243
Understanding Vertex and Fragment Shaders	232	There's more…	243
		Implementing a Glass Shader	244
Getting ready	232	Getting ready	244
How to do it…	234	How to do it…	245
How it works…	236	How it works…	247
There's more…	238	There's more…	248
See also	239	Implementing a Water Shader for 2D games	248
Using grab passes to draw behind objects	240	Getting ready	249
Getting ready	240	How to do it…	251
How to do it…	240	How it works…	254

9
Mobile Shader Adjustment

Technical requirements	258	How to do it...	270
Techniques to make shaders more efficient	258	How it works...	276
		There's more...	277
Getting ready	258	**Modifying our shaders for mobile**	**277**
How to do it...	261		
How it works...	265	Getting ready	277
Profiling your shaders	**268**	How to do it...	278
Getting ready	268	How it works...	282

10
Screen Effects with Unity Render Textures

Technical requirements	284	How it works...	305
Setting up a screen effects script system	284	Using basic Photoshop-like Blend Modes with screen effects	306
Getting ready	285		
How to do it...	286	Getting ready	306
How it works...	293	How to do it...	307
There's more...	294	How it works...	311
Using brightness, saturation, and contrast with screen effects	298	There's more...	312
		Using the Overlay Blend Mode with screen effects	316
Getting ready	299	How to do it...	316
How to do it...	300	How it works...	319

11
Gameplay and Screen Effects

Technical requirements	322	How to do it...	326
Creating an old movie screen effect	322	How it works...	334
		See also	337
Getting ready	323		

Creating a night-vision screen effect	**337**	How to do it...	340
		How it works...	348
Getting ready	338	There's more...	349

12
Advanced Shading Techniques

Technical requirements	352	How it works...	365
Using Unity's built-in CgInclude files	**352**	**Implementing a Fur Shader**	**366**
		Getting ready	366
Getting ready	353	How to do it...	367
How to do it...	354	How it works...	372
How it works...	356	There's more...	374
There's more...	357		
Making your shader work in a modular way with CgInclude	**358**	**Implementing Heatmaps with arrays**	**375**
		Getting ready	376
Getting ready	359	How to do it...	377
How to do it...	361	How it works...	385

13
Shader Graph – 2D

Technical requirement	388	**Exposing properties to the Inspector via Shader Graph**	**400**
Creating a URP-based Shader Graph project	**388**	Getting ready	400
How to do it...	388	How to do it...	401
How it works...	392	How it works...	404
Implementing a simple Shader Graph	**393**	**Creating a Sprite Outline Shader**	**405**
Getting ready	393	Getting ready	405
How to do it...	394	How to do it...	408
How it works...	399	How it works...	426

14
Shader Graph – 3D

Technical requirements	430	How to do it...	442
Implementing a glowing highlight system	430	How it works...	448
Getting ready	431	Creating custom Shader Graph functions	448
How to do it...	432	Getting ready	448
How it works...	441	How to do it...	449
Portal Shaders in Unity	441	How it works...	452
Getting ready	441		

Other Books You May Enjoy

Index

Preface

Unity 2021 Shaders and Effects Cookbook is your guide to becoming familiar with the creation of shaders and post-processing effects in Unity 2021. You will start your journey at the beginning, exploring the Post Processing Stack to see some of the possible ways you can use shaders to affect what you see without having to write scripts at all. Afterward, we will learn how to create shaders from scratch, starting by creating the most basic shaders and learning how the shader code is structured. This foundational knowledge will arm you with the means to progress further through each chapter, learning advanced techniques such as volumetric explosions and fur shading. We also explore the newly added Shader Graph editor to see how you can create shaders through a drag-and-drop interface as well! This edition of the book is written specifically for Unity 2021 and will help you to master physically based rendering and global illumination to get as close to photorealism as possible.

By the end of each chapter, you will have gained new skills that will increase the quality of your shaders and even make your shader writing process more efficient. These chapters have been tailored so that you can jump into each section and learn a specific skill, going from beginner to expert. For those who are new to shader writing in Unity, you can progress through each chapter, one at a time, to build on your knowledge. Either way, you will learn the techniques that make modern games look the way they do.

Once you have completed this book, you will have a set of shaders that you can use in your Unity 3D games as well as an understanding of how to add to them, accomplish new effects, and address performance needs. So, let's get started!

Who this book is for

Unity 2021 Shaders and Effects Cookbook is written for Game developers who want to create their first shaders in Unity 2021 or wish to take their game to a whole new level by adding professional post-processing effects. A solid understanding of Unity is required.

What this book covers

Chapter 1, Post Processing Stack, introduces you to the Post Processing Stack, which will allow users to tweak their game's appearance without having to write any additional scripts.

Chapter 2, Creating Your First Shader, introduces you to the world of shader coding in Unity. You will build some basic shaders and learn how to introduce tweakable properties in your shaders to make them more interactive.

Chapter 3, Working with Surface Shaders, covers the most common and useful techniques that you can implement with Surface Shaders, including how to use textures and normal maps for your models.

Chapter 4, Working with Texture Mapping, will show how to use textures to animate, blend, and drive any other property that you like.

Chapter 5, Understanding Lighting Models, gives you an in-depth explanation of how shaders model the behavior of light. This chapter teaches you how to create custom lighting models used to simulate special effects, such as toon shading.

Chapter 6, Physically Based Rendering, shows you that physically based rendering is the standard technology used by Unity 5 to bring realism to your games. This chapter explains how to make the most out of it by mastering transparencies, reflective surfaces, and global illumination.

Chapter 7, Vertex Functions, teaches you how shaders can be used to alter the geometry of an object. This chapter introduces vertex modifiers and uses them to bring volumetric explosions, snow shaders, and other effects to life.

Chapter 8, Fragment Shaders and Grab Passes, explains how to use grab passes to make materials that emulate the deformations generated by semi-transparent materials.

Chapter 9, Mobile Shader Adjustment, helps you optimize your shaders to get the most out of any device.

Chapter 10, Screen Effects with Unity Render Textures, shows you how to create special effects and visuals that would otherwise be impossible to achieve.

Chapter 11, Gameplay and Screen Effects, tells you how post-processing effects can be used to complement your gameplay, simulating, for instance, a night-vision effect.

Chapter 12, Advanced Shading Techniques, introduces the most advanced techniques in this book, such as fur shading and heatmap rendering.

Chapter 13, Shader Graph – 2D, explains how to set up a project to use Unity's newly added Shader Graph editor. We cover how to create a simple Shader Graph, how to expose properties, and explore the ways that we can use Shader Graph for 2D games.

Chapter 14, Shader Graph – 3D, expands on the knowledge from the previous chapter and shows how to use Shader Graph for 3D games with examples such as how to interact with the Shader Graph through code using a glow highlight system, creating a portal shader, and using custom Shader Graph functions.

To get the most out of this book

You are expected to have experience of working with Unity and some scripting experience (C# is fine). The book is written with Unity 2021.1.9f1 but should work with future versions of the engine with some minor tweaks.

Software/hardware covered in the book	OS requirements
Unity 2021.1.9f1	Windows, macOS, or Linux

If you are using the digital version of this book, we advise you to type the code yourself or access the code via the GitHub repository (link available in the next section). Doing so will help you avoid any potential errors related to the copying and pasting of code.

Download the example code files

You can download the example code files for this book from GitHub at `https://github.com/PacktPublishing/Unity-2021-Shaders-and-Effects-Cookbook-Fourth-Edition`. In case there's an update to the code, it will be updated on the existing GitHub repository.

We also have other code bundles from our rich catalog of books and videos available at `https://github.com/PacktPublishing/`. Check them out!

Download the color images

We also provide a PDF file that has color images of the screenshots/diagrams used in this book. You can download it here: `https://static.packt-cdn.com/downloads/9781839218620_ColorImages.pdf`.

Conventions used

There are a number of text conventions used throughout this book.

`Code in text`: Indicates code words in text, database table names, folder names, filenames, file extensions, pathnames, dummy URLs, user input, and Twitter handles. Here is an example: "Use the vertex color data from our `Input` struct to be assigned to the `o.Albedo` parameters in the built-in `SurfaceOutput` struct."

A block of code is set as follows:

```
void surf (Input IN, inout SurfaceOutput o)
{
    o.Albedo = IN.vertColor.rgb * _MainTint.rgb;
}
```

When we wish to draw your attention to a particular part of a code block, the relevant lines or items are set in bold:

```
struct Input
{
    float2 uv_MainTex;
    float4 vertColor;
};
```

Bold: Indicates a new term, an important word, or words that you see onscreen. For example, words in menus or dialog boxes appear in the text like this. Here is an example: "From its **Inspector** tab, make sure that **Filter Mode** is set to **Bilinear**."

> **Tips or important notes**
> Appear like this.

Sections

In this book, you will find several headings that appear frequently (*Getting ready*, *How to do it...*, *How it works...*, *There's more...*, and *See also*).

To give clear instructions on how to complete a recipe, use these sections as follows:

Getting ready

This section tells you what to expect in the recipe and describes how to set up any software or any preliminary settings required for the recipe.

How to do it...

This section contains the steps required to follow the recipe.

How it works...

This section usually consists of a detailed explanation of what happened in the previous section.

There's more...

This section consists of additional information about the recipe in order to make you more knowledgeable about the recipe.

See also

This section provides helpful links to other useful information for the recipe.

Get in touch

Feedback from our readers is always welcome.

General feedback: If you have questions about any aspect of this book, mention the book title in the subject of your message and email us at customercare@packtpub.com.

Errata: Although we have taken every care to ensure the accuracy of our content, mistakes do happen. If you have found a mistake in this book, we would be grateful if you would report this to us. Please visit www.packtpub.com/support/errata, selecting your book, clicking on the Errata Submission Form link, and entering the details.

Piracy: If you come across any illegal copies of our works in any form on the Internet, we would be grateful if you would provide us with the location address or website name. Please contact us at copyright@packt.com with a link to the material.

If you are interested in becoming an author: If there is a topic that you have expertise in and you are interested in either writing or contributing to a book, please visit authors.packtpub.com.

Share Your Thoughts

Once you've read *Unity 2021 Shaders and Effects Cookbook*, we'd love to hear your thoughts! Scan the QR code below to go straight to the Amazon review page for this book and share your feedback.

https://packt.link/r/<1839218622>

Your review is important to us and the tech community and will help us make sure we're delivering excellent quality content.

1
Post Processing Stack

It's great to write your own shaders and effects and fine-tune your project so that it looks just the way that you want it to, and this is what we will be spending the majority of the book looking into. However, it's also good to point out that Unity already comes with some prebuilt ways to get some of the more common effects that users like to have; users can implement these effects by using the Post Processing Stack.

For those who just want to get something up and running, the Post Processing Stack can be an excellent way for you to tweak the appearance of your game without having to write any additional code. Using the Post Processing Stack can also be useful in showing you what shaders can do and how they can improve your game projects as, behind the scenes, the Post Processing Stack provides several shaders as well as scripts that are applied to the screen via the aptly named screen shader.

In this chapter, we will cover the following recipes:

- Installing the Post Processing Stack
- Getting a filmic look using grain, vignetting, and depth of field
- Mimicking real life with bloom and anti-aliasing
- Setting the mood with color grading
- Creating a horror game look with fog

Technical requirements

You can find the code files for this chapter on GitHub at `https://github.com/PacktPublishing/Unity-2021-Shaders-and-Effects-Cookbook-Fourth-Edition/tree/main/Shaders-and-Effects-Cookbook-2021/Assets/Chapter%2001`.

Installing the Post Processing Stack

Before we can use the Post Processing Stack, we must get it from the Package Manager. A Unity package is a single file that contains various assets that can be used in Unity, similar to a `ZIP` file. Previously, Unity used the Asset Store to share these files with users, but with time, the Package Manager has been added to give users an easy way to get free content from Unity. We will be using the Package Manager again in *Chapter 13*, *Shader Graph – 2D*, but for now, we will be using it for the Post Processing package that it contains.

Getting ready

To get started with this recipe, you will need to have Unity running and have created a new project with the 3D template. This chapter also requires you to have an environment to work from. The code files provided with this book contain a `.unitypackage` file called `Chapter1_StartingPoint.unitypackage` in the Unity Packages folder. It contains a basic scene and content for creating the scene with Unity's Standard Assets.

Open the `Chapter 1 | Starting Point` scene inside the `Asset | Chapter 01 | Scenes` folder from the **Project** browser. If all goes well, you should see something like this from the **Game** tab:

Figure 1.1 – Starting point scene

This is a simple environment that will allow us to easily see how changes that have been made with post-processing effects can modify how things are drawn on the screen.

> **Note**
>
> If you are interested in learning how to create the environment we've used here, check out my previous book, *Unity 5.x Game Development Blueprints*, also available from Packt Publishing.

4   Post Processing Stack

How to do it...

To get started, follow these steps:

1. Open **Package Manager** by going to **Window | Package Manager**:

Figure 1.2 – The Package Manager

2. From the **Packages** dropdown at the top left, select the **Unity Registry** option to display a list of all of the possible packages that are there. Once the list populates with all of the choices, select the **Post Processing** option:

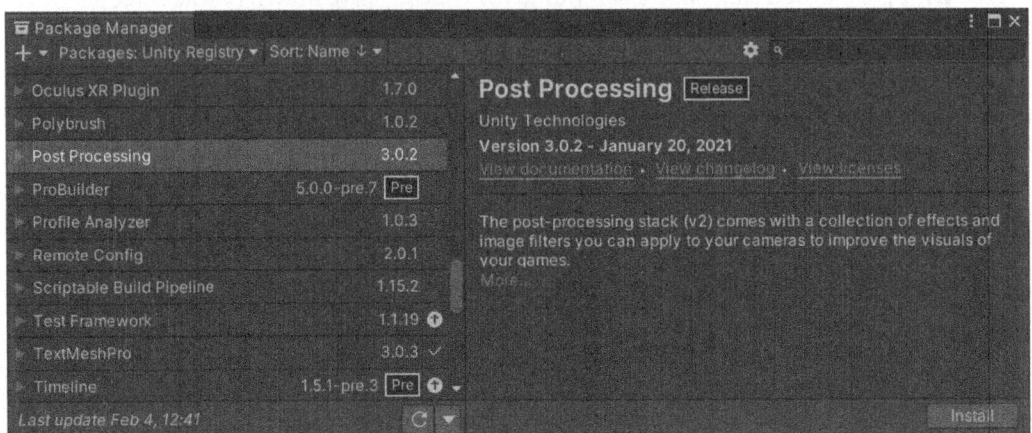

Figure 1.3 – Post Processing selected

> **Note**
>
> If you know the name of the package you are looking for, you can also find packages by typing their name in the search bar at the top right of the menu.
>
>
>
> Figure 1.4 – Search bar of Package Manager

3. From there, at the bottom right of the menu, click on the **Install** button. You may need to wait for a while for it to finish downloading the content. Once it has finished downloading, you should see a checkmark to the right of the **Post Processing** option, which shows that it has been installed:

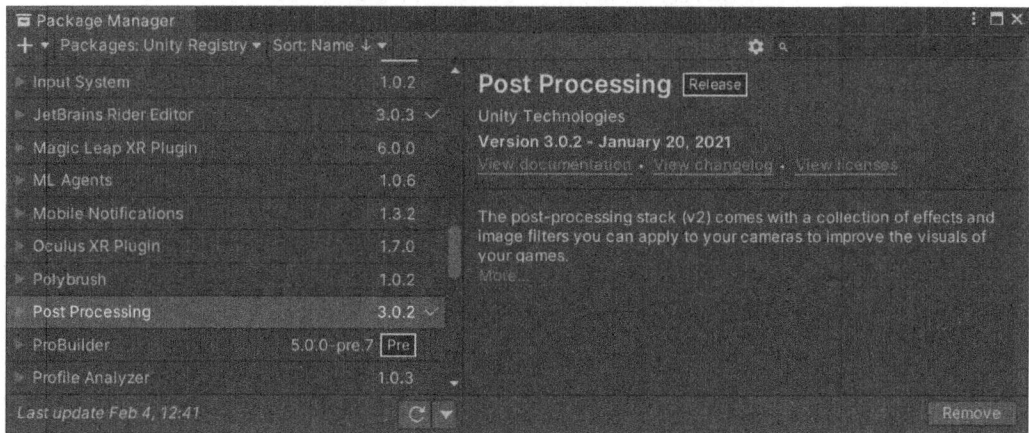

Figure 1.5 – Post Processing package installed

6   Post Processing Stack

4. Close the **Packages** tab and go back to the **Scene** window to see the level. Then, from the **Hierarchy** window, select the object that has our **Camera** component attached to it. We are doing this because the Post Processing Stack needs to know which screen we want to modify. If you are using your own project, you can select the **MainCamera** object that comes with the default Unity scene, but the example project that is being used has **Camera** located as a child of the `FPSController` object. To select it, go to the **Hierarchy** window and then click on the arrow next to the name to extend the object's children. Then, select the `FirstPersonCharacter` object:

Figure 1.6 – FirstPersonCharacter selected

5. Upon selecting this object, you should see that the **Inspector** window is now showing information about the `FirstPersonCharacter` object, including what components are attached to it:

Installing the Post Processing Stack   7

Figure 1.7 – The Inspector window with FirstPersonCharacter selected

8 Post Processing Stack

This object has a **Camera** component attached to it, which is in charge of drawing what it is pointing at to the **Game** tab when the game starts:

> **Note**
> You can double-click on a game object in the **Hierarchy** tab to zoom the camera from the **Scene** tab onto the object's location. This makes it very easy to find things, even in a large game level.

Figure 1.8 – The Scene view after double-clicking on the FirstPersonCharacter object

6. With the object selected and our **Camera** component attached to it, we need to add the **Post-processing Behavior** component to the object by going to **Component | Rendering | Post-process Layer**. Once added, you should be able to see the component in the **Inspector** window if you scroll down:

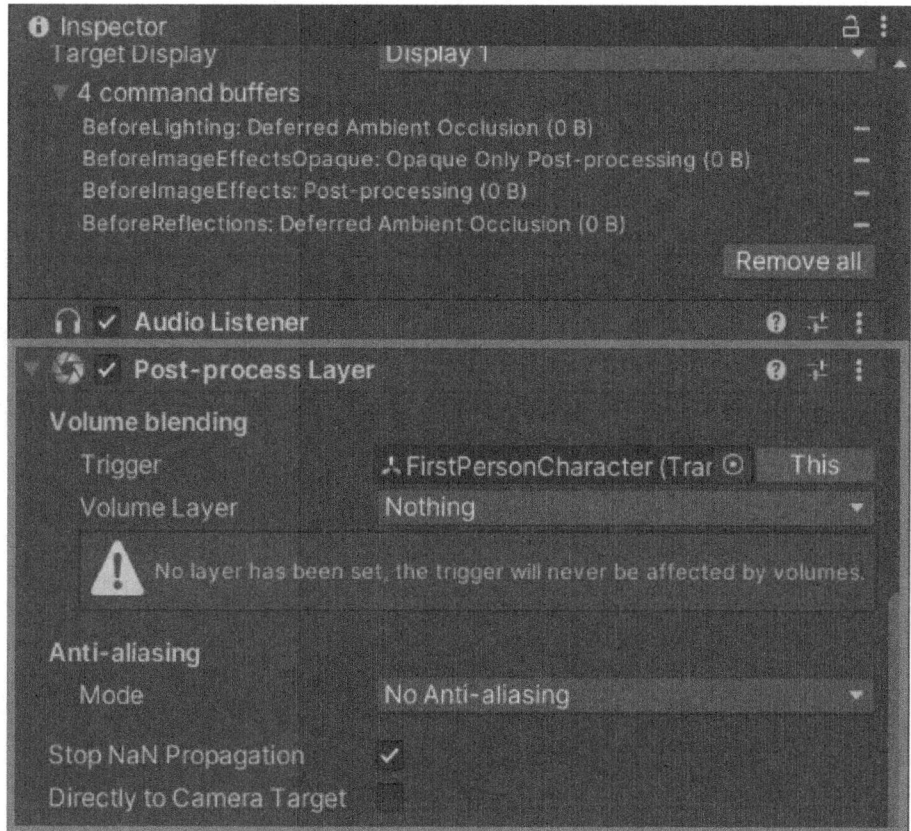

Figure 1.9 – The Post-process Layer component

The **Post-process Layer** component is responsible for rendering post-processing effects to a camera so that they're visible in our game. It requires us to be inside of a **Post-process Volume** that has a **Layer** defined on it.

7. With that in mind, go to the top right of the Unity interface and select the **Layers** dropdown. This will show a list of all of the current layers in the game. From there, select **Add Layers…**.

8. The **Inspector** window will now show the **Tags & Layers** menu. Once opened, click on the arrow to expand the **Layers** section. From there, under one of the empty **User Layer** options, type in `PostProcessing`:

Figure 1.10 – Adding a custom User Layer

> **Note**
> It is possible to type in any name you would want for this layer, so long as you assign that same layer to the volumes later.

9. From the **Hierarchy** window, select the `FirstPersonCharacter` object once again to update the **Inspector** window. From the **Inspector** window, scroll down to the **Post-Process Layer** component, select the dropdown to the right of the **Layer** property, and select `PostProcessing`:

Figure 1.11 – Assigning Volume Layer

This tells the component which objects we want to affect the screen with post-processing effects. When setting this, an object must have its **Layer** property set to `PostProcessing` to have its effects visible by this camera.

10. To create a **Post-process Volume**, go to the **GameObject** menu and select **3D Object | Post-process Volume**:

Figure 1.12 – Creating a Post-process Volume

11. From there, go to the **Inspector** window and change the **Layer** property to `PostProcessing`. Finally, to make it easier to work with, change **Position** to 0, 0, 0. Then, under the **Post-process Volume** component, check the **Is Global** property:

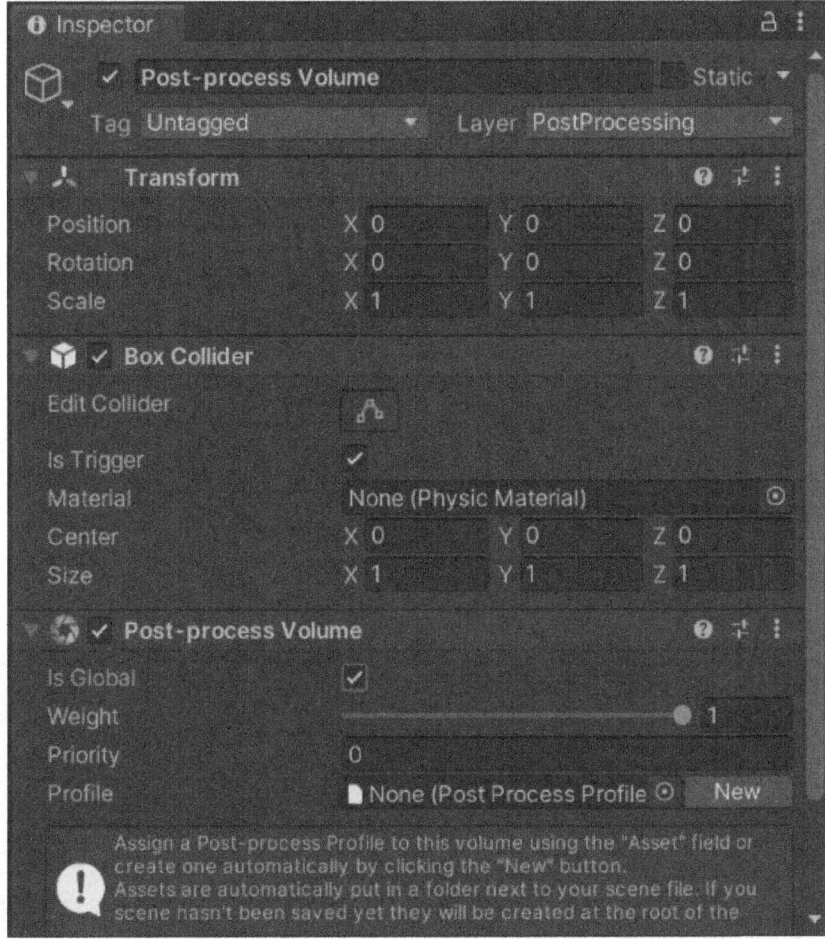

Figure 1.13 – Assigning the Is Global property

Notice that there is a **Profile** property for the volume. This property will contain information about how we wish to modify the screen. By checking **Is Global**, we are saying that this information should always be drawn by the **Post-process Layer** object. By unchecking it, the effects would only be visible from a certain distance from where the volume has been placed, as dictated by the trigger collider attached to the object. Depending on the game, this could allow you to drastically modify how the game appears in certain areas, but we only care about getting the visual effect at this point.

Getting a filmic look using grain, vignetting, and depth of field

Now that we have installed the Post Processing Stack, we can create our first post-processing volume. The new Post Processing Stack relies on using volumes that describe how things should be drawn, either globally or within a certain area.

One of the most common appearances people like projects to have is that of a film. This is used quite frequently in titles such as the *Uncharted* series and *Grand Theft Auto V*. It's also used quite effectively in the *Left 4 Dead* series as its creators were trying to emulate the B-movie zombie films that the games are based on:

Figure 1.14 – The final result of the filmic look

Getting ready

Make sure you have completed the *Installing the Post Processing Stack* recipe before starting this one.

How to do it...

Follow these steps to get a filmic look using grain, vignetting, and depth of field:

1. First, we must create a new **Post Processing Profile** by going to the **Project** window. From there, right-click within the `Assets | Chapter 1` folder and selecting **Create | Post-processing Profile**. Once selected, we can rename the item. Go ahead and set the name to `FilmicProfile`:

Getting a filmic look using grain, vignetting, and depth of field   15

Figure 1.15 – Creating FilmicProfile

> **Note**
> If you don't enter the name correctly, you can rename an item from the **Project** tab by clicking on the name and then clicking it again. Alternatively, you can right-click on the item and select **Rename** or hit *F2* on your keyboard.

2. Once the profile is created, you will notice that, when selected, the **Inspector** window now contains a button that says **Add effect...**, which will allow us to augment what is normally drawn on the screen.

3. From the **Hierarchy** tab, select the **Post-process Volume** object again. Then, from the **Inspector** tab, go to the **Post-process Volume** component and assign the **Profile** property to `FilmicProflie`, which we just created, by dragging and dropping it from the **Project** window over the property and then letting go:

Figure 1.16 – Assigning the Profile of Post-process Volume

> **Note**
> Once the **Profile** has been set, the **Add effect...** button shows up here as well.
> We can use this at either place and the changes will be saved in the file.

4. To get started, click on the **Add effect...** button and select the **Unity | Grain** option. By default, you'll only see the **Grain** option with a check, so click on the arrow to expand its contents:

Figure 1.17 – Adding the Grain effect to Post-process Volume

By default, you'll see that everything is grayed out. To have the options affect anything, you have to click on the checkbox on the left-hand side of the options to enable them. You can quickly turn them all on or off by pressing the **All** or **None** buttons at the top left of the option.

5. To see the differences in what we are doing, switch to the **Game** view by selecting that tab. In our case, check the **Intensity** option and set it to 1.0. Then, check the **Size** property and set it to 1.0. Afterward, switch to the **Game** tab to see a representation of what our tweaks have done:

Getting a filmic look using grain, vignetting, and depth of field   17

Figure 1.18 – Representation of the Grain effect

You will notice that the screen has become much fuzzier than before.

6. We want to have a more subtle effect here, so we will decrease **Intensity** to 0.2, set **Size** to 0.3, and uncheck the **Colored** option:

Figure 1.19 – Altering the Grain effect

This will change the effect of the grain effect so that it looks like this:

Figure 1.20 – Changing the Grain effect

> **Note**
> Unlike how users typically work in Unity, due to Post Processing Profiles being files, you can modify them while playing your game and, upon stopping the game, the values are still saved. This can be useful for tweaking values to achieve the exact look that you're after.

7. The next property we want to tweak is the **Vignette** property, which will add blackened edges around the screen. Click on **Add effect...** and select **Unity | Vignette**. Open the properties, enable the **Intensity** property, and set it to 0.5. Afterward, enable and set **Smoothness** to 0.35:

Figure 1.21 – Creating a Vignette effect

Adding this effect will make the screen look like this:

Figure 1.22 – Visual of the Vignette effect

8. Next, select **Add effect...** again and, this time, select **Unity | Depth of Field**. Expand the **Depth of Field** option if needed. It may be difficult to see the change right off the bat, but change **Focus Distance** to 6 and **Focal Length** to 80:

Figure 1.23 – Adjusting the Depth of Field values

Afterward, if you look at the **Scene** view, you should notice that the grass in front of the background and the mountain in the distance is now blurred:

Figure 1.24 – Adding the Depth of Field effect

9. Now, if we go into the game itself and move around, we should see our filmic look in action:

Figure 1.25 – The final result of the filmic look

And with that, we now have a scene that looks much more like a film than what we had to begin with!

How it works...

Each time we add an effect to a post-processing volume, we are overriding what would normally be put onto the screen.

If you've been to a movie theater that still uses film, you may have noticed how there were little specks in the filmstock while the film was playing. The grain effect simulates this film grain, causing the effect to become more pronounced the more the movie is played. This is often used in horror games to obscure the player's vision.

> **Note**
>
> For more information about the grain effect, check out `https://github.com/Unity-Technologies/PostProcessing/wiki/Grain`.

In the film world, vignetting can be an unintended effect of using the wrong type of lens for the type of shot you are trying to achieve or the aspect ratio that you are shooting for. In game development, we typically use vignetting for dramatic effect or to have players focus on the center of the screen by darkening and/or desaturating the edges of the screen compared to the center.

> **Note**
>
> For more information about the vignette effect, check out `https://github.com/Unity-Technologies/PostProcessing/wiki/Vignette`.

The depth of field setting determines what is blurry and what isn't. The idea is to have items of importance in focus while items in the background are not.

> **Note**
>
> For more information about the depth of field effect, check out `https://github.com/Unity-Technologies/PostProcessing/wiki/Depth-of-Field`.

Mimicking real life with bloom and anti-aliasing

The bloom optical effect aims to mimic the imaging effects of real-world cameras, where things in areas with lights will glow along the edges, thus overwhelming the camera. The bloom effect is very distinctive and you've likely seen it employed in areas in a game that are magical or heaven-like:

Figure 1.26 – The final result of using bloom and anti-aliasing

Getting ready

Make sure you have completed the *Installing the Post Processing Stack* recipe before starting this one.

How to do it...

To add the bloom and anti-aliasing effect, follow these steps:

1. First, we must create a new **Post-processing Profile** by right-clicking within the `Assets` folder in the **Project** window and then selecting **Create | Post-processing Profile**. Once selected, we can rename the item. Go ahead and set the name to `BloomProfile`.

2. Select the `Post-process volume` object and, from the **Inspector** window, go to the **Post Processing Volume** component and assign the **Profile** property to `BloomProfile`.

24   Post Processing Stack

3. Afterward, select the **Game** tab (if it hasn't been selected already) to see the results of the changes we are about to make.

4. Select the **Add effect...** button and select **Unity | Bloom**. Once the effect has been added to the **Overrides** section of the **Post-process Volume** component, select the arrow to open its properties. Check the **Intensity** property and set it to 3. Afterward, check and set **Threshold** to 0.75 and **Soft Knee** to 0.1:

Figure 1.27 – Adding a Bloom effect

Mimicking real life with bloom and anti-aliasing 25

This will give us the following effect:

Figure 1.28 – Visual of the Bloom effect

5. Next, select the object with the **Post Process Layer** component attached to it (in this example, it is the `FPSController | FirstPersonCharacter` object) and, from the **Inspector** tab, scroll down to the **Post-process Layer** component. From there, change the **Anti-aliasing** property's dropdown to `Fast Approximate Anti-aliasing (FXAA)`:

Figure 1.29 – Adjusting the Mode value of Anti-aliasing

6. Afterward, save your scene and hit the **Play** button to check out your project:

Figure 1.30 – The final result of using bloom and anti-aliasing

How it works...

As we mentioned previously, the bloom filter will make bright things even brighter while adding a glow to lighter areas. In this recipe, you may have noticed that the path is much lighter than it was previously. We can do this to ensure that players will follow the path to get to the next section of gameplay.

> **Note**
> For more information about bloom, check out `https://github.com/Unity-Technologies/PostProcessing/wiki/Bloom`.

Anti-aliasing attempts to reduce the appearance of aliasing, which is the effect of lines appearing jagged on the screen. Any time anything is sampled below the Nyquist frequency, aliasing will occur. This is because the display the player is using to play the game doesn't have a high enough resolution to be displayed properly. Anti-aliasing will combine colors with nearby lines to remove their prominence, but at the cost of the game appearing somewhat blurry.

> **Note**
> For more information about anti-aliasing and what each mode means, check out `https://github.com/Unity-Technologies/PostProcessing/wiki/Anti-aliasing`.

Setting the mood with color grading

One of the best ways to easily change the mood of a scene is by changing the colors a scene uses. One of the best examples of this can be seen in the *Matrix* series of films, where the real world is always blue-tinted, while the computer-generated world is always tinted green. We can emulate this in our games by using color grading:

Figure 1.31 – The final result of using color grading

Getting ready

Make sure you have completed the *Installing the Post Processing Stack* recipe before starting this one.

How to do it...

To add color grading, follow these steps:

1. First, we must create a new **Post-processing Profile** by right-clicking within the `Assets` folder in the **Project** window and then selecting **Create | Post-processing Profile**. Once selected, we can rename the item. Go ahead and set it to `ColorProfile`.
2. Select the `Post-process Volume` object in the **Hierarchy** window and, from the **Inspector** window, go to the **Post-processing Volume** component and assign the **Profile** property to `ColorProfile`.
3. Afterward, select the **Game** tab (if it hasn't been selected already) to see the results of the changes to be made.
4. Select the **Add effect...** button and select **Unity | Color Grading**.
5. Check the **Mode** property at the very top of the **Color Grading** section and set it to **Low Definition Range**:

Figure 1.32 – Assigning Low Definition Range for Mode

6. From there, you'll see several properties that can be used to adjust the colors on the screen, similar to how Photoshop's hue/saturation menu works. Check the **Temperature** property and set it to `30`. Afterward, set **Hue Shift** to `-20` and **Saturation** to `15`:

Figure 1.33 – Adjusting the properties of Color Grading

30   Post Processing Stack

From the **Scene** view, we will see the following output:

Figure 1.34 – Visual effect of the Color Grading properties

7. After making these changes, dive into the game and move around to see what it looks like when playing it:

Figure 1.35 – The final result of using color grading

Notice how the previously very green environment is now much warmer and more yellow than before. Using techniques like this, environments can simulate different times of the year, such as fall, with minimal effort when it comes to creating new art assets.

> **Note**
> For more information about the color grading effect, check out `https://github.com/Unity-Technologies/PostProcessing/wiki/Color-Grading`.

Creating a horror game look with fog

One of the types of games that best utilizes the features of the Post Processing Stack is the horror genre. Using things such as depth of field to hide scary objects, as well as static to make the screen more menacing, can help set your game firmly in the right place and provide the mood you are going for.

Getting ready

Make sure you have completed the *Installing the Post Processing Stack* recipe before starting this one.

How to do it...

1. First, we must create a new **Post-processing Profile** by right-clicking within the `Assets` folder in the **Project** window and then selecting **Create | Post-processing Profile**. Once selected, we can rename the item. Go ahead and name it `HorrorProfile`.

2. Select the `Post-process volume` object and, from the **Inspector** window, go to the **Post-processing Volume** component and assign the **Profile** property to `HorrorProfile`.

3. Unlike the previous settings, though, the fog settings are located in the **Lighting** window, which can be accessed by going to **Window | Rendering | Lighting Settings**.

> **Tip**
> You may see the **Lighting** window open as a separate window on your screen. If you would like, you can drag and drop the top tab into another section of the Unity editor to dock it to another section. I place it next to the **Inspector** window so that I can easily switch between the various options.

4. From there, select the **Environment** option at the top. Scroll to the bottom until you reach the **Other Settings** option. Once there, check **Fog** and set the **Color** property to a value that is close to the skybox. I used the following settings:

Figure 1.36 – The Color menu

> **Note**
> If you know the hex values of the color from your graphic editing software, such as Photoshop, you can just type it in the **Hexadecimal** property of the **Color** window.

5. Next, change **Mode** to Exponential and **Density** to 0.03:

Figure 1.37 – Enabling Fog in our scene

As you can see, it's already much more spooky than it was previously, but there are still more options that we can change:

Figure 1.38 – Visual of Fog in our scene

6. Open **HorrorProfile** again by selecting it from the **Project** window and go to the **Inspector** window. Press the **Add effect...** button and select **Unity | Ambient Occlusion**. Check the **Mode** option and select Scalable Ambient Obscurance. Afterward, change **Intensity** to 2 and **Radius** to 20:

Figure 1.39 – Adding an Ambient Occlusion effect

This will provide us with the following visual change:

Figure 1.40 – Effect after adding Ambient Occlusion

7. Lighting often has a big effect on the theme of a scene as well. If you are using the example map, select the `Directional Light` object in the **Hierarchy** tab and, from the **Inspector** tab, under the **Light** component, change **Intensity** to `0.5` and adjust **Color** to something darker. (I used the same color that I did in *Step 4*, with a **HEX** of `576E92`.)

8. Save your game and then start it to see the effect of all of these changes:

Figure 1.41 – The final result of our horror look

How it works...

Ambient occlusion is a shading and rendering technique that's used to calculate how exposed each point in a scene is to ambient lighting. In this instance, the **Ambient Occlusion** option will calculate areas that should have additional shadows. Since our scene is filled with trees, this will make the undersides much darker than they were previously.

> **Note**
>
> For more information about the Ambient Occlusion effect, check out `https://github.com/Unity-Technologies/PostProcessing/wiki/Ambient-Occlusion`. If you are interested in looking into the other options that the Post Processing Stack has, check out `https://github.com/Unity-Technologies/PostProcessing/wiki`. If you're interested in looking at the most up-to-date version of the code, check out `https://github.com/Unity-Technologies/Graphics/tree/master/com.unity.postprocessing`.

2
Creating Your First Shader

This chapter will cover some of the more common diffuse techniques found in today's game development shading pipelines. Let's imagine a cube that has been painted white uniformly in a 3D environment with directional light. Even if the color that's been used is the same on each face, they will all have different shades of white on them, depending on the direction that the light is coming from and the angle that we are looking at it from. This extra level of realism is achieved in 3D graphics through the use of shaders, special programs that are mostly used to simulate how light works. A wooden cube and a metal one may share the same 3D model, but what makes them look different is the shader that they use.

This chapter will introduce you to shader coding in Unity. If you have little to no previous experience with shaders, this chapter is what you need to understand what shaders are, how they work, and how to customize them. By the end of this chapter, you will have learned how to build basic shaders that perform basic operations. This chapter also covers some debugging information to help in case there are errors in your shaders. Armed with this knowledge, you will be able to create just about any Surface Shader.

In this chapter, we will cover the following recipes:

- Creating a basic Standard Shader
- Adding properties to a shader
- Using properties in a Surface Shader

Technical requirements

The code files for this chapter can be found at `https://github.com/PacktPublishing/Unity-2021-Shaders-and-Effects-Cookbook-Fourth-Edition/tree/main/Shaders-and-Effects-Cookbook-2021/Assets/Chapter%2002`.

Creating a basic Standard Shader

In Unity, when we create a GameObject, we attach additional functionality through the use of **components**. Every GameObject is required to have a **Transform** component; there are several components included in Unity already, and we create components of our own when we write scripts that extend from `MonoBehaviour`.

All the objects that are part of a game contain several components that affect their look and behavior. While scripts determine how objects should behave, renderers decide how they should appear on the screen. Unity comes with several renderers, depending on the type of object that we are trying to visualize; every 3D model typically has a `MeshRenderer` component attached to it. An object should have only one renderer, but the renderer itself can contain several materials. Each material is a wrapper for a single shader, which is the final ring in the food chain of 3D graphics. The relationships between these components can be seen in the following diagram:

Figure 2.1 – Relationship between shaders, models, materials, and objects

Note that the preceding diagram mentions Cg code. Cg is only the default for the built-in renderer. URP/HDRP defaults to using HLSL code.

Understanding the difference between these components is essential for understanding how shaders work.

Getting ready

To get started with this recipe, you will need to have Unity running and must have a project opened using the built-in renderer. (In my case, I am using the 3D template. If you're using Unity Hub 3, go to **Core | 3D**.) As we mentioned previously, a Unity project has been included with this cookbook, so you can use that one as well and simply add custom shaders to it as you step through each recipe. Once you've done this, you will be ready to step into the wonderful world of real-time shading!

> **Note**
> If you are using the Unity project that came with this cookbook, you can open the `Chapter 2 | Scenes | Starting Point` scene instead of completing the *Getting ready* section as it has been set up already.

Before we create our first shader, let's create a small scene for us to work with:

1. Let's create a scene by navigating to **File | New Scene**. A dialog window will appear, asking what template should be used. Select **3D** and then click on the **Create** button:

Figure 2.2 – New Scene window

40   Creating Your First Shader

2. Once you've created the scene, create a plane that will act as the ground by going to the Unity Editor and selecting **GameObject | 3D Object | Plane** from the top menu bar:

Figure 2.3 – Creating a Plane

3. Next, select the object in the **Hierarchy** tab and then go into the **Inspector** tab. From there, right-click on the **Transform** component and select the **Reset Property | Position** option:

Figure 2.4 – Resetting the position of the object

This will reset the **Position** property of the object to 0, 0, 0, which is the center of our game world.

4. To make it easier to see what our shaders will look like when applied, let's add some shapes to visualize what each of our shaders will do. Create a sphere by going to **GameObject | 3D Object | Sphere**. Once created, select it and go to the **Inspector** tab. Next, change **Position** to 0, 1, 0 so that it is above the origin of the world (which is at 0, 0, 0) and our previously created plane:

Creating a basic Standard Shader 41

Figure 2.5 – Adding a sphere

5. Once this sphere has been created, create two more spheres and place them to the left and right of the sphere at -2, 1, 0 and 2, 1, 0, respectively:

Figure 2.6 – Completing our scene

> **Note**
> One quick way to do this is to duplicate the objects by hitting the *Ctrl + D* keys while having the object selected in the **Hierarchy** window. You can rename the objects via the top textbox in the **Inspector** window.

6. Confirm that you have directional light (it should be in the **Hierarchy** tab). If not, you can add it by selecting **GameObject | Light | Directional Light** to make it easier to see your changes and how your shaders react to light.

7. The example code for this book can be found in a folder called `Chapter 2`. This folder holds all the code for this chapter. To organize your code, create a folder by going to the **Project** tab in the Unity Editor, right-clicking, and selecting **Create | Folder**. Rename the folder `Chapter 2`.

How to do it...

With our scene generated, we can start writing the shader:

1. In the **Project** tab in the Unity Editor, right-click on the `Chapter 2` folder and select **Create | Folder**.

2. Rename the folder that you created to `Shaders` by right-clicking on it and selecting **Rename** from the drop-down list, or by selecting the folder and hitting *F2* on the keyboard.

3. Create another folder and rename it `Materials`. Place this folder inside the `Chapter 2` folder as well.

4. Right-click on the `Shaders` folder and select **Create | Shader | Standard Surface Shader**. Then, right-click on the `Materials` folder and select **Create | Material**.

5. Rename both the shader and material to `StandardDiffuse`.

6. Launch the `StandardDiffuse` shader by double-clicking on the file. This will automatically launch a scripting editor for you (Visual Studio, by default) and display the shader's code.

> **Note**
> You will see that Unity has already populated our shader with some basic code. This, by default, will get you a basic shader that accepts one texture in the `Albedo (RGB)` property. We will be modifying this base code so that you can learn how to quickly start developing custom shaders.

7. Now, let's give our shader a custom folder that it can be selected from. The very first line of code in the shader is the custom description that we have to give the shader so that Unity can make it available in the shader drop-down list when assigning it to materials. We have renamed our path to `Shader "CookbookShaders/Chapter 02/StandardDiffuse"`, but you can name it whatever you want and rename it at any time, so don't worry about any dependencies at this point.

8. Save the shader in your script editor and return to the Unity Editor. Unity will automatically compile the shader when it recognizes that the file has been updated. This is what the top of your shader file should look like at this point:

```
Shader "CookbookShaders/Chapter 02/StandardDiffuse"
{
    Properties
    {
        _Color ("Color", Color) = (1,1,1,1)
        _MainTex ("Albedo (RGB)", 2D) = "white" {}
        _Glossiness ("Smoothness", Range(0,1)) = 0.5
        _Metallic ("Metallic", Range(0,1)) = 0.0
    }
    SubShader
    {
        // Rest of file...
```

9. Technically speaking, this is a Surface Shader based on **physically based rendering** (**PBR**). As the name suggests, this type of shader achieves realism by simulating how light physically behaves when hitting objects.

44   Creating Your First Shader

10. Once you've created your shader, you need to connect it to a material. Select the `StandardDiffuse` material that we created in *Step 4* and look at the **Inspector** tab. From the **Shader** drop-down list, select **CookbookShaders/Chapter 02/StandardDiffuse** (your shader path might be different if you chose to use a different pathname):

Figure 2.7 – The StandardDiffuse shader has been set as the shader to use on this material

11. This will assign your shader to your material so that you can assign it to an object.

> **Note**
> To assign a material to an object, you can simply click and drag your material from the **Project** tab to the object in your scene. You can also drag the material to the **Inspector** tab of an object in the Unity Editor to assign it.

Creating a basic Standard Shader

The following screenshot shows what we have done so far:

Figure 2.8 – The created material

There's not much to look at at this point, but our shader development environment has been set up, which means we can start to modify the shader so that it suits our needs.

How it works...

Unity has made the task of getting your shader environment up and running very easy. It is simply a matter of a few clicks and you are good to go. There are a lot of elements working in the background concerning the Surface Shader itself. Unity has taken the Cg shader language and made it more efficient to write by doing a lot of the heavy Cg code lifting for you. The Surface Shader language is a more component-based way of writing shaders. Tasks such as processing texture coordinates and transformation matrices have already been done for you, so you don't have to start from scratch anymore.

In the past, we would have to start a new shader and rewrite a lot of code over and over again. As you gain more experience with Surface Shaders, you will want to explore more of the underlying functions of the Cg language and how Unity is processing all of the low-level **graphics processing unit (GPU)** tasks for you.

> **Note**
> All the files in a Unity project are referenced independently from the folder that they are in. We can move shaders and materials from within the editor without the risk of breaking any connections. Files, however, should never be moved from outside the editor as Unity will not be able to update their references.

So, by simply changing the shader's pathname to a name of our choice, we have got our basic diffuse shader working in the Unity environment, along with lights and shadows, just by changing one line of code!

There's more...

The source code of the built-in shaders is typically hidden in Unity. You cannot open this from the editor as you do with your own shaders. For more information on where to find a large portion of the built-in Cg functions for Unity, go to your Unity install directory (visible in the **Installs** section of Unity Hub, if you have it installed; select the three dots next to **Installs** (a gear icon in Unity Hub 3) and select the **Show in Explorer** option):

Figure 2.9 – The Show in Explorer option

From the installation location, navigate to the `Editor | Data | CGIncludes` folder:

Figure 2.10 – The location of the CGIncludes folder

In this folder, you can find the source code for the shaders that were shipped with Unity. Over time, they have changed a lot; you can visit the **Unity download archive** (`https://unity3d.com/get-unity/download/archive`) if you need to access the source code of a shader that's been used in a different version of Unity. After choosing the right version, select **Built in shaders** from the drop-down list, as shown in the following screenshot:

Figure 2.11 – Unity download archive

There are three files that that are important at this point: `UnityCG.cginc`, `Lighting.cginc`, and `UnityShaderVariables.cginc`. Our current shader is making use of all these files at the moment. In *Chapter 12, Advanced Shading Techniques*, we will explore how to use CGInclude for a modular approach to shader coding.

Adding properties to a shader

The properties of a shader are very important for the shader pipeline as you use them to let the artist or user of the shader assign textures and tweak your shader values. Properties allow you to expose GUI elements in a material's **Inspector** tab, without you having to use a separate editor, which provides us with visual ways to tweak a shader. With your shader open in your IDE of choice, look at lines three through nine. This is called the `Properties` block of the script. Currently, it will have one texture property called `_MainTex`.

If you look at your material that has this shader applied to it, you will notice that there is one **texture** GUI element in the **Inspector** tab. These lines of code in our shader are creating this GUI element for us. Again, Unity has made this process very efficient in terms of coding and the amount of time it takes to change your properties.

Getting ready

Let's see how this works in our current shader, called `StandardDiffuse`, by creating some properties and learning more about the syntax involved. For this example, we will refit the shader we created previously. Instead of using a texture, it will only use its color and some other properties that we will be able to change directly from the **Inspector** tab. Start by duplicating the `StandardDiffuse` shader. You can do this by selecting it from the **Inspector** tab and pressing *Ctrl + D*. This will create a copy called `StandardDiffuse 1`. Go ahead and rename it `StandardColor`.

> **Note**
>
> You can give a friendlier name to your shader in its first line. For instance, `Shader "CookbookShaders/StandardDiffuse"` tells Unity to call this shader `StandardDiffuse` and move it to a group called `CookbookShaders`. Adding additional groups, as we did in our previous example, works similarly to how folders work within a project. If you duplicate a shader using *Ctrl + D*, your new file will share the same name. To avoid confusion, make sure that you change the first line of each new shader so that it uses a unique alias in this and future recipes.

How to do it...

Once the `StandardColor` shader is ready, we can start changing its properties:

1. In the first line of the script, update the name to the following:

   ```
   Shader "CookbookShaders/Chapter 02/StandardColor"
   ```

   > **Downloading the example code**
   >
   > As we mentioned at the beginning of this chapter, it is possible to download the example code from this book via this book's GitHub page at https://github.com/PacktPublishing/Unity-2021-Shaders-and-Effects-Cookbook-Fourth-Edition.

2. In the `Properties` block of our shader, remove the current property by deleting the following code from our current shader:

   ```
   _MainTex ("Albedo (RGB)", 2D) = "white" {}
   ```

3. After removing this, we should remove all of the other references to `_MainTex` as well. Let's remove this other line inside of the `SubShader` section:

   ```
   sampler2D _MainTex;
   ```

4. The original shader used `_MainTex` to color the model. Let's change this by replacing the first line of code of the `surf()` function with this:

   ```
   fixed4 c = _Color;
   ```

   Just like you may be used to the `float` type being used for floating-point values when writing code in C# and other programming languages, `fixed` is used for fixed-point values and is the type that's used when writing shaders. You may also see the `half` type being used as well, which is like the `float` type but takes up half the space. This is useful for saving memory but is less precise in how it is presented. We will discuss this in much greater detail in the *Techniques to make shaders more efficient* recipe in *Chapter 9, Mobile Shader Adjustment*.

   > **Note**
   >
   > For more information on fixed-point values, check out https://en.wikipedia.org/wiki/Fixed-point_arithmetic.

4 in `fixed4` stands for the fact that the color is a single variable that contains four `fixed` values: red, green, blue, and alpha. You will learn more about how this works and how to modify these values in more detail in the next chapter, *Chapter 3, Working with Surface Shaders*.

5. When you save and return to Unity, the shader will compile. Now, we will need to create a material that will use our new shader. From the **Project** window, go to the **Chapter 02 | Materials** folder, duplicate the **StandardDiffuse** material, and rename the newly created material `StandardColor`. From the **Inspector** window, change the shader to **CookbookShaders/Chapter 02/StandardColor**:

Figure 2.12 – The Standard Color (Material) shader

6. As you can see, our material's **Inspector** tab doesn't have a texture swatch anymore. To refit this shader, let's add one more property to the `Properties` block and see what happens. Go back into your code editor of choice and enter the following code shown in bold:

```
Properties
{
    _Color("Color", Color) = (1,1,1,1)
```

```
    _AmbientColor("Ambient Color", Color) = (1,1,1,1)
    _Glossiness("Smoothness", Range(0,1)) = 0.5
    _Metallic("Metallic", Range(0,1)) = 0.0
}
```

7. We have added another color swatch to the material's **Inspector** tab. Now, let's add one more to get a feel for other kinds of properties that we can create. Add the following code to the `Properties` block:

```
_MySliderValue ("This is a Slider", Range(0,10)) = 2.5
```

8. With that, we have created another GUI element that allows us to visually interact with our shader. This time, we created a slider called **This is a Slider**, as shown in the following screenshot:

Figure 2.13 – Properties added to the shader

Properties allow you to tweak shaders without having to change the values in the shader code itself. The next recipe will show you how these properties can be used to create a more interesting shader.

> **Note**
> While properties belong to shaders, the values associated with them are stored in materials. The same shader can be safely shared between many different materials. On the other hand, changing the property of a material will affect the look of all the objects that are currently using it.

How it works...

Every Unity shader has a built-in structure that it is looking for in its code. The **Properties** block is one of those functions that is expected by Unity. The reason behind this is to give you, the shader programmer, a means of quickly creating GUI elements that tie directly into your shader code. These properties (variables) that you declare in the **Properties** block can then be used in your shader code to change values, colors, and textures. The syntax for defining a property is as follows:

```
Properties
{
    _AmbientColor ("Ambient Color", Color) = (1,1,1,1)
}
```

Variable Name | Inspector GUI Name | Type | Default Value

Figure 2.14 – Properties syntax

Let's take a look at what is going on under the hood here. When you first start writing a new property, you will need to give it a **variable name**. The variable name is going to be the name that your shader code is going to use to get the value from the GUI element. This saves us a lot of time because we don't have to set up this system ourselves.

The next elements of a property are the **inspector GUI name** and the **type** of the property, which are contained within parentheses. The inspector GUI name is the name that is going to appear in the material's **Inspector** tab when the user is interacting with and tweaking the shader. The type is the type of data that this property is going to control. There are many types that we can define for properties inside Unity shaders.

The following table describes the types of variables that we can have in our shaders:

Surface Shader Property Types	Description
Range (min, max)	This creates a `float` property as a slider from the minimum value to the maximum value.
Color	This creates a color swatch in the **Inspector** tab that opens `color picker = (float,float,float,float)`.
2D	This creates a texture swatch that allows a user to drag a texture into the shader.
Rect	This creates a non-power-of-two texture swatch and functions the same as the 2D GUI element.
Cube	This creates a Cubemap swatch in the **Inspector** tab and allows a user to drag and drop a Cubemap into the shader.
`float`	This creates a float value in the **Inspector** tab but without a slider.
Vector	This creates a four-float property that allows you to create directions or colors.
3D	This is a texture that contains information in three dimensions rather than the standard two.
`int`	This creates an integer value in the **Inspector** tab.

Finally, there is the default value. This simply sets the value of this property to the value that you placed in the code. So, in the previous example diagram, the default value for the `_AmbientColor property`, which is of the `Color` type, is set to a value of 1, 1, 1, 1. As this is a `Color` property expecting a color that is RGBA or `float4` or r, g, b, a = x, y, z, w, this `Color` property, when it's created, is set to white.

> **Note**
> Default values are only set the first time a shader is assigned to a new material. After that, the material's values are used. Changing the default value will not affect the values of existing materials that use the shader. This is a good thing, of course, but often forgotten. So, if you change a value and notice something not changing, this could be the reason for this.

See also

These properties are documented in the Unity manual at `http://docs.unity3d.com/Documentation/Components/SL-Properties.html`.

Using properties in a Surface Shader

Now that we have created some properties, let's hook them up to the shader so that we can use them as tweaks and make the material process much more interactive. We can use the **Properties** values from the material's **Inspector** tab because we have attached a variable name to the property itself, but in the shader code, you have to set up a couple of things before you can start calling the value by its variable name.

How to do it...

The following steps show you how to use the properties in a Surface Shader:

1. Continuing from the previous example, let's create another shader called `ParameterExample`. Remove the `_MainTex` property, just like we did in the *Adding properties to a shader* recipe of this chapter:

   ```
   // Inside the Properties block
   _MainTex ("Albedo (RGB)", 2D) = "white" {}
   ```

   ```
   // Below the CGPROGRAM line
   sampler2D _MainTex;
   ```

   ```
   // Inside of the surf function
   fixed4 c = tex2D (_MainTex, IN.uv_MainTex) * _Color;
   ```

2. Afterward, update the `Properties` section so that it contains the following code:

   ```
   Properties
   {
       _Color("Color", Color) = (1,1,1,1)
       _AmbientColor("Ambient Color", Color) = (1,1,1,1)
       _Glossiness("Smoothness", Range(0,1)) = 0.5
       _Metallic("Metallic", Range(0,1)) = 0.0
       _MySliderValue("This is a Slider", Range(0,10)) =
           2.5
   }
   ```

3. Next, add the following lines of code to the shader, below the `CGPROGRAM` line:

   ```
   float4 _AmbientColor;
   float _MySliderValue;
   ```

4. With *Step 3* complete, we can now use the values from the properties in our shader. Let's do this by adding the value from the `_Color` property to the `_AmbientColor` property and giving the result of this to the `o.Albedo` line of code. So, let's add the following code to the shader in the `surf()` function:

   ```
   void surf(Input IN, inout SurfaceOutputStandard o)
   {
       // We can then use the properties values in our
       // shader
       fixed4 c = pow((_Color + _AmbientColor),
                     _MySliderValue);

       // Albedo comes from property values given from
       // slider and colors
       o.Albedo = c.rgb;

       // Metallic and smoothness come from slider
       // variables
       o.Metallic = _Metallic;
       o.Smoothness = _Glossiness;
       o.Alpha = c.a;
   }
   ```

5. Finally, your shader should look like the following shader code. If you save your shader and reenter Unity, your shader will compile. If there were no errors, you will now have the ability to change the ambient and emissive colors of the material, as well as increasing the saturation of the final color, using the slider value. This is pretty neat:

   ```
   Shader "CookbookShaders/Chapter 02/ParameterExample"
   {
       Properties
       {
           _Color("Color", Color) = (1,1,1,1)
   ```

```
        _AmbientColor("Ambient Color", Color) =
            (1,1,1,1)
        _Glossiness("Smoothness", Range(0,1)) = 0.5
        _Metallic("Metallic", Range(0,1)) = 0.0
        _MySliderValue("This is a Slider",
                    Range(0,10)) = 2.5
    }
    SubShader
    {
        Tags { "RenderType" = "Opaque" }
        LOD 200

        CGPROGRAM

        float4 _AmbientColor;
        float _MySliderValue;


        // Physically based Standard lighting model,
        // and enable shadows on all light types
        #pragma surface surf Standard
            fullforwardshadows

        // Use shader model 3.0 target, to get nicer
        // looking lighting
        #pragma target 3.0

        struct Input
        {
            float2 uv_MainTex;
        };

        half _Glossiness;
        half _Metallic;
        fixed4 _Color;
```

```
            // Add instancing support for this shader. You
            // need to check 'Enable Instancing' on
            // materials that use the shader.
            // See https://docs.unity3d.com/Manual/
            // GPUInstancing.html  for more information
            // about instancing.
            // #pragma
            // instancing_optionsassumeuniformscaling
            UNITY_INSTANCING_BUFFER_START(Props)
                // put more per-instance properties here
            UNITY_INSTANCING_BUFFER_END(Props)

            void surf(Input IN, inoutSurfaceOutputStandard
                    o)
            {
                // We can then use the properties values
                // in our shader
                fixed4 c = pow((_Color + _AmbientColor),
                            _MySliderValue);

                // Albedo comes from property values given
                // from slider and colors
                o.Albedo = c.rgb;

                // Metallic and smoothness come from
                // slider variables
                o.Metallic = _Metallic;
                o.Smoothness = _Glossiness;
                o.Alpha = c.a;
            }

        ENDCG

    }
FallBack "Diffuse"
}
```

> **Note**
>
> The pow(arg1, arg2) function is a built-in function that will perform the equivalent math function of power. So, the arg1 argument is the value that we want to raise to a power, while the arg2 argument is the power that we want to raise it to.
>
> To find out more about the pow() function, look at the Cg tutorial. It is a great free resource that you can use to learn more about shading. There is also a glossary of all the functions available to you in the Cg shading language: http://http.developer.nvidia.com/CgTutorial/cg_tutorial_appendix_e.html.

6. When you save and return to Unity, the shader will compile. Now, we need to create a material that will use our new shader. From the **Project** window, go to the **Chapter 02 | Materials** folder, duplicate one of the previous materials, and rename the newly created material ParameterExample.

7. From the **Inspector** window, change the shader to the **CookbookShaders | Chapter 02 | ParameterExample** option. Then, assign the material to the spheres in the scene by dragging and dropping the material on top of them in the **Scene** view and releasing the mouse:

Figure 2.15 – Attaching the ParameterExample shader

8. After doing this, modify the parameters of the material and see how it affects the objects within the scene.

   The following screenshot shows the result that was obtained by using our properties to control our material's colors and saturation from within the material's **Inspector** tab:

Figure 2.16 – Tweaking the ParameterExample properties

How it works...

When you declare a new property in the `Properties` block, you are allowing the shader to retrieve the tweaked value from the material's **Inspector** tab. This value is stored in the variable name portion of the property. In this case, `_AmbientColor`, `_Color`, and `_MySliderValue` are the variables where we are storing the tweaked values.

For you to be able to use the value in the `SubShader` block, you need to create three new variables with the same names as the property's variable name. This automatically sets up a link between these two so that they know they have to work with the same data. Additionally, it declares the type of data that we want to store in our `SubShader` variables, which will come in handy when we look at optimizing shaders in a later chapter. Once you have created the `SubShader` variables, you can then use the values in the `surf()` function. In this case, we want to add the `_Color` and `_AmbientColor` variables together and take it to a power of whatever the `_MySliderValue` variable is equal to in the material's **Inspector** tab. The vast majority of shaders start as Standard Shaders and are modified until they match the desired look. With that, we have created the foundation for any Surface Shader you will create that requires a diffuse component.

> **Note**
> Materials are assets. This means that any changes that are made to them while your game is running in the editor are permanent. If you have changed the value of a property by mistake, you can undo it using *Ctrl + Z*.

There's more...

Like any other programming language, Cg does not allow mistakes. As such, your shader will not work if you have a typo in your code. When this happens, your materials will be rendered in unshaded magenta:

Figure 2.17 – Example of ErrorShader

When a script does not compile, Unity prevents your game from being exported or even executed. Conversely, errors in shaders do not stop your game from being executed. If one of your shaders is magenta, it is time to investigate where the problem is. If you select the incriminated shader, you will see a list of errors in its **Inspector** tab:

Figure 2.18 – Errors example

> **Note**
> Shader errors are also shown within the **Console** window.

Despite showing the line that raised the error, this rarely means that this is the line that must be fixed. The error message shown in the previous screenshot was generated by deleting the `sampler2D _MainTex` variable from the `SubShader{}` block. However, the error is raised by the first line that tries to access such a variable. Finding and fixing what's wrong with code is a process called **debugging**. The most common mistakes that you should check for are as follows:

- A missing bracket. If you forgot to add a curly bracket to close a section, the compiler is likely to raise errors at the end of the document, at the beginning of the document, or in a new section.
- A missing semicolon. This is one of the most common mistakes but luckily one of the easiest to spot and fix. When looking at the error definition, check whether the line above it contains a semicolon or not.

- A property that has been defined in the Properties section but has not been coupled with a variable in the SubShader{} block.
- Compared to what you might be used to in C# scripts, the floating-point values in Cg do not need to be followed by an f. It's 1.0, not 1.0f.

> **Tip**
> The error messages raised by shaders can be very misleading, especially due to their strict syntactic constraints. If you are in doubt about their meaning, it is best to search the internet. The Unity forums are filled with other developers who are likely to have encountered (and fixed) your problem before.

See also

More information on how to master Surface Shaders and their properties can be found in *Chapter 3, Working with Surface Shaders*.

If you are curious to see what shaders can do when they're used at their full potential, have a look at *Chapter 12, Advanced Shading Techniques,* for some of the most advanced techniques that will be covered in this book.

3
Working with Surface Shaders

In this chapter, we will explore the topic of Surface Shaders in greater detail than in the previous chapter. We will start by building a very simple matte material and end with holographic projections.

In this chapter, we will cover the following recipes:

- Implementing diffuse shading
- Accessing and modifying packed arrays
- Creating a shader with normal mapping
- Creating a Holographic Shader

Surface Shaders were introduced in *Chapter 2*, *Creating Your First Shader*, as one of the types of shader that can be used in Unity. This chapter will show you what these are and how they work. Generally speaking, two essential steps need to be done when creating any Surface Shader:

1. First, you have to specify certain physical properties of the material that you want to describe, such as its diffuse color, smoothness, and transparency. These properties are initialized in a function called the **surface function** and are stored in a structure called `SurfaceOutput`.

2. Secondly, `SurfaceOutput` is passed to a lighting model. This is a special function that will also take information about the nearby lights in the scene. Both of these parameters are then used to calculate the final color for each pixel of your model. The lighting function is the piece of code that determines how light should behave when it touches a material.

The following diagram loosely summarizes how a Surface Shader works. Custom lighting models will be explored in *Chapter 5*, *Understanding Lighting Models*, while *Chapter 7*, *Vertex Functions*, will focus on vertex modifiers:

Figure 3.1 – Summary of how a Surface Shader works

Technical requirements

The code files and folders required for this chapter are present here: `https://github.com/PacktPublishing/Unity-2021-Shaders-and-Effects-Cookbook-Fourth-Edition/tree/main/Shaders-and-Effects-Cookbook-2021/Assets/Chapter%2003`.

Implementing diffuse shading

Before we start our journey into texture mapping, it is important to understand how diffuse materials work. Certain objects might have a uniform color and smooth surface but are not smooth enough to shine in reflected light. These matte materials are best represented with a Diffuse Shader. While in the real world pure diffuse materials do not exist, Diffuse Shaders are relatively cheap to implement and are largely applied in games with low-poly aesthetics, so they're worth learning about.

There are several ways in which you can create a Diffuse Shader. A quick way is to start with Unity's Standard Surface Shader and edit it to remove any additional texture information.

Getting ready

Before starting this recipe, you should have created a Standard Surface Shader called `SimpleDiffuse`. For instructions on creating a Standard Surface Shader, look at the *Creating a basic Standard Shader* recipe of *Chapter 2, Creating Your First Shader*, if you haven't done so already.

How to do it...

Follow these steps to apply Diffuse Shading to a model:

1. To create a copy of the original shader, I duplicated the `SimpleDiffuse` file from the `Chapter 02/Shaders` folder by selecting it in the **Project** window and pressing *Ctrl + D* on my computer. From there, I moved the duplicate to the `Chapter 03/Shaders` folder and then renamed the duplicated file from `SimpleDiffuse 1` to `SimpleDiffuse`.

2. By opening the `SimpleDiffuse` shader you created, we can differentiate it between the `Chapter 02` version by renaming the first line to the following:

   ```
   Shader "CookbookShaders/Chapter 03/StandardDiffuse"
   ```

   After that, we can then make a few changes.

3. In the `Properties` section, remove all of the variables except for `_Color`:

   ```
   Properties
   {
       _Color ("Color", Color) = (1,1,1,1)
   }
   ```

4. From the `SubShader{}` section, remove the `_MainTex`, `_Glossiness`, and `_Metallic` variables. You should not remove the reference to `uv_MainTex` as Cg does not allow the `Input` struct to be empty. The value will simply be ignored.
5. Also, remove the `UNITY_INSTANCING_BUFFER_START/END` macros and the comments used with them.
6. Remove the content of the `surf()` function and replace it with the following:

```
void surf (Input IN, inout SurfaceOutputStandard o)
{
    o.Albedo = _Color.rgb;
}
```

7. Your shader should look as follows:

```
Shader "CookbookShaders/Chapter 03/StandardDiffuse"
{
    Properties
    {
        _Color ("Color", Color) = (1,1,1,1)
    }
    SubShader
    {
        Tags { "RenderType"="Opaque" }
        LOD 200

        CGPROGRAM
        // Physically based Standard lighting model,
        // and enable shadows on all light types
        #pragma surface surf Standard
            fullforwardshadows

        // Use shader model 3.0 target, to get nicer
        // looking lighting
        #pragma target 3.0
```

```
        struct Input
        {
            float2 uv_MainTex;
        };


        fixed4 _Color;

        void surf (Input IN, inout
                SurfaceOutputStandard o)
        {
        o.Albedo = _Color.rgb;
        }
        ENDCG
    }
    FallBack "Diffuse"
}
```

> **Note**
> There are two comments in this file (lines with // in front of them) that are actually one line in the actual file but are broken apart as two lines due to the size of this book.

As this shader has been refitted with a Standard Shader, it will use physically-based rendering to simulate how light behaves on your models.

> **Note**
> If you are trying to achieve a non-photorealistic look, you can change the first `#pragma` directive so that it uses `Lambert` rather than `Standard`. If you do so, you should also replace the `SurfaceOutputStandard` parameter of the `surf` function with `SurfaceOutput`. For more information on this and the other lighting models that Unity supports, Jordan Stevens put together a very nice article about it, which you can see here: http://www.jordanstevenstechart.com/lighting-models.

8. Save the shader and dive back into Unity. Using the same instructions that were provided in the *Creating a basic Standard Shader* recipe of *Chapter 2, Creating Your First Shader*, create a new material called `SimpleDiffuseMat` and apply our newly created shader to it. Change the color to something different, such as red, by clicking on the window next to the **Color** property in the **Inspector** window while it's selected.

9. Then, create a new scene by going to **File | New Scene**. From the template menu that pops up, go ahead and create a **Basic (Built In)** scene and press **Create**.

10. Go into the `Models` folder of this book's example code and bring the bunny object into our scene by dragging and dropping it from the **Project** window into the **Hierarchy** window.

> **Note**
> You can double-click on an object in the **Hierarchy** tab to center the camera on the object that's been selected.

11. From there, assign the `SimpleDiffuseMat` material to the object:

Figure 3.2 –SimpleDiffuseMat applied to the bunny model

How it works...

Shaders allow you to communicate the rendering properties of your material to their lighting model by their `SurfaceOutput`. This is a wrapper around all the parameters that the current lighting model needs. It should not surprise you that different lighting models have different `SurfaceOutput` structs. The following table shows the three main output structs that are used in Unity and how they can be used:

Type of Shader	Standard	Physically Based Lighting Models
Diffuse	Any Surface Shader `SurfaceOutput`	Standard `SurfaceOutputStandard`
Specular	Any Surface Shader `SurfaceOutput`	Standard (Specular setup) `SurfaceOutputStandardSpecular`

The `SurfaceOutput` struct has the following properties:

- `fixed3 Albedo;`: This is the diffuse color of the material.
- `fixed3 Normal;`: This is the tangent space, normal, if written.
- `fixed3 Emission;`: This is the color of the light that's emitted by the material (this property is declared as `half3` in Standard Shaders).
- `fixed Alpha;`: This is the transparency of the material.
- `half Specular;`: This is the specular power from 0 to 1.
- `fixed Gloss;`: This is the specular intensity.

The `SurfaceOutputStandard` struct has the following properties:

- `fixed3 Albedo;`: This is the base color of the material (whether it's diffuse or specular).
- `fixed3 Normal;`.
- `half3 Emission;`: This property is declared as `half3`, while it was defined as `fixed3` in `SurfaceOutput`.
- `fixed Alpha;`.
- `half Occlusion;`: This is the occlusion (default 1).
- `half Smoothness;`: This is the smoothness (0 = rough, 1 = smooth).
- `half Metallic;`: 0 = non-metal, 1= metal.

The `SurfaceOutputStandardSpecular` struct has the following properties:

- `fixed3 Albedo;`.
- `fixed3 Normal;`.
- `half3 Emission;`.
- `fixed Alpha;`.
- `half Occlusion;`.
- `half Smoothness;`.
- `fixed3 Specular;`: This is the specular color. This is very different from the `Specular` property in `SurfaceOutput` as it allows you to specify a color rather than a single value.

Using a Surface Shader correctly is a matter of initializing `SurfaceOutput` with the correct values.

> **Note**
>
> For more information on creating Surface Shaders, check out the following link: `https://docs.unity3d.com/Manual/SL-SurfaceShaders.html`.

Accessing and modifying packed arrays

Loosely speaking, the code inside a shader has to be executed for at least every pixel on your screen. This is the reason why GPUs are highly optimized for parallel computing; they can execute multiple processes at the same time. This philosophy is also evident in the standard type of variables and operators available in Cg. Understanding them is essential, not just so that you can use the shaders correctly, but also so that you can write highly optimized ones.

How to do it...

There are two types of variables in Cg: single values and packed arrays. The latter can be identified because their type ends with a number such as `float3` or `int4`. As their names suggest, these types of variables are similar to structs, which means that they each contain several single values. Cg calls them packed arrays, though they are not exactly *arrays* in the traditional sense.

The elements of a packed array can be accessed as a normal struct. They are typically called x, y, z, and w. However, Cg also provides you with other aliases for them, that is, r, g, b, and a. Despite there being no difference between using x or r, it can make a huge difference to your readers. Shader coding often involves making calculations with positions and colors. You might have seen this in the Standard Shaders:

```
o.Alpha = _Color.a;
```

Here, o was a struct and _Color was a packed array. This is also why Cg prohibits the mixed usage of these two syntaxes: you cannot use _Color.xgz.

There is also another important feature of packed arrays that has no equivalent in C#: **swizzling**. Cg allows you to address and reorder elements within packed arrays in just a single line. Once again, this appears in the Standard Shader:

```
o.Albedo = _Color.rgb;
```

Albedo is fixed3, which means that it contains three values of the fixed type. However, _Color is defined as a fixed4 type. A direct assignment would result in a compiler error as _Color is bigger than Albedo. The C# way of doing this would be as follows:

```
o.Albedo.r = _Color.r;
o.Albedo.g = _Color.g;
o.Albedo.b = _Color.b;
```

However, it can be compressed in Cg into the following:

```
o.Albedo = _Color.rgb;
```

Cg also allows you to reorder elements; for instance, using _Color.bgr to swap the red and blue channels.

Lastly, when a single value is assigned to a packed array, it is copied to all of its fields:

```
o.Albedo = 0; // Black = (0,0,0)
o.Albedo = 1; // White = (1,1,1)
```

This is referred to as **smearing**.

Swizzling can also be used on the left-hand side of an expression, allowing only certain components of a packed array to be overwritten:

```
o.Albedo.rg = _Color.rg;
```

This is called **masking**.

There's more...

Where swizzling shows its full potential is when it's applied to packed matrices. Cg allows types such as `float4x4`, which represents a matrix of floats with four rows and four columns. You can access a single element of the matrix using the _mRC notation, where *R* is the row and *C* is the column:

```
float4x4 matrix;
// ...
float first = matrix._m00;
float last = matrix._m33;
```

The _mRC notation can also be chained:

```
float4 diagonal = matrix._m00_m11_m22_m33;
```

An entire row can be selected using squared brackets:

```
float4 firstRow = matrix[0];
// Equivalent to
float4 firstRow = matrix._m00_m01_m02_m03;
```

See also

In addition to being easier to write, the swizzling, smearing, and masking properties have performance benefits as well.

However, using swizzling inappropriately can make your code harder to understand at first glance and may make it harder for the compiler to automatically optimize your code.

Packed arrays are one of the nicest features of Cg. You can discover more about them here: `http://http.developer.nvidia.com/CgTutorial/cg_tutorial_chapter02.html`.

Creating a shader with normal mapping

Every triangle of a 3D model has a *facing direction*, which is the direction that it is pointing toward. It is often represented with an arrow placed in the center of the triangle and is orthogonal to the surface. The facing direction plays an important role in the way light reflects on a surface. If two adjacent triangles face different directions, they will reflect lights at different angles, so they will be shaded differently. For curved objects, this is a problem: it is obvious that the geometry is made out of flat triangles.

To avoid this problem, the way the light reflects on a triangle doesn't take its facing direction into account, but its *normal direction* instead. As stated in the *Adding a texture to a shader* recipe, vertices can store data; the normal direction is the most used information after the UV data. This is a vector of unit length (which means it has a length of 1), which indicates the direction the vertex is facing.

Regardless of the facing direction, every point within a triangle has a normal direction, which is a linear interpolation of the ones stored in its vertices. This gives us the ability to fake the effect of high-resolution geometry on a low-resolution model.

The following screenshot shows the same geometric shape rendered with different per-vertex normals. On the left, the normals are orthogonal to the face represented by its vertices; this indicates that there is a clear separation between each face. On the right, the normals are interpolated along the surface, indicating that even if the surface is rough, the light should reflect as if it's smooth. It's easy to see that even if the three objects in the following screenshot share the same geometry, they reflect light differently. Despite being made out of flat triangles, the object on the right reflects light as if its surface was curved:

Figure 3.3 – Same shape with different per-vertex normals

Smooth objects with rough edges are a clear indication that per-vertex normals have been interpolated. This can be seen if we draw the direction of the normal stored in every vertex, as shown in the following screenshot. Note that every triangle has only three normals, but since multiple triangles can share the same vertex, more than one line can come out of it:

Figure 3.4 – The normal directions for each vertex

Calculating the normals from the shader is a technique that has rapidly declined in favor of a more advanced one-normal mapping. Similar to what happens with texture mapping, the normal directions can be provided using an additional texture, usually called a normal map or bump map.

Normal maps are usually images where the red, green, and blue channels of the image are used to indicate the X, Y, and Z components of the normal direction. There are many ways to create normal maps these days. Some applications, such as CrazyBump (`http://www.crazybump.com/`) and NDO Painter (`http://quixel.se/ndo/`), will take in 2D data and convert it into normal data for you. Other applications such as Zbrush 4R7 (`http://www.pixologic.com/`) and Autodesk (`http://usa.autodesk.com`) will take 3D-sculpted data and create normal maps for you. The actual process of creating normal maps is outside the scope of this book, but the links provided in this paragraph should help you get started.

Unity makes the process of adding normals to your shaders quite an easy process in the Surface Shader realm by using the `UnpackNormals()` function. Let's see how this is done.

Getting ready

To get started, follow these steps:

1. Create a new scene by selecting **File** | **New Scene**.
2. Choose the **Basic (Build-In)** template and then select **Create**.
3. Then, create a sphere game object by going to **GameObject** | **3D Object** | **Sphere**.
4. Double-click on the object in the **Hierarchy** tab to bring the object into focus in the **Scene** tab.
5. You will also need to create a new standard Surface Shader file (`NormalShader`) and material (`NormalShaderMat`).
6. Once created, set the material to the sphere that was created in *Step 3* in the **Scene** view. This will give us a clean workspace where we can look at the normal mapping technique:

Figure 3.5 – Setting the material as a sphere

You will need a normal map for this recipe, but there is also one in the Unity project included with this book.

The example normal map included with this book's content is shown here:

Figure 3.6 – Normal map

You can see it for yourself by going to the Assets | Chapter 03 | Textures folder under normalMapExample.

How to do it...

Follow these steps to create a normal map shader:

1. Let's get the `Properties` block set up so that we have a `Tint` color and texture:

   ```
   Properties
   {
       _MainTint ("Diffuse Tint", Color) = (0,1,0,1)
       _NormalTex ("Normal Map", 2D) = "bump" {}
   }
   ```

   > **Note**
   >
   > In this case, I have 1 for the green and alpha channels and 0 for red and blue, so the default color will be green. For the `_NormalTex` property, we are using a 2D type, which means we can use a 2D image to dictate what each pixel will use. By initializing the texture as `bump`, we are telling Unity that `_NormalTex` will contain a normal map (sometimes referred to as bump maps as well, hence the bump name). If the texture is not set, it will be replaced with a gray texture. The color used (0.5, 0.5, 0.5, 1) indicates no bump at all.

2. In the `SubShader{}` block, scroll below the `CGPROGRAM` statement and remove the original `_MainTex`, `_Glossiness`, `_Metallic`, and `_Color` definitions. Afterward, add our `_NormalTex` and `_MainTint`:

   ```
   CGPROGRAM
   // Physically based Standard lighting model, and
   // enable shadows on all light types
   #pragma surface surf Standard fullforwardshadows

   // Use shader model 3.0 target, to get nicer
   // looking lighting
   #pragma target 3.0

   // Link the property to the CG program
   sampler2D _NormalTex;
   float4 _MainTint;
   ```

3. We need to make sure that we update the `Input` struct with the proper variable name so that we can use the model's UVs for the normal map texture:

```
// Make sure you get the UVs for the texture in the
// struct
struct Input
{
    float2 uv_NormalTex;
};
```

4. Finally, we will extract the normal information from the normal map texture using the built-in `UnpackNormal()` function. Then, you only have to apply these new normals to the output of the Surface Shader:

```
void surf(Input IN, inout SurfaceOutputStandard o)
{
    // Use the tint provided as the base color for the
    // material
    o.Albedo = _MainTint;

    // Get the normal data out of the normal map
    // texture using the UnpackNormal function
    float3 normalMap = UnpackNormal(tex2D(_NormalTex,
                                    IN.uv_NormalTex));

    // Apply the new normal to the lighting model
    o.Normal = normalMap.rgb;
}
```

5. Save your script and return to the Unity Editor. You should notice that the sphere is now green by default:

Figure 3.7 – Normal material updated

6. More importantly, though, notice that the **Normal Map** property has been added. Drag and drop the normal map texture into this slot.

7. You may notice some changes, but it may be hard to see what is going on visually. In the **Normal Map** property, change **Tiling** to (10, 10):

Figure 3.8 – Adjusting the Tiling property

8. This way, you can see that the normal map was duplicated 10 times throughout the sphere on the *x* and *y* axes instead of only once:

Figure 3.9 – View from the Scene window

9. The following screenshot demonstrates the result of our normal map shader:

Figure 3.10 – Result of the normal map shader

> **Note**
> Shaders can have both a texture map and a normal map. It is not uncommon to use the same UV data to address both. However, it is possible to provide a second set of UVs in the vertex data (UV2), which are specifically used for the normal map.

How it works...

The math you must perform for the normal mapping effect is beyond the scope of this chapter, but Unity has done it all for us already. It has created the functions for us so that we do not have to keep doing it over and over again. This is another reason why Surface Shaders are an efficient way of writing shaders.

If you look in the `UnityCG.cginc` file, which can be found in the `Editor|Data|CGIncludes` folder in your Unity installation directory, you will find the definitions for the `UnpackNormal()` function. When you declare this function in your Surface Shader, Unity takes the normal map provided and processes it for you, giving you the correct type of data so that you can use it in your per-pixel lighting function. It's a huge time-saver! When sampling a texture, you get RGB values from 0 to 1; however, the directions of a normal vector range from -1 to 1. `UnpackNormal()` brings these components into the right range.

Once you have processed the normal map with the `UnpackNormal()` function, you can send it back to your `SurfaceOutput` struct so that it can be used in the lighting function. You can do this using `o.Normal = normalMap.rgb;`. We will learn how the normal is used to calculate the final color of each pixel in *Chapter 5*, *Understanding Lighting Models*.

There's more...

You can also add some controls to your normal map shader that let a user adjust the intensity of the normal map. You can do this by modifying the x and y components of the normal map variable and then adding them together. Add another property to the `Properties` block and name it `_NormalMapIntensity`:

```
Properties
{
    _MainTint ("Diffuse Tint", Color) = (0,1,0,1)
    _NormalTex ("Normal Map", 2D) = "bump" {}
    _NormalMapIntensity ("Normal intensity", Range(0,3)) = 1
}
```

Creating a shader with normal mapping

In this case, we are giving the property the ability to be between 0 and 3 with a default value of 1. Once created, you'll need to add the variable inside the SubShader:

```
// Link the property to the CG program
sampler2D _NormalTex;
float4 _MainTint;
float _NormalMapIntensity;
```

Once the property has been added, we can make use of it. Multiply the x and y components of the unpacked normal map and reapply this value to the normal map variable by using the following code in bold:

```
void surf (Input IN, inout SurfaceOutputStandard o)
{
    // Use the tint provided as the base color for the
    // material
    o.Albedo = _MainTint;

    // Get the normal data out of the normal map texture
    // using the UnpackNormal function
    float3 normalMap = UnpackNormal(tex2D(_NormalTex,
                                    IN.uv_NormalTex));

    normalMap.x *= _NormalMapIntensity;
    normalMap.y *= _NormalMapIntensity;

    // Apply the new normal to the lighting model
    o.Normal = normalize(normalMap.rgb);

}
```

> **Note**
>
> Normal vectors are supposed to have lengths equal to one. Multiplying them for `_NormalMapIntensity` changes their length, making normalization necessary. The `normalize` function will take the vector and adjust it so that it is pointing in the correct direction but with a length of one, which is what we are looking for.

82   Working with Surface Shaders

Now, you can let a user adjust the intensity of the normal map in the material's **Inspector** tab, as follows:

Figure 3.11 – The adjustable Normal intensity property

The following screenshot shows the result of modifying the normal map with our scalar values:

Figure 3.12 – The result of adjusting the normal map intensity

Creating a Holographic Shader

More and more space-themed games are being released every year. An important part of a good sci-fi game is the way futuristic technology is presented and integrated into gameplay. There's nothing that screams futuristic more than holograms. Despite being present in many flavors, holograms are often represented as semi-transparent, thin projections of an object. This recipe will show you how to create a shader that simulates such effects. Take this as a starting point: you can add noise, animated scan lines, and vibrations to create a truly outstanding holographic effect. The following screenshot shows an example of a holographic effect:

Figure 3.13 – Holographic effect on a bunny model

Getting ready

Create a shader called `Holographic`. Attach it to a material (`HolographicMat`) and assign it to a 3D model in your scene:

Figure 3.14 – Bunny model with the Holographic Material attached

How to do it...

Follow these steps to change our existing shader into a holographic one:

1. Remove the following properties as they will not be used:

    - `_Glossiness`
    - `_Metallic`

2. Add the following property to the shader:

    ```
    _DotProduct("Rim effect", Range(-1,1)) = 0.25
    ```

3. Add its respective variable to the `CGPROGRAM` section:

    ```
    float _DotProduct;
    ```

4. As this material is transparent, add the following tags:

    ```
    Tags
    {
        "Queue" = "Transparent"
        "IgnoreProjector" = "True"
        "RenderType" = "Transparent"
    }
    ```

5. According to the type of object that you will use, you might want its backside to appear. If this is the case, add `Cull Off` so that the back of the model won't be removed (culled):

    ```
    Tags
    {
        "Queue" = "Transparent"
        "IgnoreProjector" = "True"
        "RenderType" = "Transparent"
    }

    // turn off backface culling to make this shader
    // double-sided
    Cull Off
    ```

6. This shader is not trying to simulate a realistic material, so there is no need to use the PBR lighting model. **Lambertian reflectance**, which is very cheap, is used instead here. Signal to Cg that this is a Transparent Shader using `alpha:fade`:

   ```
   #pragma surface surf Lambert alpha:fade
   ```

   > **Note**
   > If you get lost and want to confirm the location and/or code used for any of the recipes within this book, feel free to look at the example code for the chapter you are interested in.

7. Change the `Input` structure so that Unity will fill it with the current view direction and the world normal direction:

   ```
   struct Input
   {
       float2 uv_MainTex;
       float3 worldNormal;
       float3 viewDir;
   };
   ```

8. Use the following surface function. Remember that since this shader is using Lambertian reflectance as its lighting function, the name of the `SurfaceOutput` structure should be changed accordingly to `SurfaceOutput` instead of `SurfaceOutputStandard`:

   ```
   void surf(Input IN, inout SurfaceOutput o)
   {
       float4 c = tex2D(_MainTex, IN.uv_MainTex) *
           _Color;
       o.Albedo = c.rgb;

       float border = 1 - (abs(dot(IN.viewDir,
                           IN.worldNormal)));

       float alpha = (border * (1 - _DotProduct) +
                       _DotProduct);
       o.Alpha = c.a * alpha;
   }
   ```

9. Save your script and dive into Unity. From there, change the **Color** and **Rim Effect** properties in **HolographicMat**:

Figure 3.15 – Adjusting the Color and Rim effect properties

10. Once you've done this, you should be able to see your hologram come to life:

Figure 3.16 – Material attached to a model

You can now use the **Rim effect** slider to choose the strength of the holographic effect.

How it works...

As we mentioned previously, this shader works by showing only the silhouette of an object. If we look at the object from another angle, its outline will change. Geometrically speaking, the edges of a model are those triangles whose *normal direction* is orthogonal (90 degrees) to the current *view direction*. The Input structure declares these parameters, which are worldNormal and viewDir, respectively. These new parameters are of the float3 type, which means that instead of a single float, they consist of three together, similar to Vector3 in C# Unity scripting.

The problem of understanding when two vectors are orthogonal can be solved using _DotProduct. This is an operator that takes two vectors and returns zero if they are orthogonal. We can use _DotProduct to determine how close to zero _DotProduct has to be for the triangle to fade completely.

The second aspect that is used in this shader is the gentle fading between the edge of the model (fully visible) and the angle determined by `_DotProduct` (invisible). This linear interpolation can be used as follows:

```
float alpha = (border * (1 - _DotProduct) + _DotProduct);
```

Finally, the original `alpha` from the texture is multiplied by the newly calculated coefficient to achieve the final look.

There's more...

This technique is very simple and relatively inexpensive, and yet it can be used for a large variety of effects, such as the following:

- The slightly colored atmosphere of a planet in sci-fi games
- The edge of an object that has been selected or is currently under the mouse
- A ghost or specter
- Smoke coming out of an engine
- The shockwave of an explosion
- The bubble shield of a spaceship under attack

See also

`_DotProduct` plays an important role in the way reflections are calculated. *Chapter 5, Understanding Lighting Models*, will explain how it works and why it is widely used in so many shaders.

4
Working with Texture Mapping

Textures can bring our shaders to life very quickly in terms of achieving very realistic effects. In this chapter, we will see how you can use textures to animate and blend, and how to use **C#** code to modify properties at runtime to manipulate what a shader does.

In this chapter, we will cover the following topics:

- Adding a texture to a shader
- Scrolling textures by modifying **UV** values
- Creating a transparent material
- Packing and blending textures
- Creating a circle around your terrain

Technical requirements

You can find all of the code files present in this chapter on GitHub at `https://github.com/PacktPublishing/Unity-2021-Shaders-and-Effects-Cookbook-Fourth-Edition/tree/main/Shaders-and-Effects-Cookbook-2021/Assets/Chapter%2004`.

Adding a texture to a shader

In order to effectively use textures, we need to understand how a 2D image is mapped to a 3D model. This process is called **texture mapping**, and it requires some work to be done on the shader and 3D model that we want to use. Models, in fact, are made out of triangles, which are often referred to as polygons; each vertex on the model can store data that shaders can access and use to determine what to draw.

One of the most important pieces of information that is stored in vertices is the **UV data**. This consists of two coordinates, U and V, ranging from 0 to 1 to get the full extent of the image. They represent the XY position of the pixel in the 2D image that will be mapped to the vertices. UV data is present only for vertices; when the inner points of a triangle have to be texture-mapped, the GPU interpolates the closest UV values to find the right pixel in the texture to be used. The following diagram shows you how a **2D texture** is mapped to a triangle from a 3D model:

Figure 4.1 – How UVs are projected to a polygon

The UV data is stored in the 3D model and requires modeling software to be edited. Some models lack the UV component and therefore cannot support texture mapping. For example, the *Stanford bunny* that we used in the last chapter was not originally provided with one.

Getting ready

For this recipe, you'll need a 3D model with UV data and its texture. They both need to be imported to **Unity** before starting. You can do this simply by dragging them to the editor. As the **Standard Shader** supports texture mapping by default, we'll use this and then explain how it works in detail.

How to do it...

Adding a texture to your model using the Standard Shader is incredibly simple:

1. In the sample code for this chapter that's provided with this book, you can find the `basicCharacter` model in the `Chapter 04/Models` folder, which, by default, has UV information embedded in it, making it so that when we attach a material, it will draw the texture using that information.

2. Create a new **Standard Surface Shader** by going to the **Project** window, selecting the + symbol in the top left, and then selecting **Shader | Standard Surface Shader**. Once created, you can type in a new name for the shader (I used `TexturedShader`) and then press *Enter*.

3. For organization's sake, open the shader and change the first line to the following:

   ```
   Shader "CookbookShaders/Chapter 04/TexturedShader"
   ```

   This will allow us to find the shader inside of the organization we have been using so far in this book.

4. Create a new material called `TexturedMaterial` by going to the **Project** window and then right-clicking and selecting **Create | Material**. Once created, you can type in a new name for the material and then press *Enter* to confirm the change.

92 Working with Texture Mapping

5. Assign the shader to the material by going to the **Inspector** tab and then clicking on the **Shader** dropdown before selecting `CookbookShaders/Chapter 04/TexturedShader`:

Figure 4.2 – The Shader assigned

> **Note**
> You may also do this by first selecting the material and then dragging the shader file over it in the **Project** tab.

6. After selecting the material, drag your texture to the empty rectangle called **Albedo (RGB)**. If you are missing some, there are textures located in this chapter's example code that can be used. If you have followed all of these steps correctly, your material **Inspector** tab should look like this:

Figure 4.3 – The finished Textured Shader

> **Note**
> The Standard Shader knows how to map a 2D image to a 3D model using the UV models, and the textures used in this example were created by Kenney Vleugels and Casper Jorissen. You can find these and many other public-domain game assets at `Kenney.nl`.

94　Working with Texture Mapping

7. To see the UV data in action, in the example code's `Models` folder, drag and drop the model into the **Hierarchy** tab of your scene. Once there, double-click on the newly created object to zoom in so that you can see the object:

Figure 4.4 – Placing the character in the scene

8. Once there, you may go to the **Project** tab and open up the `Chapter 4 | Materials` folder, and drag and drop `Textured Material` onto the character. Note that the model consists of different objects, each of which provides direction to draw in a particular place. This means you will need to drop the material on each part of the model (`ArmLeft1`, `ArmRight1`, `Body1`, and so on); trying to apply this to only the top level of the hierarchy (`basicCharacter`) will not work:

Figure 4.5 – The finished shader

9. It's also possible to change what the object looks like by changing the texture that's being used. For instance, if we use the other texture provided (`skin_womanAlternative`) on the material, we have a very different looking character:

Figure 4.6 – Changing the texture

> **Note**
> This is often used in games to provide different kinds of characters with minimal cost.

How it works...

When the Standard Shader is used from the **Inspector** of a material, the process behind texture mapping is completely transparent to developers. If we want to understand how it works, it's necessary to take a closer look at `TexturedShader`. From the `Properties` section, we can see that the `Albedo (RGB)` texture is actually referred to in the code as `_MainTex`:

```
_MainTex ("Albedo (RGB)", 2D) = "white" {}
```

In the `CGPROGRAM` section, this texture is defined as `sampler2D`, the standard type for 2D textures:

```
sampler2D _MainTex;
```

The following line shows a struct called `Input`. This is the input parameter for the surface function and contains a packed array called `uv_MainTex`:

```
struct Input
{
    float2 uv_MainTex;
};
```

Every time the `surf()` function is called, the `Input` structure will contain the UV of `_MainTex` for the specific point of the 3D model that needs to be rendered. The Standard Shader recognizes that the name `uv_MainTex` refers to `_MainTex` and initializes it automatically. If you are interested in understanding how the UV is actually mapped from a 3D space to a 2D texture, you can check out *Chapter 5, Understanding Lighting Models*.

Finally, the UV data is used to sample the texture in the first line of the surface function:

```
fixed4 c = tex2D (_MainTex, IN.uv_MainTex) * _Color;
```

This is done using the `tex2D()` function of Cg; it takes a texture and UV and returns the color of the pixel at that position.

> **Note**
>
> The U and V coordinates go from 0 to 1, where (0,0) and (1,1) correspond to two opposite corners. UVs can go beyond [0..1] and can be used this way to tile textures. Different implementations associate UV with different corners; if your texture happens to appear reversed, try inverting the V component.

There's more...

When you import a texture to Unity, you are setting up some of the properties that `sampler2D` will use. The most important is **Filter Mode**, which determines how colors are interpolated when the texture is sampled. It is very unlikely that the UV data will point exactly to the center of a pixel; in all other cases, you might want to interpolate between the closest pixels to get a more uniform color.

The following is a screenshot of the **Inspector** tab of an example texture:

Figure 4.7 – The location of Filter Mode, set to Bilinear

For most applications, **Bilinear** provides an inexpensive but effective way to smooth the texture. However, if you are creating a 2D game, **Bilinear** might produce blurred tiles. In this case, you can use **Point** to remove any interpolation from the texture sampling.

When a texture is seen from a steep angle, texture sampling is likely to produce visually unpleasant artifacts. You can reduce these by setting **Aniso Level** to a higher value. This is particularly useful for floor and ceiling textures, where glitches can break the illusion of continuity.

See also

If you would like to know more about the inner workings of how textures are mapped to a 3D surface, you can read the information available at the following link:

`https://developer.download.nvidia.com/CgTutorial/cg_tutorial_chapter03.html`

For a complete list of the options available when importing a 2D texture, you can refer to the following website:

`http://docs.unity3d.com/Manual/class-TextureImporter.html`

Scrolling textures by modifying UV values

One of the most common texture techniques used in today's game industry is the process of allowing you to scroll the textures over the surface of an object. This allows you to create effects such as waterfalls, rivers, and lava flows. It's also a technique that is the basis of creating animated sprite effects, but we will cover this in a subsequent recipe of this chapter. First, let's see how we will create a simple scrolling effect in a Surface Shader.

Getting ready

To begin this recipe, you will need to create a new shader file (`ScrollingUVs`) and material (`ScrollingUVMat`) in a similar manner to how we've created our shader files previously. This will set us up with a nice clean shader that we can use to study the scrolling effect by itself.

How to do it...

To begin with, we will launch our new shader file that we just created and enter the code mentioned in the following steps:

1. The shader will need two new properties that will allow us to control the speed of the texture scrolling. So, let's add a speed property for the X direction and a speed property for the Y direction, as shown in the following code:

```
Properties
{
    _Color("Color", Color) = (1,1,1,1)
    _MainTex("Albedo (RGB)", 2D) = "white" {}
    _ScrollXSpeed("X Scroll Speed", Range(0,10)) = 2
    _ScrollYSpeed("Y Scroll Speed", Range(0,10)) = 2
}
```

When working in **ShaderLab**, `Properties` has a syntax that looks like the following:

```
Properties
{
    _propertyName("Name in Inspector", Type) = value
}
```

Each property contained in the `Properties` block first has a name that is used in code to refer to the object, here specified as `_propertyName`. The underscore isn't required but is a common standard in place. Inside the parentheses, you'll see two parameters. The first is a string that defines what text will be displayed in the **Inspector** for what this property is. The second parameter is the type of data we wish to store.

In our case, for the X and Y scroll speed, we are creating a number with a possible range of 0 to 10. Lastly, we can initialize the property with a default value, which is done at the end. As we've seen before, these properties will show up in the **Inspector** if you select a material that is using this shader.

> **Note**
>
> For more information on *properties* and how to create them, check out `https://docs.unity3d.com/Manual/SL-Properties.html`.

For this example, we don't need the `Smoothness` or `Metallic` properties, so we can remove them as well.

2. Modify the Cg properties in the `CGPROGRAM` section above the definition of `_MainTex` and create new variables so that we can access the values from our properties:

```
fixed _ScrollXSpeed;
fixed _ScrollYSpeed;
sampler2D _MainTex;
```

3. We also need to remove the `_Glossiness` and `_Metallic` definitions, as we are not using them anymore.

4. Modify the surface function to change the UVs given to the `tex2D()` function. Then, use the built-in `_Time` variable to animate the UVs over time when the **Play** button is pressed in the editor:

```
void surf (Input IN, inout SurfaceOutputStandard o)
{
    // Create a separate variable to store our UVs
    // before we pass them to the tex2D() function
    fixed2 scrolledUV = IN.uv_MainTex;

    // Create variables that store the individual x
    // and y components for the UV's scaled by time
    fixed xScrollValue = _ScrollXSpeed * _Time;
    fixed yScrollValue = _ScrollYSpeed * _Time;

    // Apply the final UV offset
    scrolledUV += fixed2(xScrollValue, yScrollValue);

    // Apply textures and tint
    half4 c = tex2D(_MainTex, scrolledUV);
    o.Albedo = c.rgb * _Color;
    o.Alpha = c.a;
}
```

5. Once the script is finished, save it and then go back to the Unity Editor. Go to the `Materials` folder and assign `ScrollingUVsMat` to use our `ScrollingUVs` shader. Once that is done, under the **Albedo (RGB)** property, drag and drop the water texture from the example code provided with this book in the `Chapter 04 | Textures` folder to assign the property:

Figure 4.8 – The final version of the scrolling UV material

6. After this is created, we need to create an object that can use the shader. From a new scene, go ahead and select **GameObject | 3D Object | Plane** and drag and drop the `ScrollingUVMat` material onto it.

102   Working with Texture Mapping

7. Once applied, go ahead and play the game to see the shader in action:

Figure 4.9 – The scrolling UVs shader attached to a plane

While it is not visible in this still image, you will notice that in the Unity Editor, the object will now move in both the *x* and *y* axes! Feel free to drag the **X Scroll Speed** and **Y Scroll Speed** properties in the **Inspector** tab to see how the changes affect how the object moves. Also, feel free to move the camera to make it easier to see if you would like.

> **Note**
> If you modify a variable on a **material** during gameplay, the value will stay changed, unlike how Unity typically works.

Pretty cool! With this knowledge, we can take this concept much further to create interesting visual effects. The following screenshot demonstrates the result of utilizing the scrolling UV system with multiple materials in order to create a simple river motion for your environments:

Figure 4.10 – A simple river using scrolling UVs

How it works...

The scrolling system starts with the declaration of a couple of properties, which will allow the user of this shader to increase or decrease the speed of the scrolling effect itself. At their core, they are float values being passed from the material's **Inspector** tab to the surface function of the shader. For more information on shader properties, see *Chapter 2, Creating Your First Shader*.

Once we have these float values from the material's **Inspector** tab, we can use them to offset our UV values in the shader.

To begin this process, we first store the UVs in a separate variable called `scrolledUV`. This variable has to be `float2/fixed2` because the UV values are being passed to us from the `Input` structure:

```
struct Input
{
    float2 uv_MainTex;
}
```

Once we have access to the mesh's UVs, we can offset them using our scroll speed variables and built-in `_Time` variable. This built-in variable returns a variable of the `float4` type, meaning that each component of this variable contains different values of time as it pertains to game time.

> **Note**
> A complete description of these individual time values is described at the following link: `http://docs.unity3d.com/Manual/SL-UnityShaderVariables.html`.

This `_Time` variable will give us an incremented float value based on Unity's game time clock. So, we can use this value to move our UVs in a UV direction and scale that time with our scroll speed variables:

```
// Create variables that store the individual x and y
// components for the uv's scaled by time
fixed xScrollValue = _ScrollXSpeed * _Time;
fixed yScrollValue = _ScrollYSpeed * _Time;
```

With the correct offset being calculated by time, we can add the new offset value back to the original UV position. This is why we are using the += operator in the next line. We want to take the original UV position, add the new offset value, and then pass this to the `tex2D()` function as the texture's new UVs. This creates the effect of the texture moving on the surface. What we are really doing is manipulating the UVs to take on the effect of the texture moving:

```
scrolledUV += fixed2(xScrollValue, yScrollValue);
half4 c = tex2D (_MainTex, scrolledUV);
```

Creating a transparent material

All the shaders we have seen so far have something in common: they are used for solid materials. If you want to improve the look of your game, transparent materials are often a good way to start. They can be used for anything from a fire effect to a glass window. Unfortunately, working with them is slightly more complicated. Before rendering solid models, Unity orders them according to the distance from the camera (**Z ordering**) and skips all the triangles that are facing away from the camera (**culling**). When rendering transparent geometries, there are instances in which these two aspects can cause problems. This recipe will show you how to solve some of these issues when it comes to creating a transparent Surface Shader. This topic will be revisited in detail in *Chapter 8, Fragment Shaders and Grab Passes*, where realistic glass and water shaders will be provided.

Getting ready

This recipe requires a new shader, which we'll be calling `Transparent`, and a new material (`TransparentMat`) so that it can be attached to an object. As this is going to be a transparent glass window, a quad or plane is perfect (**GameObject | 3D Object | Quad**). If the quad shows up as invisible on your screen, rotate your camera around until it can be seen. We will also need several other non-transparent objects to test the effect:

Figure 4.11 – A quad placed in front of a cube

In this example, we will use a PNG image file for the glass texture, since it has support for an alpha channel that will be used to determine the transparency of the glass. The process of creating such an image depends on the software that you are using. However, these are the main steps that you will need to follow:

1. Find the image of the glass you want for your windows.
2. Open it with photo editing software, such as **GIMP** or **Photoshop**.
3. Select the parts of the image that you want to be semi-transparent.
4. Create a white (full opacity) layer mask on your image.
5. Use the selection previously made to fill the layer mask with a darker color. White is treated as fully visible, black will be treated as invisible, and gray will be somewhere in the middle.
6. Save the image and import it into Unity.

106   Working with Texture Mapping

The toy image used in this recipe is a picture of stained glass from the *Meaux Cathedral* in France (`https://en.wikipedia.org/wiki/Stained_glass`). If you have followed all of these steps, your image should look like this (`RGB` channels on the left, and `A` channel on the right):

Figure 4.12 – Sample image used in our recipe

You can also make use of the image file provided in the example code for this book in the `Chapter 04 | Textures` folder (`Meaux_Vitrail.psd`).

Attaching this image to the material will cause the image to show up, but we cannot see it behind the glass:

Figure 4.13 – Glass without the transparency effect

As we would like to see behind this, we can make adjustments to the shader to do exactly that.

How to do it...

As mentioned previously, there are a few aspects that we need to take care of while using a Transparent Shader:

1. Remove the `_Glossiness` and `_Metallic` variables from the `Properties` and `SubShader` sections of the code as they are not needed for this example.

2. In the `SubShader{}` section of the shader, modify the `Tags` section to match the following so that we can signal that the shader is transparent:

   ```
   Tags
   {
       "Queue" = "Transparent"
       "IgnoreProjector" = "True"
       "RenderType" = "Transparent"
   }
   ```

   Tags are used by `SubShader` to know how and when items should be rendered. Similar to the dictionary type, tags are key-value pairs where the left-hand side is the tag name and the right-hand side is the value you wish for it to be set to.

   > **Note**
   >
   > For more information on tags in ShaderLab, check out `https://docs.unity3d.com/Manual/SL-SubShaderTags.html`.

3. As this shader is designed for 2D materials, make sure that the back geometry of your model is not drawn by adding the following below the LOD 200 line:

   ```
   LOD 200

       // Do not show back
       Cull Back

   CGPROGRAM
   ```

4. Tell the shader that this material is transparent and needs to be blended with what was drawn on the screen before:

   ```
   #pragma surface surf Standard alpha:fade
   ```

5. Use this Surface Shader to determine the final color and transparency of the glass:

   ```
   void surf(Input IN, inout SurfaceOutputStandard o)
   {
       float4 c = tex2D(_MainTex, IN.uv_MainTex) * _Color;
       o.Albedo = c.rgb;
       o.Alpha = c.a;
   }
   ```

6. Afterward, save your script and dive back to the Unity Editor:

Figure 4.14 – Example of the transparency effect in use

Notice that you can now see the cube behind the glass. Perfect!

How it works...

This shader introduces several new concepts. First of all, `Tags` are used to add information about how the object is going to be rendered. The really interesting one here is `Queue`. Unity, by default, will sort your objects for you based on the distance from the camera. So, as an object gets nearer to the camera, it is going to be drawn over all the objects that are further away from the camera. For most cases, this works out just fine for games, but you will find yourself in certain situations where you will want to have more control over the sorting of your objects in your scene. Unity has provided us with some default render queues, each with a unique value that directs Unity when to draw the object to the screen. These built-in render queues are called `Background`, `Geometry`, `AlphaTest`, `Transparent`, and `Overlay`. These queues weren't just created arbitrarily; they actually serve a purpose to make our lives easier when writing shaders and interacting with the real-time renderer.

Refer to the following table for descriptions of the use of each of these individual render queues:

Render queue	Render queue description	Render queue value
`Background`	This render queue is rendered first. It is used for skyboxes and so on.	1000
`Geometry`	This is the default render queue. This is used for most objects. Opaque geometry uses this queue.	2000
`AlphaTest`	Alpha-tested geometry uses this queue. It's different from the `Geometry` queue as it's more efficient to render alpha-tested objects after all the solid objects are drawn.	2450
`Transparent`	This render queue is rendered after `Geometry` and `AlphaTest` queues in back-to-front order. Anything alpha-blended (that is, shaders that don't write to the depth buffer) should go here, for example, glass and particle effects.	3000
`Overlay`	This render queue is meant for overlay effects. Anything rendered last should go here (for example, lens flares).	4000

So, once you know which render queue your object belongs to, you can assign its built-in render queue tag. Our shader used the `Transparent` queue, so we wrote `Tags{"Queue"="Transparent"}`.

> **Note**
>
> The fact that the `Transparent` queue is rendered after `Geometry` does *not* mean that our glass will appear on top of all the other solid objects. Unity will draw the glass last, but it will not render pixels that belong to pieces of geometry hidden behind something else. This control is done using a technique called **ZBuffering**. More information on how models are rendered can be found at the following link:
>
> `http://docs.unity3d.com/Manual/SL-CullAndDepth.html`

One thing that's important to note is that transparent objects don't receive shadows in Unity. Transparent objects can cast shadows by rendering the object as opaque in a shadow pass.

The `IgnoreProjector` tag makes this object unaffected by Unity's projectors. Lastly, `RenderType` plays a role in **shader replacement**, a topic that will be covered briefly in *Chapter 11, Gameplay and Screen Effects*.

The last concept introduced is `alpha:fade`. This indicates that all the pixels from this material have to be blended with what was on the screen before according to their alpha values. Without this directive, the pixels will be drawn in the correct order, but they will not have any transparency.

Packing and blending textures

Textures are not only useful for storing loads of data or pixel colors as we generally tend to think of them, but also for multiple sets of pixels in both the X and Y directions and RGBA channels. We can actually pack multiple images into a single RGBA texture and use each of the R, G, B, and A components as individual textures themselves by extracting each of these components from the shader code.

The result of packing individual grayscale images into a single RGBA texture can be seen in the following screenshot:

Figure 4.15 – Packing

Why is this helpful? Well, in terms of the amount of actual memory that your application takes up, textures are a large portion of your application's size. We can, of course, reduce the size of the image, but then we would lose details in how it can be represented. So, to begin reducing the size of your application, we can look at all of the images that we are using in our shader and see whether we can merge these textures into a single texture. Using a single texture with multiple images in them requires fewer draw calls and less overhead than separate files. We can also use this concept to combine irregularly shaped textures (that is, those that are not squares) into a single one to take up less space than giving them their own full texture.

Any texture that is grayscale can be packed into one of the RGBA channels of another texture. This might sound a bit odd at first, but this recipe is going to demonstrate one of the uses of packing a texture and using these packed textures in a shader.

One example of using these packed textures is when you want to blend a set of textures together onto a single surface. You see this most often in terrain-type shaders, where you need to blend into another texture nicely using some sort of control texture or, in this case, the packed texture. This recipe covers this technique and shows you how to construct the beginnings of a nice four-texture blended terrain shader.

Getting ready

Let's create a new shader file in your Shaders folder (TextureBlending) and then create a new material for this shader (TextureBlendingMat). The naming convention is entirely up to you for your shader and material files, so try your best to keep them organized and easy to reference later on.

112   Working with Texture Mapping

Once you have your shader and material ready, create a new scene in which we can test our shader. Inside the scene, place the `Terrain_001` object from the `Chapter 04 | Models` folder and assign the `TextureBlendingMat` material to it:

Figure 4.16 – Terrain with material applied

You will also need to gather up four textures that you would want to blend together. These can be anything, but for a nice terrain shader, you will want grass, dirt, rocky dirt, and rock textures. You can find these assets in the `Chapter 01 | Standard Assets | Environment | TerrainAssets | SurfaceTextures` folder in the example code for this book.

Finally, we will also need a blending texture that is packed with grayscale images. This will give us the four blending textures that we can use to direct how the color textures will be placed on the object surface.

We can use very intricate blending textures to create a very realistic distribution of terrain textures over a terrain mesh, as shown in the following screenshot:

Figure 4.17 – Example of blended textures

How to do it...

Let's learn how to use packed textures by entering the code shown in the following steps:

1. We need to add a few properties to our `Properties` block. We will need five `sampler2D` objects, or textures, and two `Color` properties:

   ```
   Properties
   {
       _MainTint("Diffuse Tint", Color) = (1,1,1,1)

       // Add the properties below so we can input all of
       // our textures
       _ColorA("Terrain Color A", Color) = (1,1,1,1)
       _ColorB("Terrain Color B", Color) = (1,1,1,1)
       _RTexture("Red Channel Texture", 2D) = ""{}
       _GTexture("Green Channel Texture", 2D) = ""{}
       _BTexture("Blue Channel Texture", 2D) = ""{}
       _ATexture("Alpha Channel Texture", 2D) = ""{}
       _BlendTex("Blend Texture", 2D) = ""{}
   }
   ```

   > **Note**
   > As always, in our code, remove the properties we are not using from the base shader.

2. We then need to create the `SubShader{}` section variables that will be our link to the data in the `Properties` block:

   ```
   CGPROGRAM
   #pragma surface surf Lambert

   // Use shader model 3.5 target, to support enough
   // textures
   #pragma target 3.5
   float4 _MainTint;
   float4 _ColorA;
   float4 _ColorB;
   sampler2D _RTexture;
   ```

Working with Texture Mapping

```
sampler2D _GTexture;
sampler2D _BTexture;
sampler2D _BlendTex;
sampler2D _ATexture;
```

3. Due to the number of items inside of our shader, we will need to update the target level version of our shader model to 3.5.

> **Note**
> For more information on **Shader compilation target levels**, check out https://docs.unity3d.com/Manual/SL-ShaderCompileTargets.html.

4. So, now we have our texture properties and we are passing them to our `SubShader{}` function. In order to allow the user to change the tiling rates on a per-texture basis, we will need to modify our `Input` struct. This will allow us to use the tiling and offset parameters on each texture:

```
struct Input
{
    float2 uv_RTexture;
    float2 uv_GTexture;
    float2 uv_BTexture;
    float2 uv_ATexture;
    float2 uv_BlendTex;
};
```

5. In the `surf()` function, get the texture information and store it in its own variables so that we can work with the data in a clean, easy-to-understand way:

```
void surf (Input IN, inout SurfaceOutput o)
{
    // Get the pixel data from the blend texture
    // we need a float 4 here because the texture
    // will return R,G,B,and A or X,Y,Z, and W
    float4 blendData = tex2D(_BlendTex,
        IN.uv_BlendTex);

    // Get the data from the textures we want to blend
```

```
        float4 rTexData = tex2D(_RTexture,
            IN.uv_RTexture);
        float4 gTexData = tex2D(_GTexture,
            IN.uv_GTexture);
        float4 bTexData = tex2D(_BTexture,
             IN.uv_BTexture);
        float4 aTexData = tex2D(_ATexture,
            IN.uv_ATexture);
```

> **Note**
>
> Remember that due to us using **Lambert**, we will be using `SurfaceOutput` instead of `SurfaceOutputStandard` for the `surf` function.

6. Let's blend each of our textures together using the `lerp()` function. It takes three arguments: `lerp(value : a, value : b, and blend: c)`. The `lerp()` function takes in two textures and blends them with the float value given in the last argument:

```
// Now we need to construct a new RGBA value and add
// all the different blended texture back together
float4 finalColor;
finalColor = lerp(rTexData, gTexData, blendData.g);
finalColor = lerp(finalColor, bTexData, blendData.b);
finalColor = lerp(finalColor, aTexData, blendData.a);
finalColor.a = 1.0;
```

7. Finally, we multiply our blended texture by the color tint values and use the red channel to determine where the two different terrain tint colors go:

```
// Add on our terrain tinting colors
float4 terrainLayers = lerp(_ColorA, _ColorB,
blendData.r);
finalColor *= terrainLayers;
finalColor = saturate(finalColor);

o.Albedo = finalColor.rgb * _MainTint.rgb;
o.Alpha = finalColor.a;
}
```

116   Working with Texture Mapping

8. Save your script and go back into Unity. Once there, you can assign the `TerrainBlend` texture to the **Blend Texture** property. Once you've done that, place different textures in the different channels:

Figure 4.18 – Assigning the textures to be blended

Packing and blending textures | 117

9. After it has been finished, in order to see our script in action all we need to do is return to our terrain object:

Figure 4.19 – Final result

10. This effect can be taken even further by using different textures and terrain tinting to create some great-looking terrains with minimal effort. The result of blending together four terrain textures and creating a terrain tinting technique can be seen in the following screenshot:

Figure 4.20 – Further example of the blended textures

How it works...

This might seem like quite a few lines of code, but the concept behind blending is actually quite simple. For the technique to work, we have to employ the built-in `lerp()` function from the CgFX standard library. This function allows us to pick a value between *argument one* and *argument two*, using *argument three* as the blend amount:

Function	Description
`lerp(a, b, f)`	This involves linear interpolation: $(1-f)*a + b*f$ Here, a and b are matching vector or scalar types. The f parameter can be either a scalar or vector of the same type as a and b.

So, for example, if we wanted to find the mid-value between `1` and `2`, we could feed the `0.5` value as the third argument to the `lerp()` function and it would return `1.5`. This works perfectly for our blending needs, as the values of an individual channel in an RGBA texture are single float values, usually in the range of `0` to `1`.

In the shader, we simply take one of the channels from our **Blend Texture** and use it to drive the color that is picked in a `lerp()` function for each pixel. For instance, we take our grass texture and dirt texture, use the red channel from our blending texture, and feed this to a `lerp()` function. This will give us the correct blended color result for each pixel on the surface.

A more visual representation of what is happening when using the `lerp()` function is shown in the following diagram:

Figure 4.21 – Example of the lerp function

The shader code simply uses the four channels of the **Blend Texture** and all the color textures to create a final **Blended Texture**. This final texture then becomes the color that we can multiply with our diffuse lighting.

Creating a circle around your terrain

Many **real-time strategy (RTS)** games display distances (range attack, moving distance, sight, and so on) by drawing a circle around the selected unit. If the terrain is flat, this can be done simply by stretching a quad with the texture of a circle. If that's not the case, the quad will most likely be clipped behind a hill or another piece of geometry. This recipe will show you how to create a shader that allows you to draw circles around an object of arbitrary complexity. If you want to be able to move or animate your circle, you will need both a shader and C# script.

The following screenshot shows an example of drawing a circle in a hilly region using a shader:

Figure 4.22 – Example of a circle in your region

Getting ready...

Despite working with every piece of geometry, this technique is oriented to terrains. Hence, the first step is setting up a terrain in Unity, but instead of using a model, we will create one within the Unity Editor:

1. Let's start by creating a new shader called `RadiusShader` and the respective material, `RadiusMat`.
2. Create a GameObject to represent your character; we will draw a circle around it later on.
3. From the menu, navigate to **GameObject | 3D Object | Terrain** to create a new terrain.
4. Create the geometry for your terrain. You can either import an existing one or draw your own using the tools available (**Raise/Lower Terrain**, **Paint Height**, **Smooth Height**):

Figure 4.23 – Terrain example

5. Terrains are special objects in Unity, and the way texture mapping works on them is different from traditional 3D models. You cannot provide `_MainTex` from a shader as it needs to be provided directly from the terrain itself. To do this, you will first need to go to the **Raise or Lower Terrain** dropdown and select **Paint Texture**:

Figure 4.24 – Adding Paint Texture

122   Working with Texture Mapping

6. Afterward, in the **Terrain Layers** section, select **Edit Terrain Layers...** and then **Add Layer**. Select a material and apply it:

Figure 4.25 – An example of the terrain with the initial texture

> **Note**
> The creation of a terrain isn't covered in this book, but if you would like to learn more about it, check out the following link:
>
> `https://docs.unity3d.com/Manual/terrain-UsingTerrains.html`

7. Now that the texture is set, you have to change the material of the terrain so that a custom shader can be provided. From **Terrain Settings**, change the **Material** property to the **Radius** material:

Figure 4.26 – Applying the RadiusMat property

You are now ready to create your shader. As you can see, there is a warning in the preceding screenshot stating the shader may be unsuitable for use with terrains. We will fix that shortly.

How to do it...

Let's start by editing the `RadiusShader` file:

1. In the new shader, remove the `_Glossiness` and `_Metallic` properties and add these four properties:

    ```
    _Center("Center", Vector) = (200,0,200,0)
    _Radius("Radius", Float) = 100
    _RadiusColor("Radius Color", Color) = (1,0,0,1)
    _RadiusWidth("Radius Width", Float) = 10
    ```

2. Add their respective variables to the CGPROGRAM section, remembering to remove the declaration of _Glossiness and _Metallic:

```
float3 _Center;
float _Radius;
fixed4 _RadiusColor;
float _RadiusWidth;
```

3. The Input to our surface function requires not only the UV of the texture but also the position (in world coordinates) of every point of the terrain. We can retrieve this parameter by changing struct Input as follows:

```
struct Input
{
    float2 uv_MainTex; // The UV of the terrain texture
    float3 worldPos;   // The in-world position
};
```

4. Next, to get rid of the warning from earlier, we would need to add an additional tag:

```
Tags
{
    "RenderType"="Opaque"
    "TerrainCompatible"="True"
}
```

5. Lastly, we use this surface function:

```
void surf(Input IN, inout SurfaceOutputStandard o)
{
    // Get the distance between the center of the
    // place we wish to draw from and the input's
    // world position
    float d = distance(_Center, IN.worldPos);

    // If the distance is larger than the radius and
    // it is less than our radius + width change the
    // color
    if ((d > _Radius) && (d < (_Radius + _RadiusWidth)))
    {
```

```
            o.Albedo = _RadiusColor;
    }
    // Otherwise, use the normal color
    else
    {
            o.Albedo = tex2D(_MainTex, IN.uv_MainTex).rgb;
    }
}
```

These steps are all it takes to draw a circle on your terrain.

Return to the Unity Editor, go back to your `RadiusMat` material, and assign an **Albedo** texture to use. Afterward, also assign the **Tiling** value higher to make the terrain look good:

Figure 4.27 – Setting properties of the RadiusMat component

After this, zoom out and you should be able to see the circle drawn within the terrain:

Figure 4.28 – Radius Mat's default look

How it works...

The relevant parameters to draw a circle are its center, radius, and color. They are all available in the shader with the names `_Center`, `_Radius`, and `_RadiusColor`. By adding the `worldPos` variable to the `Input` structure, we are asking Unity to provide us with the position of the pixel that we are drawing expressed in world coordinates. This is the actual position of an object in the editor.

The `surf()` function is where the circle is actually drawn. It calculates the distance from the point being drawn and the center of the radius, and then it checks whether it is between `_Radius` and `_Radius + _RadiusWidth`; if this is the case, it uses the chosen color. In the other case, it just samples the texture map like all the other shaders we have seen so far.

There's more...

This is great, but you'll likely also want to change where the circle is at runtime, which we can do via code. If you want the circle to follow your character, other steps are necessary:

1. Create a new C# script called `SetRadiusProperties`.
2. Since you may wish to see this change both in the game and outside, we can add a tag to the top of the class saying to execute this code while in the editor, in addition to when the game is being played, by adding the following tag:

```
[ExecuteInEditMode]
public class SetRadiusProperties :MonoBehaviour
```

3. Add these properties to the script:

   ```
   public Material radiusMaterial;
   public float radius = 1;
   public Color color = Color.white;
   ```

4. In the `Update()` method, add these lines of code:

   ```
   if(radiusMaterial != null)
   {
   radiusMaterial.SetVector("_Center", transform.position);
   radiusMaterial.SetFloat("_Radius", radius);
   radiusMaterial.SetColor("_RadiusColor", color);
   }
   ```

5. Attach the script to the object you wish to have the circle drawn around.
6. Finally, drag the `RadiusMat` material to the **Radius Material** slot of the script:

Figure 4.29 – Default options with the cube attached to it

128   Working with Texture Mapping

You can now move your character around and this will create a nice circle around it. Changing the properties of the `Radius` script will change the radius as well.

Figure 4.30 – Tweaking the properties of the SetRadiusProperties component

5
Understanding Lighting Models

In the previous chapters, we introduced Surface Shaders and explained how we can change physical properties (such as Albedo and Specular) to simulate different materials. So, how does this actually work? Well, at the heart of every Surface Shader is its **lighting model**. This is the function that takes these properties and calculates the final shade of each pixel. Usually, Unity hides this from developers because, in order to write a lighting model, you have to understand how light reflects and refracts onto surfaces. This chapter will finally show you how lighting models work and present you with the basics that you need to create your own.

Simulating the way light works is a very challenging and resource-consuming task. For many years, video games have used very simple lighting models, which, despite lacking in realism, were very believable. Even if most 3D engines are now using physically based renderers, it is worth exploring some simpler techniques. The ones presented in this chapter are reasonably realistic and have been widely adopted on devices with low resources such as mobile phones. Understanding these simple lighting models is also essential if you want to create your own.

In this chapter, we will cover the following recipes:

- Creating a custom diffuse lighting model
- Creating a toon shader
- Creating a Phong Specular type
- Creating a Blinn-Phong Specular type
- Creating an Anisotropic Specular type

Technical requirements

You can find all of the code files present in this chapter on GitHub at https://github.com/PacktPublishing/Unity-2021-Shaders-and-Effects-Cookbook-Fourth-Edition/tree/main/Shaders-and-Effects-Cookbook-2021/Assets/Chapter%2005.

Creating a custom diffuse lighting model

If you are familiar with Unity 4, you might know that the default shader it provided was based on a lighting model called **Lambertian reflectance**. This recipe will show you how it is possible to create a shader with a custom lighting model. Additionally, we will explain the mathematics involved and the implementation. The following diagram shows the same geometry rendered with a Standard Shader (on the right-hand side) and a diffuse Lambert one (on the left-hand side):

Figure 5.1 – A diffuse Lambert shader (left) versus a standard shader (right)

Shaders based on the Lambertian reflectance are classified as non-photorealistic; no object in the real world actually looks like this. However, Lambert shaders are still often used in low-poly games, as they produce a neat contrast between the faces of complex geometries. The lighting model used to calculate the Lambertian reflectance is also very efficient, making it perfect for mobile games.

Unity has already provided us with a lighting function that we can use for our shaders. It is called the Lambertian lighting model. It is one of the more basic and efficient forms of reflectance, which you can find in a lot of games even today. As it is already built in the Unity Surface Shader language, we thought it best to start with this first and then build on it. You can also find an example in the Unity reference manual; however, here, we will go into more depth and explain where the data is coming from and why it is working the way it is. This will help you to get a nice grounding in how to set up custom lighting models so that we can build on this knowledge in the future recipes within this chapter.

Getting ready

Let's start by carrying out the following steps:

1. Create a new Scene by navigating to **File | New Scene**. Select the **Basic (Built-in)** Scene and then hit **Create**.
2. Create a new shader and give it a name (for example, `SimpleLambert`).
3. Create a new material, give it a name (for example, `SimpleLambertMat`), and assign the new shader to its `shader` property.
4. Then, create a sphere object and place it roughly in the center of the scene. Attach the new material to it.
5. Finally, let's create a directional light to cast some light on our object if one hasn't been created already.

Once your assets have been set up in Unity, you should have a scene that resembles the following screenshot:

Figure 5.2 – The initial scene

How to do it...

The Lambertian reflectance can be achieved via the following changes to the shader:

1. Begin by replacing the shader's `Properties` block with the following:

   ```
   Properties
   {
       _MainTex ("Texture", 2D) = "white"
   }
   ```

2. Since we are removing all of the other properties, remove the `_Glossiness`, `_Metallic`, and `_Color` declarations inside the `SubShader` section.

3. Change the `#pragma` directive of the shader so that, instead of `Standard`, it uses our custom lighting model:

   ```
   #pragma surface surf SimpleLambert
   ```

Creating a custom diffuse lighting model

> **Note**
> If you try to run the script now, it will complain that it doesn't know what the `SimpleLambert` lighting model is. We will need to create a function called `Lighting` along with the name that we have given here and instructions on how to light the object, which we will be writing later on in this recipe. In this case, it would be `LightingSimpleLambert`.

4. Use a very simple surface function that just samples the texture according to its UV data:

```
void surf(Input IN, inout SurfaceOutput o)
{
    o.Albedo = tex2D(_MainTex, IN.uv_MainTex).rgb;
}
```

5. Add a function called `LightingSimpleLambert()` that will contain the following code for the Lambertian reflectance:

```
// Allows us to use the SimpleLambert lighting mode
half4 LightingSimpleLambert (SurfaceOutput s, half3
                             lightDir, half atten)
{
    // First calculate the dot product of the light
    // direction and the surface's normal
    half NdotL = dot(s.Normal, lightDir);

    // Next, set what color should be returned
    half4 color;

    color.rgb = s.Albedo * _LightColor0.rgb * (NdotL *
        atten);
    color.a = s.Alpha;

    // Return the calculated color
    return color;
}
```

134   Understanding Lighting Models

6. Save your script and return to the Unity Editor. You should observe that it looks somewhat different from what was there before:

Figure 5.3 – The initial effect of the simple Lambert shader

7. The effect is even easier to view if we use the sphere object included within the `Assets | Chapter 05 | Models` folder within the example code for this book:

Figure 5.4 – A simple Lambert shader (left) versus a normal diffuse shader (right)

Additionally, you can observe an even greater difference if you view it isometrically by clicking on the gray box on the Scene gizmo in the upper-right corner of the **Scene** view:

Figure 5.5 – The same view with an isometric camera

How it works...

As discussed in *Chapter 2, Creating Your First Shader*, the `#pragma` directive is used to specify which surface function to use. Choosing a different lighting model works in a similar fashion: `SimpleLambert` forces Cg to look for a function called `LightingSimpleLambert()`. Pay attention to the `Lighting` at the beginning, which is omitted in the directive.

The `Lighting` function takes three parameters: the *surface output* (which contains physical properties such as the albedo and transparency), the *direction* the light is coming from, and its *attenuation*, which also has shadow information.

According to the Lambertian reflectance, the amount of light a surface reflects depends on the angle between the incident light and the surface normal. If you have played pool or billiards, you are surely familiar with this concept; the direction of a ball depends on its incident angle against the wall. If you hit a wall at a 90-degree angle, the ball will come back at you; if you hit it with a very low angle, its direction will be mostly unchanged. The Lambertian model makes the same assumption; if the light hits a triangle at a 90-degree angle, all the light gets reflected back. The lower the angle, the less light that is reflected back to you. This concept is shown in the following diagram:

Figure 5.6 – A demonstration of the Lambertian model

This simple concept has to be translated into a mathematical form. In vector algebra, which is a part of the study of linear algebra, the angle between two unit vectors can be calculated via an operator called the **dot product**. When the dot product is equal to zero, the two vectors are orthogonal. This means that they make a 90-degree angle. When it is equal to one (or minus one), they are parallel to each other. Cg has a function called dot(), which implements the dot product extremely efficiently. It is important to note that the vectors need to be normalized for this to work correctly.

The following diagram shows a light source (the sun) shining on a complex surface. **L** indicates the light direction (called lightDir in the shader) and **N** is the normal to the surface. The light is reflected with the same angle that it hits the surface with:

Figure 5.7 – A light source shining on a complex surface

> **Note**
> For more information on normals and what they mean mathematically, please refer to https://en.wikipedia.org/wiki/Normal_(geometry).

The Lambertian reflectance simply uses the `NdotL` dot product as a multiplicative coefficient for the intensity of light:

$$I = N \cdot L$$

When *N* and *L* are parallel, all the light is reflected back to the source, causing the geometry to appear brighter. The `_LightColor0` variable contains the color of the light that is calculated.

> **Note**
> Prior to Unity 5, the intensity of the lights was different. If you are using an old diffuse shader based on the Lambertian model, you might notice that `NdotL` is multiplied by two: for instance, (`NdotL * atten * 2`) rather than (`NdotL * atten`). If you are importing a custom shader from Unity 4, you will need to correct this manually. Legacy shaders, however, have already been designed taking this aspect into account.

When the dot product is negative, the light is coming from the opposite side of the triangle. This is not a problem for opaque geometries, as triangles that are not facing the camera frontally are culled (that is, discarded) and not rendered.

This basic Lambert is a great starting point when you are prototyping your shaders. This is because you can get a lot accomplished in terms of writing the core functionality of the shader while not having to worry about the basic `Lighting` functions.

Unity has provided us with a lighting model that has already taken the task of creating a Lambert lighting for you. If you take a look at the `UnityCG.cginc` file, which can be found in your Unity's installation directory under the `Data` folder, you will notice that you have Lambert and Blinn-Phong lighting models available for you to use. The moment you compile your shader with `#pragma surface surf Lambert`, you are telling the shader to utilize Unity's implementation of the Lambert `Lighting` function in the `UnityCG.cginc` file. This is so that you don't have to write that same code over and over again. We will explore how the Blinn-Phong model works later in this chapter.

Creating a toon shader

One of the most commonly used effects in games is **toon shading**, which is also known as **celluloid** (**CEL**) shading. This is a non-photorealistic rendering technique that makes 3D models appear flat. Many games use it to give the illusion that the graphics are being drawn by hand rather than modeled in 3D. In the following diagram, you can view a sphere rendered with a toon shader (on the left-hand side) and a sphere rendered with a standard shader (on the right-hand side):

Figure 5.8 – A toon shader (left) versus a standard shader (right)

Achieving this effect using just surface functions is not impossible, but it would be extremely expensive and time-consuming. In fact, the surface function only works on the properties of the material, not its actual lighting condition. As toon shading requires us to change the way light reflects, we need to create a custom lighting model instead.

Getting ready

Let's start this recipe by creating a shader and its material and importing a special texture. Perform the following steps:

1. Create a new Scene by going to **File | New Scene**. Select the **Basic (Built-in)** scene and then hit **Create**.

2. Then, create a sphere object and place it roughly within the center of the scene.

3. Next, create a new shader; in this example, we will duplicate the one that we made in the *Creating a custom diffuse lighting model* recipe (that is, `SimpleLambert`) by selecting it in the **Project** tab and then hitting *Ctrl + D*. We will change the name of this new shader to `ToonShader`.

   > Note
   > You can rename an object in the **Project** window by clicking once on the name or by selecting it and hitting *F2* on the keyboard.

4. Create a new material for the shader (`ToonShaderMat`) and attach it to a 3D model. Toon shading works best on curved surfaces.

5. This recipe requires an additional texture called a **ramp map**, which will be used to dictate when we want to use certain colors depending on the shade received:

Figure 5.9 – An example of a ramp map

Our ramp maps were made in Adobe Photoshop, but they can be made using any image editing application such as GIMP.

6. An example texture can be found in the `Chapter 5 | Textures` folder of this book. If you decide to import your own, it is important that you select your next texture and, from the **Inspector** tab, change the ramp map's **Wrap Mode** property to **Clamp**. If you want the edges between the colors to be sharp, the **Filter Mode** option should also be set to **Point (no filter)**.

140   Understanding Lighting Models

Finally, hit the **Apply** button:

Figure 5.10 – Setup for the ToonRamp texture

> **Note**
> The example project included with this book already has this step completed in the `Assets | Chapter 5 | Texture | ToonRamp` file, but it is a good idea to verify that this is the case before moving forward.

How to do it...

The toon aesthetic can be achieved by making the following changes to the shader:

1. Add a new property for a texture called `_RampTex`:

   ```
   Properties
   {
       _MainTex ("Texture", 2D) = "white"
       _RampTex ("Ramp", 2D) = "white" {}
   }
   ```

2. Add its relative variable to the `CGPROGRAM` section:

   ```
   sampler2D _RampTex;
   ```

3. Change the `#pragma` directive so that it points to a function called `LightingToon()`:

   ```
   #pragma surface surf Toon
   ```

4. Replace the `LightingSimpleLambert` function with the following function instead:

   ```
   fixed4 LightingToon(SurfaceOutput s, fixed3 lightDir,
   fixed atten)
   {
       // First calculate the dot product of the light
       // direction and the surface's normal
       half NdotL = dot(s.Normal, lightDir);

       // Remap NdotL to the value on the ramp map
       NdotL = tex2D(_RampTex, fixed2(NdotL, 0.5));

       // Next, set what color should be returned
   ```

```
        half4 color;

        color.rgb = s.Albedo * _LightColor0.rgb * (NdotL *
            atten);
        color.a = s.Alpha;

        // Return the calculated color
        return color;
    }
```

5. Save the script, open up `ToonShaderMat`, and assign the **Ramp** property to your ramp map. If all goes well, you should see something similar to the following in your scene:

Figure 5.11 – The Toon Shader material with the Ramp texture applied

Creating a toon shader   143

This effect can be modified by the lighting in the scene. You can change the illumination of the scene by navigating to **Window | Rendering | Lighting**. From the tabs at the top, click on the **Environment** option. From there, in the **Environment Lighting** section, set the **Intensity Multiplier** property to 0:

Figure 5.12 – Reducing Intensity Multiplier

After making the changes, you'll get the following result:

Figure 5.13 – The final result

How it works...

The main characteristic of toon shading is the way the light is rendered; surfaces are not shaded uniformly. To achieve this effect, we need a ramp map. Its purpose is to remap the Lambertian light intensity, `NdotL`, to another value. Using a ramp map without a gradient, we can force the lighting to be rendered in steps. The following diagram shows how the ramp map is used to correct the light intensity:

Figure 5.14 – How a ramp map is used to correct the light intensity

Any negative values from `NdotL` are clamped to the border pixel because the **Texture Wrap** mode is set to **Clamp**.

There's more...

There are many different ways whereby you can achieve a toon shading effect. Using different ramps can produce dramatic changes to the way your models look, so you should experiment in order to find the best one.

An alternative to ramp textures is to **snap** the `NdotL` light intensity so that it can only assume a certain number of values equidistantly sampled from 0 to 1:

```
fixed _CelShadingLevels;

half4 LightingCustomLambert (SurfaceOutput s, half3
    lightDir, half3 viewDir, half atten)
{
  half NdotL = max(0, dot(s.Normal, lightDir));
  
  // Snap instead
  half cel = floor(NdotL * _CelShadingLevels) /
            (_CelShadingLevels - 0.5);
  
  // Next, set what color should be returned
  half4 color;
  
  color.rgb = s.Albedo * _LightColor0.rgb * (cel * atten );
  color.a = s.Alpha;
  
  // Return the calculated color
  return color;
}
```

To snap a number, first, we multiply `NdotL` by the `_CelShadingLevels` variable, round the result to an integer through the `floor` function, and then divide it back. This rounding is done by the `floor` function, which will effectively remove the decimal point from a number. By doing this, the `cel` quantity is forced to assume one of the `_CelShadingLevels` equidistant values from `0` to `1`. This removes the need for a ramp texture and makes all of the color steps the same size. If you are going for this implementation, remember to add a property called `_CelShadingLevels` to your shader. You will also need to rename the lighting function in `#pragma` or rename the lighting function itself. You can find an example of this in the example code for this chapter. Try dragging the **Levels** property to view how it affects the object, as shown in the following screenshot:

Figure 5.15 – Adjusting the Levels property

You can also observe what it looks like, in the **Scene** view, on the object that we attached it to:

Figure 5.16 – The effect on the scene

Creating a Phong Specular type

The specularity of an object's surface simply describes how shiny it is. In the shader world, these types of effects are often referred to as view-dependent effects. This is because, in order to achieve a realistic Specular effect in your shaders, you need to include the direction of the camera or the user who is facing the object's surface. The most basic and performance-friendly Specular type is the Phong Specular effect. It is the calculation of the light direction reflecting off the surface compared to the user's view direction. It is a common Specular model used in many applications, from games to movies. While it is not the most realistic in terms of accurately modeling the reflected Specular, it gives a great approximation of what is expected of the shininess that performs well in most situations. Additionally, if your object is further away from the camera and there is no need for a perfectly accurate Specular, this is a great way to provide a Specular effect to your shaders.

In this recipe, we will be covering how to implement the per-vertex version of the shader and also the per-pixel version using some new parameters in the Surface Shader's `Input` struct. We will observe the differences and discuss when and why you should use these two different implementations for different situations.

Getting ready

To start with this recipe, perform the following steps:

1. Create a new Standard Surface Shader (`Phong`), material (`PhongMat`), and a new Scene with a sphere in it and a **Plane** object underneath (**GameObject | 3D Objects | Plane**).

2. Attach the shader to the material and the material to the object. To finish off your new Scene, create a new directional light if there is not one already. Select it and under the **Inspector** tab, change the **Light** component's **Intensity** property to **0.5** to make it easier to view your Specular effect as you code it:

Figure 5.17 – The Scene setup

How to do it...

Follow these steps to create a Phong lighting model:

1. At this point, you might be noticing a pattern, but we always like to start with the most basic part of the shader writing process: the creation of properties. So, let's remove all of the current properties with their definitions in the `SubShader` block and then add the following properties to the shader:

   ```
   Properties
   {
       _MainTint ("Diffuse Tint", Color) = (1,1,1,1)
       _MainTex ("Base (RGB)", 2D) = "white" {}
       _SpecularColor ("Specular Color", Color) = (1,1,1,1)
       _SpecPower ("Specular Power", Range(0,30)) = 1
   }
   ```

2. We then need to add the corresponding variables to our `CGPROGRAM` block in our `SubShader{}` block:

   ```
   float4 _SpecularColor;
   sampler2D _MainTex;
   float4 _MainTint;
   float _SpecPower;
   ```

3. Now, we have to add our custom lighting model so that we can compute our own Phong Specular. Don't worry if it doesn't make sense at this point; we will cover each line of code in the *How it works...* section of this recipe. Add the following code to the shader's `SubShader{}` function:

   ```
   fixed4 LightingPhong (SurfaceOutput s, fixed3
       lightDir, half3 viewDir, fixed atten)
   {
       // Reflection
       float NdotL = dot(s.Normal, lightDir);
       float3 reflectionVector = normalize(2.0 * s.Normal *
           NdotL - lightDir);

       // Specular
       float spec = pow(max(0, dot(reflectionVector,
           viewDir)), _SpecPower);
   ```

```
            float3 finalSpec = _SpecularColor.rgb * spec;

    // Final effect
    fixed4 c;
    c.rgb = (s.Albedo * _LightColor0.rgb * max(0,NdotL)
        * atten) + (_LightColor0.rgb * finalSpec * atten);
    c.a = s.Alpha;
    return c;
}
```

4. Next, we have to tell the CGPROGRAM block that it needs to use our custom lighting function instead of one of the built-in ones. We can do this by changing the #pragma statement to the following:

```
CGPROGRAM
#pragma surface surf Phong
```

5. Finally, let's update the surf function to the following:

```
void surf (Input IN, inout SurfaceOutput o)
{
    half4 c = tex2D (_MainTex, IN.uv_MainTex) *
        _MainTint;
    o.Albedo = c.rgb;
    o.Alpha = c.a;
}
```

The following screenshot displays the result of our custom Phong lighting model using our own custom reflection vector:

Figure 5.18 – The resulting effect

> **Note**
> Try changing the **Specular Power** property of the material and make a note of the effect that you see.

How it works…

Let's break down the lighting function by itself, as at this point, the rest of the shader should be pretty familiar to you.

In the previous recipes, we used a lighting function that only provided the light direction, `lightDir`. Unity comes with a set of lighting functions that you can use, including one that provides the view direction, `viewDir`.

Understanding Lighting Models

To figure out how to write your own custom lighting mode, please refer to the following table and replace `NameYouChoose` with the lighting function name that you gave in the `#pragma` statement. Alternatively, you can go to `https://docs.unity3d.com/Manual/SL-SurfaceShaderLighting.html` for further details:

Not view-dependent	`half4 LightingNameYouChoose (SurfaceOutput s, half3 lightDir, half atten);`
View-dependent	`half4 LightingNameYouChoose (SurfaceOutput s, half3 lightDir, half3 viewDir, half atten);`

In our case, we are using a Specular shader, so we need to have the view-dependent `Lighting` function structure. We need to write the following:

```
CPROGRAM
#pragma surface surf Phong
fixed4 LightingPhong (SurfaceOutput s, fixed3 lightDir, half3 viewDir, fixed atten)
{
    // ...
}
```

This will tell the shader that we want to create our own view-dependent shader. Always ensure that your lighting function name is the same in your `Lighting` function declaration and the `#pragma` statement; otherwise, Unity will not be able to find your lighting model.

The components that play a role in the `Phong` model are described in the following diagram. We have the light direction, **L** (coupled with its perfect reflection, **R**), and the normal direction, **N**. We have encountered each one before in the Lambertian model, with the exception of **V**, which is the **view direction**:

Figure 5.19 – The components within the Phong model

The `Phong` model assumes that the final light intensity of a reflective surface is given by two components, its diffuse color and Specular value, as follows:

$$I = D + S$$

The diffuse component, D, remains unchanged from the Lambertian model:

$$D = N \cdot L$$

The Specular component, S, is defined as follows:

$$S = (R \cdot V)^p$$

Here, p is the Specular power defined as `_SpecPower` in the shader.

In our code, the `max` function is used to pick the larger of the numbers between this result and 0. This is because, without it, there will be visible artifacts when specular is added in the calculation.

The only unknown parameter is *R*, which is the reflection of *L* according to *N*. In vector algebra, this can be calculated as follows:

$$R = 2N \cdot (N \cdot L) - L$$

This is exactly what is calculated in the following:

```
float3 reflectionVector = normalize(2.0 * s.Normal * NdotL -
                                    lightDir);
```

This has the effect of bending the normal toward the light; as a vertex, the normal is pointing away from the light, so it is forced to look at the light. Please refer to the following diagram for a more visual representation. The script that produces this debug effect is included on GitHub at https://github.com/PacktPublishing/Unity-2021-Shaders-and-Effects-Cookbook-Fourth-Edition/blob/main/Shaders-and-Effects-Cookbook-2021/Assets/Chapter%2005/Scripts/ShowRays.cs:

Figure 5.20 – Debug reflection vector example

The following diagram displays the final result of our Phong Specular calculation isolated in the shader:

Figure 5.21 – The final result of our Phong Specular calculation

Creating a Blinn-Phong Specular type

Blinn is another more efficient way of calculating and estimating specularity. It is done by getting the half vector from the view direction and the light direction. It was brought into the world of Cg by Jim Blinn. Blinn found that it was far more efficient to simply get the half vector instead of calculating our own reflection vectors. This cut down on the code and processing time. If you actually look at the built-in Blinn-Phong lighting model included in the `UnityCG.cginc` file, you will notice that it is using the half vector as well; hence, it is named Blinn-Phong. It is just a simpler version of the full Phong calculation.

Getting ready

To begin, perform the following steps:

1. This time, instead of creating a whole new Scene, let's just use the objects and scene that we already have by navigating to **File | Save Scene As...**. Then, create a new shader (`Blinn-Phong`) and material (`BlinnPhongMat`):

Figure 5.22 – The completed setup of the Scene

2. Once you have a new shader, double-click on it to launch your **Integrated Development Environment** (**IDE**) of choice so that you can start editing your shader.

How to do it...

Perform the following steps to create a Blinn-Phong lighting model:

1. First, let's remove all of the current properties with their definitions in the `SubShader` block. Then, we need to add our own properties to the `Properties` block so that we can control the look of the Specular highlight:

```
Properties
{
```

```
    _MainTint ("Diffuse Tint", Color) = (1,1,1,1)
    _MainTex ("Base (RGB)", 2D) = "white" {}
    _SpecularColor ("Specular Color", Color) = (1,1,1,1)
    _SpecPower ("Specular Power", Range(0.1,60)) = 3
}
```

2. Then, we need to make sure that we have created the corresponding variables in our CGPROGRAM block. This is so that we can access the data from our Properties block inside our subshader:

```
sampler2D _MainTex;
float4 _MainTint;
float4 _SpecularColor;
float _SpecPower;
```

3. Now, it's time to create our custom lighting model that will process our diffuse and Specular calculations. The code is as follows:

```
fixed4 LightingCustomBlinnPhong(SurfaceOutput s,
                                fixed3 lightDir,
                                half3 viewDir,
                                fixed atten)
{
    float NdotL = max(0, dot(s.Normal, lightDir));

    float3 halfVector = normalize(lightDir + viewDir);
    float NdotH = max(0, dot(s.Normal, halfVector));
    float spec = pow(NdotH, _SpecPower) *
        _SpecularColor;

    float4 color;
    color.rgb = (s.Albedo * _LightColor0.rgb * NdotL)
        + (_LightColor0.rgb * _SpecularColor.rgb *
            spec) * atten;
    color.a = s.Alpha;
    return color;
}
```

4. Update the `surf` function to the following:

```
void surf(Input IN, inoutSurfaceOutput o)
{
    half4 c = tex2D(_MainTex, IN.uv_MainTex) *
        _MainTint;
    o.Albedo = c.rgb;
    o.Alpha = c.a;
}
```

5. To complete our shader, we will need to tell our `CGPROGRAM` block to use our custom lighting model rather than a built-in one by modifying the `#pragma` statement with the following code:

```
CPROGRAM
#pragma surface surf CustomBlinnPhong
```

The following screenshot demonstrates the results of our Blinn-Phong lighting model:

Figure 5.23 – The results of the Blinn-Phong lighting model

How it works...

The Blinn-Phong Specular is almost exactly like the Phong Specular, except that it is more efficient because it uses less code to achieve almost the same effect. Before the introduction of physically based rendering, this approach was the default choice for Specular reflection in Unity 4.

Calculating the reflection vector, **R**, is generally expensive. The Blinn-Phong Specular replaces it with the half vector, **H**, between the view direction, **V**, and the light direction, **L**:

Figure 5.24 – The components of the Blinn-Phong model

Instead of calculating our own reflection vector, we are simply going to get the vector halfway between the view direction and the light direction, essentially simulating the reflection vector. In fact, it has been found that this approach is more physically accurate than the last approach, but we thought it necessary to show you all of the possibilities:

$$S_{\text{Phong}} = (R \cdot V)^p, \quad S_{\text{Blinnphong}} = (N \cdot H)^p$$

According to vector algebra, the half vector can be calculated as follows:

$$H = \frac{V + L}{|V + L|}$$

Here, $|V + L|$ is the length of the vector, $V + L$. In Cg, we simply need to add the view direction and the light direction together and then normalize the result into a unit vector:

```
float3 halfVector = normalize(lightDir + viewDir);
```

Then, we simply need to dot the vertex normal with this new half vector to get our main Specular value. Following this, we just take it to a power of `_SpecPower` and multiply it by the Specular color variable. It's much lighter on the code and math; however, it still gives us a nice Specular highlight that will work for many real-time situations.

See also

The light models that you have viewed in this chapter are extremely simple; no real material is perfectly matte or perfectly specular. Moreover, it is not uncommon for complex materials such as clothing, wood, and skin to require knowledge of how light scatters in the layers beneath the surface. Use the following table to recap the different lighting models that we have encountered so far:

Technique	Type	Light Intensity (I)
Lambertian	Diffuse	$I = N \cdot L$
Phong	Specular	$I = N \cdot L + (R \cdot V)^p$ $R = 2N \cdot (N \cdot L) - L$
Blinn-Phong	Specular	$I = N \cdot L + (N \cdot H)^p$ $H = \dfrac{V + L}{|V + L|}$

There are other interesting lighting models such as the Oren-Nayar, Ward, Cook-Torrance, and Ashikhmin-Shirley lighting models for rough surfaces. For more information, please refer to `https://www1.cs.columbia.edu/CAVE/projects/oren/`.

Creating an Anisotropic Specular type

Anisotropic is a type of Specular or reflection that simulates the directionality of grooves in a surface and modifies/stretches the Specular in a perpendicular direction. This is very useful when you want to simulate brushed metals, not metals with a clear, smooth, and polished surface. Imagine the Specular that you see when you look at the data side of a CD or DVD or the way the Specular is shaped at the bottom of a pot or pan. Note that if you carefully examine the surface, there is a direction to the grooves, usually in the way that the metal was brushed. When you apply a Specular to this surface, you get a Specular stretched in a perpendicular direction.

This recipe will introduce you to the concept of augmenting your Specular highlights to achieve different types of brushed surfaces. In future recipes, we will look at the various ways in which we can use the concepts of this recipe to achieve other effects, such as stretched reflections and hair; however, first, you are going to learn about the fundamentals of this technique. We will be using a shader as a reference for our own custom Anisotropic shader, which you can find at `http://wiki.unity3d.com/index.php?title=Anisotropic_Highlight_Shader`.

The following diagram shows examples of different types of Specular effects that you can achieve using Anisotropic shaders in Unity:

Figure 5.25 – Specular effects

Getting ready

Let's start this recipe by creating a shader, its material, and some lights for our scene:

1. Create a new Scene with some objects and lights so that we can visually debug our shader. In this case, we will be using some capsules, a sphere, and a cylinder.

2. Following this, create a new shader (`Anisotropic`) and material (`AnisotropicMat`). Then, hook them up to your objects:

Figure 5.26 – The Scene setup

3. Finally, we will need some sort of a normal map that will indicate the directionality of our Anisotropic Specular highlight.

The following screenshot shows the Anisotropy normal map that we will be using for this recipe. It is available from this book's support page at https://www.packtpub.com/books/content/support:

Figure 5.27 – Anisotropy normal map

How to do it...

To create an Anisotropic effect, we need to make the following changes to the shader created earlier:

1. First, we need to remove the old properties and then add the properties that we are going to need for our shader. This will allow a lot of artistic control over the final appearance of the surface:

```
Properties
{
    _MainTint("Diffuse Tint", Color) = (1,1,1,1)
    _MainTex("Base (RGB)", 2D) = "white" {}
    _SpecularColor("Specular Color", Color) =
        (1,1,1,1)
    _Specular("Specular Amount", Range(0,1)) = 0.5
    _SpecPower("Specular Power", Range(0,1)) = 0.5
    _AnisoDir("Anisotropic Direction", 2D) = "" {}
    _AnisoOffset("Anisotropic Offset", Range(-1,1)) =
        -0.2
}
```

2. Then, we need to make the connection between our `Properties` block and our `SubShader{}` block. This is so that we can use the data being provided by the `Properties` block:

```
sampler2D _MainTex;
sampler2D _AnisoDir;
float4 _MainTint;
float4 _SpecularColor;
float _AnisoOffset;
float _Specular;
float _SpecPower;
```

3. Now, we can create our `Lighting` function that will produce the correct Anisotropic effect on our surface. We will use the following code for this:

```
fixed4 LightingAnisotropic(SurfaceAnisoOutput s,
                    fixed3 lightDir, half3
                       viewDir, fixed atten)
{
    fixed3 halfVector = normalize(normalize(lightDir)
                        + normalize(viewDir));

    // The vertex normal dotted with the light vector
    // or direction
    float NdotL = saturate(dot(s.Normal, lightDir));

    // The normalized sum of the vertex normal and
    // per-pixel vectors from our Anisotropic normal
    //map
    fixed3 H = normalize(s.Normal + s.AnisoDirection);
    fixed HdotA = dot(H, halfVector);

    float aniso = max(0, sin(radians((HdotA +
        _AnisoOffset) * 180)));

    float spec = saturate(pow(aniso, s.Gloss * 128) *
            s.Specular);
```

```
            fixed3 albedoColor = s.Albedo * _LightColor0.rgb *
                NdotL;
            fixed3 specColor = _LightColor0.rgb *
                _SpecularColor.rgb * spec;

            fixed4 c;
            c.rgb = (albedoColor + specColor) * atten;
            c.a = s.Alpha;
            return c;
        }
```

4. In order to use this new `Lighting` function, we need to tell the subshader's `#pragma` statement to look for it instead of using one of the built-in `Lighting` functions:

```
CGPROGRAM
#pragma surface surf Anisotropic
```

5. We have also given the Anisotropic normal map its own UVs by declaring the following code in `struct Input`. This isn't entirely necessary, as we could just use the UVs from the main texture; however, this does give us independent control over the tiling of our brushed metal effect so that we can scale it to any size we want:

```
struct Input
{
    float2 uv_MainTex;
    float2 uv_AnisoDir;
};
```

6. We also need to add `struct SurfaceAnisoOutput`, which can be added right after the input struct:

```
struct SurfaceAnisoOutput
{
    fixed3 Albedo;
    fixed3 Normal;
    fixed3 Emission;
    fixed3 AnisoDirection;
    half Specular;
    fixed Gloss;
```

166　Understanding Lighting Models

```
        fixed Alpha;
};
```

7. Finally, we need to use the `surf()` function to pass the correct data to our `Lighting` function. Therefore, we will get the per-pixel information from our Anisotropic normal map and set our Specular parameters as follows:

```
void surf(Input IN, inout SurfaceAnisoOutput o)
{
    half4 c = tex2D(_MainTex, IN.uv_MainTex) *
        _MainTint;
    float3 anisoTex = UnpackNormal(tex2D(_AnisoDir,
                                    IN.uv_AnisoDir));

    o.AnisoDirection = anisoTex;
    o.Specular = _Specular;
    o.Gloss = _SpecPower;
    o.Albedo = c.rgb;
    o.Alpha = c.a;
}
```

8. Save your script and return to the Unity Editor. Select the `AnisotropicMat` material and assign the **Anisotropic Direction** property to the texture we talked about in the *Getting ready* section of this recipe. Afterward, adjust the **Anisotropic Offset** property using the slider and make a note of the changes.

   The Anisotropic normal map allows us to give the surface direction and helps us to disperse the Specular highlight around the surface.

9. Next, try adjusting the other properties to observe how this will affect the final result. For instance, the following settings are what I used within the example code for this book:

Figure 5.28 – Tweaked parameters within the Anisotropic Material

The following screenshot demonstrates the result of our Anisotropic shader:

Figure 5.29 – Tweaking the values of the material provides the following result

How it works...

Let's break down this shader into its core components and explain why we are getting this effect. We will mostly be covering the custom lighting function here, as, at this point, the rest of the shader should be pretty self-explanatory.

First, we start by declaring our `SurfaceAnisoOutput` struct. We need to do this in order to get the per-pixel information from the Anisotropic normal map, and the only way we can do this in a Surface Shader is to use a `tex2D()` function in the `surf()` function. The following code shows the custom surface output structure used in our shader:

```
struct SurfaceAnisoOutput
{
    fixed3 Albedo;
    fixed3 Normal;
    fixed3 Emission;
    fixed3 AnisoDirection;
```

```
        half Specular;
        fixed Gloss;
        fixed Alpha;
};
```

We can use the `SurfaceAnisoOutput` struct as a way of interacting between the lighting function and the surface function. In our scenario, we are storing the per-pixel texture information in the variable called `anisoTex` in our `surf()` function and then passing this data to the `SurfaceAnisoOutput` struct by storing it in the `AnisoDirection` variable. Once we have this, we can use the per-pixel information in the `Lighting` function using `s.AnisoDirection`.

With this data connection set up, we can move on to our actual lighting calculations. This begins by getting the usual out of the way, that is, the half vector. This is so that we don't have to do the full reflection calculation and diffuse lighting, which is the vertex normal dotted with the light vector or direction. The `saturate` function clamps the value within it so that it is never larger than 1.0 and never smaller than 0.0. This is done in Cg with the following lines:

```
fixed3 halfVector = normalize(normalize(lightDir) +
                    normalize(viewDir));
float NdotL = saturate(dot(s.Normal, lightDir));
```

Then, we start the actual modification to the Specular to get the right look. First, we dot the normalized sum of the vertex normal and per-pixel vectors from our Anisotropic normal map with the `halfVector` value that was calculated in the previous step. This gives us a float value that shows a value of 1 as the surface normal, which is modified by the Anisotropic normal map as it becomes parallel with `halfVector` and 0 as it is perpendicular. Finally, we modify this value with a `sin()` function so that, essentially, we can get a darker middle highlight and, ultimately, a ring effect based on `halfVector`. All of the previously mentioned operations are summarized in the following lines of Cg code:

```
fixed3 H = normalize(s.Normal + s.AnisoDirection);
fixed HdotA = dot(H, halfVector);

float aniso = max(0, sin(radians((HdotA + _AnisoOffset) *
                        180)));
```

Finally, we scale the effect of the `aniso` value by taking it to a power of `s.Gloss`, and then globally decrease its strength by multiplying it with `s.Specular`:

```
float spec = saturate(pow(aniso, s.Gloss * 128) * s.Specular);
```

This effect is great for creating more advanced metal types of surfaces, especially the ones that are brushed and appear to have some directionality to them. It also works well for hair or any sort of soft surface with directionality.

6
Physically Based Rendering

Introduced in Unity 5, **physically based rendering** or **PBR** is a shading model that seeks to render graphics in a way that acts similarly to how light works in the real world. All the lighting models we encountered in *Chapter 5*, *Understanding Lighting Models*, were very primitive descriptions of how light behaves. The most important aspect while creating them was *efficiency*. Real-time shading is expensive, and techniques such as Lambertian or Blinn-Phong are a compromise between computational cost and realism.

Having a more powerful GPU has allowed us to write progressively more sophisticated lighting models and rendering engines to simulate how light behaves. This is, in a nutshell, the philosophy behind PBR. As the name suggests, it tries to get as close as possible to the physics behind the processes to give us a unique look at each material. Despite this, the term PBR has been widely used in marketing campaigns and is more of a synonym for **state-of-the-art rendering** rather than a well-defined technique.

Unity implements PBR in two main ways, as follows:

- The first is a completely new lighting model (called Standard). Surface Shaders allow developers to specify the physical properties of a material, but they do not impose actual physical constraints on them. PBR fills this by gap using a lighting model that enforces principles of physics such as **energy conservation** (an object cannot reflect more light than the amount it receives), **microsurface scattering** (rough surfaces reflect light more erratically compared to smooth ones), **Fresnel reflectance** (specular reflections appear at grazing angles), and **surface occlusion** (darkening corners and other geometries that are hard to light). All these aspects, and many others, are used to calculate the Standard lighting model.

- The second aspect that makes PBR so realistic is called **global illumination** (GI) and is the simulation of physically based light transportation. This means that objects are not drawn in the scene as if they were separate entities. They all contribute to the final rendering as light can reflect on them before hitting something else. This aspect is not captured in the shaders themselves but is an essential part of how the rendering engine works. Unfortunately, accurately simulating how light rays bounce over surfaces in real time is beyond the capabilities of modern GPUs. Unity makes some clever optimizations that allow us to retain visual fidelity without sacrificing performance. Some of the most advanced techniques (such as reflections), however, require user input.

All of these aspects will be covered in this chapter. It is important to remember that PBR and GI do not automatically guarantee that your game will be photorealistic. Achieving photorealism is a very challenging task and, like every art, it requires great expertise and exceptional skills.

Previous chapters have repeatedly mentioned PBR without revealing too much about it. If you want to understand not only how PBR works, but also how to get the most out of it, this is the chapter you should read. In this chapter, you will learn how to utilize PBR and the properties it gives us.

In this chapter, we will cover the following recipes:

- Understanding the metallic setup
- Adding transparency to PBR
- Creating mirrors and reflective surfaces
- Baking lights into your scene

By the end of this chapter, you will have a better understanding of what PBR is, how it works, and how it can be utilized through several shader examples.

Technical requirements

You can find all of the code files present in this chapter on GitHub at https://github.com/PacktPublishing/Unity-2021-Shaders-and-Effects-Cookbook-Fourth-Edition/tree/main/Shaders-and-Effects-Cookbook-2021/Assets/Chapter%2006.

Understanding the metallic setup

Unity provides three different types of PBR shaders; they are referred to in the drop-down menu of the material's **Inspector** tab as **Standard**, **Standard (Roughness Setup)**, and **Standard (Specular setup)**. The main difference is that **Standard** and **Standard (Roughness Setup)** expose the **Metallic** property, but **Standard** contains a **Smoothness** property while the second replaces **Smoothness** with **Roughness**. **Standard (Specular setup)** contains **Smoothness** but replaces the **Metallic** property with **Specular**. **Smoothness** and **Roughness** are opposites of each other, so a **Smoothness** value of 1 means a **Roughness** value of 0 and vice versa. You can generally get the same result no matter which shader you use, so it mostly comes down to personal preference.

These setups represent different ways in which you can initialize PBR materials. One of the concepts that has driven PBR is the ability to provide meaningful, physically related properties that artists and developers can tweak and play with. The properties of some materials are easier to represent, indicating how *metallic* they are. For others, it is more important to specify how they reflect light directly through their **specularity**. This recipe will show you how to use the **metallic setup** effectively. It's important to remember that the metallic workflow is not just for metallic materials; it is also a way of defining how materials will look according to how metallic or non-metallic their surface is.

174　Physically Based Rendering

Despite being presented as two different types of shaders, both the **Metallic** and **Specular** setups are generally equally expressive. As shown in the Unity documentation at `http://docs.unity3d.com/Manual/StandardShaderMetallicVsSpecular.html`, and as mentioned earlier, the same materials can usually be recreated with both setups (see the following screenshot):

Figure 6.1 – Standard shader (left) versus Standard (Specular setup) shader (right)

Getting ready

This recipe will use the Standard Shader, so there is no need to create a new one. Follow these steps:

1. Create a new material (`MetallicMat`).
2. From its **Inspector** tab, make sure that **Standard** is selected from its **Shader** drop-down menu.

3. You will also need a textured 3D model. The basic character we used previously (basicCharacter, which is located in the Chapter 03/Models folder of the project) will work perfectly. Drag and drop it into the scene. Afterward, drag and drop the MetallicMat material onto each of the parts of the character. Also, assign the texture for the **material** (skin_man or skin_woman, both of which are located in the Chapter 04/Textures folder) to the **Albedo** property:

Figure 6.2 – Setup for the scene

How to do it...

Two main textures need to be configured in the Standard Shader: **Albedo** and **Metallic**. To use the metallic workflow effectively, we need to initialize these maps correctly. Follow these steps:

1. The **Albedo** map should be initialized with the unlit texture of the 3D model.
2. To create the **Metallic** map, start by duplicating the file for your **Albedo** map. You can do this by selecting the map from the **Project** tab and pressing *Ctrl + D*.
3. Use white (#ffffff) to color the regions of the map that correspond to materials that are made of pure metal.
4. Use black (#000000) for all the other colors. Shades of gray should be used for dusty, weathered, or worn-out metal surfaces, including rust, scratched paint, and so on. Unity only uses the red channel to store the metallic value; the green and blue ones are ignored.

5. Use the alpha channel of the image to provide information about the **Smoothness** property of the material:

Figure 6.3 – An example of a Metallic map opened in Photoshop

For our simple character, the belt and the little ends of the hoodie are the only parts we need to be metallic. I've also made the opacity 55% for the main character, with the belt having a higher opacity of 80%.

6. Assign the **Metallic** map to the material. The **Metallic** slider will disappear as these two properties are now controlled by the map. You may use the **Smoothness** slider to provide a modifier for the map you've provided:

Figure 6.4 – Adjusting the Smoothness property of Metallic Mat (Material)

How it works...

Metals are known to conduct electricity; light is measured in the form of electromagnetic waves, meaning that almost all metals behave similarly compared to non-conductors (often referred to as **insulators**). Conductors tend to reflect most photons (70-100%), resulting in high reflectance. The remaining light is absorbed, rather than diffused, suggesting that conductors have a very dark diffuse component. Insulators, on the other hand, have a low reflectance (4%); the rest of the light is scattered on the surface, contributing to their diffused looks.

In the Standard Shader, purely metallic materials have dark diffuse components, and the color of their specular reflections is determined by the **Albedo** map. Conversely, the diffuse components of purely non-metallic materials are determined by the **Albedo** map; the color of their specular highlights is determined by the color of the incoming light. Following these principles allows the metallic workflow to combine **Albedo** and specular into the **Albedo** map, enforcing physically accurate behaviors. This also lets you save more space, resulting in a significant speed increase at the expense of reduced control over the look of your materials.

See also

For more information about the metallic setup, you can refer to these links:

- **Calibration chart**: How to calibrate a metallic material (`https://docs.unity3d.com/uploads/Main/StandardShaderCalibrationChartMetallic.png`)
- **Material chart**: How to initialize the Standard Shader parameters for common materials (`http://docs.unity3d.com/Manual/StandardShaderMaterialCharts.html`)
- **Quixel Megascans**: A vast library of materials, including textures and PBR parameters (`https://quixel.com/megascans/home`)
- **PBR Texture Conversion**: How traditional shaders can be converted into PBR shaders (`https://marmoset.co/posts/pbr-texture-conversion/`)
- **Substance Designer**: A node-based software for working with PBR (`https://www.substance3d.com/products/substance-designer`)
- **The Theory of Physically-Based Rendering**: A complete guide to PBR (`https://academy.substance3d.com/courses/the-pbr-guide-part-1`)

Adding transparency to PBR

Transparency is such an important aspect in games that the Standard Shader supports three different ways of doing this. This recipe will be useful to you if you need to have realistic materials with transparent or semi-transparent properties. Glasses, bottles, windows, and crystals are good candidates for PBR transparent shaders. This is because you can still have all the realism that's introduced by PBR but with the addition of a transparent or translucent effect. If you need transparency for something different, such as UI elements or pixel art, there are more efficient alternatives. These were explored in the *Creating a transparent material* recipe of *Chapter 4, Working with Texture Mapping*.

> **Important Information**
> To have a transparent standard material, changing the alpha channel of its **Albedo** color property is not enough. Unless you set its **Rendering Mode** property, your material will not appear transparent.

Getting ready

This recipe will use the Standard Shader, so there is no need to create a new one:

1. Create a new material (`TransparencyMat`).
2. Make sure that the **Shader** property is set to either **Standard** or **Standard (Specular setup)** from the material's **Inspector** tab.
3. Assign the newly created material to the 3D object that you want to be transparent:

Figure 6.5 – Project setup

How to do it...

The Standard Shader provides three different types of transparencies. Despite being very similar, they have subtle differences and are used in different contexts.

Semi-transparent materials

Some materials such as clear plastics, crystals, and glass are semi-transparent. This means that they require all the realistic effects of PBR (such as specular highlights and Fresnel refraction and reflection) but allow the geometry behind an object with the material attached to be seen. If this is what you need, follow these steps:

1. From the material's **Inspector** tab, set **Rendering Mode** to **Transparent**.
2. The amount of transparency is determined by the alpha channel of the **Albedo** color or the **Albedo** map (if any). If you click on the box to the right of the **Albedo** section, you'll bring up a **Color** menu. Adjusting the **A** channel will make the item more or less visible:

Figure 6.6 – Changing the Albedo color of the material

3. Set the **A** channel to 4, 6 to create the following effect:

Figure 6.7 – The result of altering the alpha

4. The following screenshot shows the Unity calibration scene with four different highly polished plastic spheres. From left to right, their transparency is increasing. The last sphere is fully transparent, but retains all the added effects of PBR:

Figure 6.8 – Transparent Rendering Mode – Alpha Effect

The **Transparent** rendering mode is perfect for windows, bottles, gems, and headsets.

> **Important Information**
> Note that many transparent materials don't usually project shadows. On top of this, the **Metallic** and **Smoothness** properties of a material can interfere with the transparency effect. A mirror-like surface can have the alpha set to zero, but if it reflects all the incoming light, it won't appear transparent.

Fading objects

Sometimes, you want an object to fully disappear with a fading effect. In this case, specular reflections and Fresnel refraction and reflection should disappear as well. When a fading object is fully transparent, it should also be invisible. To do this, follow these steps:

1. From the material's **Inspector** tab, set **Rendering Mode** to **Fade**.
2. As we did previously, use the alpha channel of the **Albedo** color or map to determine the final transparency:

Figure 6.9 – Changing Rendering Mode to Fade

3. The following screenshot shows four fading spheres. Here, we can see that the PBR effects fade with the sphere as well. As you can see, the last one on the right is almost invisible:

Figure 6.10 – Fade Rendering Mode – Alpha Effect

This rendering mode works best for non-realistic objects, such as holograms, laser rays, faux lights, ghosts, and particle effects.

Solid geometries with holes

Most of the materials that are encountered in a game are solid, meaning that they don't allow light to pass through them. At the same time, many objects have a very complex (yet flat) geometry. Modeling leaves and grass with 3D objects is often overkill. A more efficient approach is to use a quad (rectangle) with a leaf texture. While the leaf itself is solid, the rest of the texture should be fully transparent. If this is what you want, then follow these steps:

1. From the material's **Inspector** tab, set **Rendering Mode** to **Cutout**.
2. Use the **Alpha Cutoff** slider to determine the cutoff threshold. All the pixels in the **Albedo** map with an alpha value less than or equal to **Alpha Cutoff** will be hidden.

   The following screenshot, taken from *Unity Official Tutorials* on PBR (`https://www.youtube.com/watch?v=fD_ho_ofY6A`), shows you how the effect of the **Cutout** rendering mode can be used to create a hole in the geometry:

Figure 6.11 – The effect of the Cutout rendering mode

It's worth noticing that **Cutout** does not allow the back of the geometry to be seen. In the previous example, you can't see the inner volume of the sphere. If you need to do this, you need to create a shader and make sure that the back geometry is not culled.

See also

More information about Albedo and transparency can be found at `http://docs.unity3d.com/Manual/StandardShaderMaterialParameterAlbedoColor.html`.

Creating mirrors and reflective surfaces

Specular materials reflect light when objects are viewed from certain angles. Unfortunately, even the Fresnel reflection, which is one of the most accurate models, does not reflect light from nearby objects correctly. The lighting models we examined in the previous chapters only took light sources into account; they ignored light that is reflected from other surfaces. With what you've learned about shaders so far, making a mirror is simply not possible.

GI makes this possible by providing PBR shaders with information about their surroundings. This allows objects to have not just specular highlights, but also real reflections, which depend on the other objects around them. Real-time reflections are very costly and must be set up and tweaked to work. When done properly, they can be used to create mirror-like surfaces, as shown in the following screenshot:

Figure 6.12 – Mirror-like reflection

Getting ready

This recipe will not feature a new shader. Instead, most of the work will be done directly in the editor. Follow these steps:

1. Create a new scene and place an object(s) into the scene to be reflected. I used the bunny model that's located in the `Chapter 03/Models` folder.
2. Create a quad (**GameObject | 3D Object | Quad**); this will serve as a mirror. I've scaled it up to (`10, 10, 1`), moved it to (`-10, 3 -11`), and rotated it to `-65` in the Y axis to make it easy to see.
3. Create a new material (`MirrorMat`) and attach it to the mirror.
4. Create a new reflection probe by going to **GameObject | Light | Reflection Probe** and place it in front of the quad:

Creating mirrors and reflective surfaces   185

Figure 6.13 – Recipe setup

How to do it...

If you followed the preceding steps correctly, you should have a quad in the middle of your scene, close to a reflection probe. To make it into a mirror, some changes need to be made:

1. Double-check that the shader of the material is set to **Standard** and that **Rendering Mode** is set to **Opaque**.

2. Change its **Metallic** and **Smoothness** properties to 1. You should see the material reflecting the sky more clearly in the **Inspector** view. However, on the main scene, you may see the material within the **Scene** view change to black:

Figure 6.14 – Material settings updated

3. Select the reflection probe and change **Type** to **Realtime** and **Refresh Mode** to **Every frame**. Also, make sure that **Culling Mask** is set to **Everything**.

4. Next, check the **Box Projection** property and then change its **Box Size** and **Box Offset** properties until it is in front of the quad and it encloses all the objects that you want to reflect.

5. To make the item clearer, under **Cubemap capture settings**, change **Resolution** to 2048.

Your reflection probe should now be configured, as shown in the following screenshot:

Figure 6.15 – Settings for Reflection Probe

6. Using these settings, you should see something similar to this:

Figure 6.16 – The mirror image is now working

You may notice that the bunny seems larger in the reflection compared to what's beside it. If your probe is being used for a real mirror, you should check the **Box Projection** flag (in this example, setting the box size to 1, 1, 1 does a pretty good job of making it look like a mirror). If it is used for other reflective surfaces, such as shiny pieces of metal or glass tables, you can uncheck it.

How it works...

When a shader wants information about its surroundings, it is usually provided in a structure called **cube maps**. These were briefly mentioned in *Chapter 2, Creating Your First Shader*, as one of the shader property types, among Color, 2D, Float, and Vector. Loosely speaking, cube maps are the 3D equivalent of 2D textures; they represent a 360-degree view of the world, as seen from a center point.

Unity previews cube maps with a spherical projection, as shown in the following figure:

Figure 6.17 – Cube maps example

When cube maps are attached to a camera, they are referred to as **skyboxes**, since they are used to provide a way to reflect the sky. They can be used to reflect geometries that are not in the actual scene, such as nebulae, clouds, and stars.

The reason why they are called cube maps is because of the way they are created: a cube map is made up of six different textures, each one attached to the face of a cube. You can create a cube map manually or delegate it to a **reflection probe**. You can imagine a reflection probe as a collection of six cameras, creating a 360-degree mapping of the surrounding area. This also gives you an idea as to why probes are so expensive. By creating one in our scene, we allow Unity to know which objects are around the mirror. If you need more reflective surfaces, you can add multiple probes. You don't need to do anything else for the reflection probes to work. The Standard Shaders will use them automatically.

You should notice that when they are set to **Realtime**, they render their cube map at the beginning of every frame. There is a trick to make this faster; if you know that part of the geometry that you want to reflect does not move, you can bake the reflection. This means that Unity can calculate the reflection before starting the game, allowing for more precise (and computationally expensive) calculations. To do this, your reflection probe must be set to **Baked** and will only work for objects that are flagged as **Static**. Static objects cannot move or change, which makes them perfect for terrain, buildings, and props. Every time a static object is moved, Unity will regenerate the cube maps for its baked reflection probes. This might take a few minutes to several hours.

You can mix **Realtime** and **Baked** probes to increase the realism of your game. Baked probes will provide very high-quality reflections and environmental reflections, while the real-time ones can be used to move objects such as cars or mirrors. The *Baking lights into your scene* section will explain how light baking works.

See also

If you are interested in learning more about reflection probes, you should check out these links:

- Unity manual about the reflection probe: `http://docs.unity3d.com/Manual/class-ReflectionProbe.html`
- Box projection and other advanced reflection probe settings: `https://docs.unity3d.com/Manual/AdvancedRefProbe.html`

Baking lights into your scene

Rendering lighting is a very expensive process. Even with state-of-the-art GPUs, accurately calculating the **light transport** (which is how light bounces between surfaces) can take hours. To make this process feasible for games, real-time rendering is essential. Modern engines compromise between realism and efficiency; most of the computation is done beforehand in a process called **light baking**. This recipe will explain how light baking works and how you can get the most out of it.

Getting ready

Light baking requires you to have a scene ready. It should contain geometries and, obviously, lights. For this recipe, we will rely on Unity's standard features so that there is no need to create additional shaders or materials. We will be reusing the map that we used in *Chapter 1*, *Post Processing Stack*. For better control, you might want to access the **Lighting** window. If you don't see it, select **Window** | **Rendering** | **Lighting** from the menu and dock it somewhere that is more convenient for you.

How to do it...

Light baking requires some manual configuration. There are three essential, yet independent, steps that you need to follow.

Configuring the static geometry

Follow these steps to configure the static geometry:

1. Identify all the objects in your scene that do not change position, size, and material. Possible candidates include buildings, walls, terrain, props, trees, and others. In our case, it will be all of the objects aside from `FPSController` and its children.

2. Select these objects and check the **Static** box from the **Inspector** tab, as shown in the following screenshot. If any of the selected objects have children, Unity will ask if you want them to be considered static as well. If they meet the requirements (fixed position, size, and material), select **Yes, change children** in the pop-up box:

Figure 6.18 – Setting the Static property

> **Tip**
> If a light qualifies as a static object but illuminates non-static geometry, make sure that its **Baking** property is set to **Mixed**. If it will only affect static objects, set it to **Baked**.

Configuring the light probes

There are objects in your game that will move, such as the main character, enemies, and the other **non-playable characters** (**NPCs**). If they enter a static region that is illuminated, you might want to surround it with light probes. To do this, follow these steps:

1. From the menu, navigate to **GameObject | Light | Light Probe Group**. A new object called **Light Probe Group** will appear in the **Hierarchy** window.

2. Once selected, eight interconnected spheres will appear. Click and move them around the scene so that they enclose the static region that your characters can enter. The following screenshot shows an example of how light probes can be used to enclose the volume of a static office space:

Figure 6.19 – How light probes can be used to enclose the volume of a static office space

For our example, it would just be the center area that the player can enter:

Figure 6.20 – Adjusting the size of Light Probe Group

3. Select the moving objects that will enter the light probe region.
4. From their **Inspector** tabs, expand their **renderer component** (usually, this is **Mesh Renderer**) and make sure that **Light Probes** is not set to **Off checked** (see the following screenshot):

Figure 6.21 – Ensuring the Light Probes property is not set to Off

Deciding where and when to use light probes is a critical problem; more information about this can be found in the *How it works...* section of this recipe.

Baking the lights

To bake the lights, follow these steps:

1. First, select the lights you'd like to bake. From the **Inspector** tab, confirm that **Mode** is set to **Baked** in the **Light** component:

Figure 6. 22 – Setting the light's Mode to Baked

2. To bake the lights, open the **Lighting** window by going to **Window | Rendering | Lighting**. Once there, select the **Scene** tab.

3. If the **Auto Generate** checkbox is enabled, Unity will automatically execute the baking process in the background. If not, click on **Generate Lighting**.

> **Tip**
> Light baking can take several hours, even for a relatively small scene. If you are constantly moving static objects or lights, Unity will restart the process from scratch, causing a severe slowdown in the editor. You can uncheck the **Auto Generate** checkbox from the **Window | Rendering | Lighting** window to prevent this so that you can decide when to start the process manually.

How it works...

The most complicated part of rendering is transporting the light. During this phase, the GPU calculates how the rays of light bounce between objects. If an object and its lights don't move, this calculation can be done only once as it will never change during the game. Flagging an object as **Static** is how to tell Unity that such an optimization can be made.

Loosely speaking, light baking refers to the process of calculating the GI of a static object and saving it in what is called a **lightmap**. Once baking has been completed, the lightmaps can be seen in the **Baked Lightmaps** tab of the **Lighting** window:

Figure 6.23 – The Baked Lightmaps menu

Clicking on the **Open Preview** button will allow you to see the other maps that were generated, including the **Baked Directionality** map:

Figure 6.24 – A Baked Directionality map

Light baking comes at a great expense: memory. Every static surface is retextured so that it already includes its lighting condition. Let's imagine that you have a forest of trees, all sharing the same texture. Once they have been made static, each tree will have its very own texture. Light baking not only increases the size of your game but can also take up a lot of texture memory if used indiscriminately.

The second aspect that was introduced in this recipe was **light probing**. Light baking produces extremely high-quality results for static geometries but does not work on moving objects. If your character is entering a static region, it can look somehow *detached* from the environment. Its shading will not match the surroundings, resulting in an aesthetically unpleasant result. Other objects, such as **skinned mesh renderers**, will not receive GI, even if they're made static. Baking lights in real time is not possible, although light probes offer an effective alternative. Every light probe samples the GI at a specific point in space. A light probe group can sample several points in space, allowing GI to be interpolated within a specific volume. This allows us to cast a better light on moving objects, even though GI has only been calculated for a few points. It is important to remember that light probes need to enclose a volume to work. It is best to place light probes in regions where there is a sudden change in light conditions. Similar to lightmaps, probes consume memory and should be placed wisely; remember that they only exist for non-static geometry. Since there are no visible objects in the demo scene, this was done purely for demonstration purposes.

Even while using light probes, there are a few aspects that Unity's GI cannot capture. Non-static objects, for instance, cannot reflect light on other objects.

See also

You can read more about light probes at `http://docs.unity3d.com/Manual/LightProbes.html`.

7
Vertex Functions

The term *shader* originates from the fact that **C for Graphics** (**Cg**) has been mainly used to simulate realistic lighting conditions (shadows) on **three-dimensional** (**3D**) models. Despite this, shaders are now much more than that. They not only define the way objects are going to look, but they can also redefine their shapes entirely. If you want to learn how to manipulate the geometry of a 3D object via shaders, this is the chapter for you.

In *Chapter 2*, *Creating Your First Shader*, we explained that 3D models are not just a collection of triangles. Each vertex can contain data that is essential to render the model itself correctly. This chapter will explore how to access this information in order to use it in a shader. We will also explore in detail how the geometry of an object can be deformed simply by using Cg code.

In this chapter, you will learn the following recipes:

- Accessing a vertex color in a Surface Shader
- Animating vertices in a Surface Shader
- Extruding your models
- Implementing a snow shader
- Implementing a volumetric explosion

By the end of this chapter, you will have seen several different ways that you can manipulate the geometry of a 3D object via shaders rather than by manipulating the mesh of the object itself.

Technical requirements

This chapter was created with Unity 2021.1.9f1 but should work in future versions of Unity with minimal revisions.

You can find the code files present in this chapter on GitHub at `https://github.com/PacktPublishing/Unity-2021-Shaders-and-Effects-Cookbook-Fourth-Edition/tree/main/Shaders-and-Effects-Cookbook-2021/Assets/Chapter%2007`.

Accessing a vertex color in a Surface Shader

Let's start this chapter by taking a look at how we can access the information of a model's vertex using the vertex function in a Surface Shader. This will arm us with the knowledge to start utilizing the elements contained within a model's vertex to create really useful and visually appealing effects.

A vertex in a vertex function can return information about itself that we need to be aware of. You can actually retrieve the vertices' normal directions as a `float3` value and the position of the vertex as `float3`, and you can even store color values in each vertex and return that color as `float4`. This is what we will take a look at in this recipe. We need to see how to store color information and retrieve this stored color information inside each vertex of a Surface Shader.

Getting ready

In order to write this shader, we need to prepare a few assets.

To view the colors of a vertex, we need to have a model that has had color applied to its vertices. While you could use Unity to apply colors, you would have to write a tool to allow an individual to apply the colors or write some scripts to achieve the color application.

In the case of this recipe, you can use a 3D modeling tool such as Maya or Blender to apply the colors to our model. There is a model available in the example code provided with the book in the `Chapter 07 | Models` folder (`VertexColorObject.fbx`), which you can obtain at the book's GitHub page at `https://github.com/PacktPublishing/Unity-2021-Shaders-and-Effects-Cookbook-Fourth-Edition`.

The following steps will set us up to create this Vertex Shader:

1. Create a new scene and place the imported model (`VertexColorObject`) in the scene.
2. Create a new **Shader** (`SimpleVertexColor`) and **Material** (`SimpleVertexColorMat`).
3. When completed, assign the shader to the material and then the material to the imported model.

Your scene should now look similar to this:

Figure 7.1 – Recipe setup

How to do it...

With our scene, shader, and material created and ready to go, we can begin to write the code for our shader. Launch the shader by double-clicking on it in the **Project** tab in the Unity Editor. Perform the following steps:

1. As we are creating a very simple shader, we will not need to include any properties in our `Properties` block. We will still include a `Global Color Tint`, just to stay consistent with the other shaders in this book. Replace the code within the `Properties` block of your shader with the following:

   ```
   Properties
   {
       _MainTint("Global Color Tint", Color) = (1,1,1,1)
   }
   ```

2. This next step tells Unity that we will be including a vertex function in our shader. To do this, we will replace the Standard `fullforwardshadows` part of our `#pragma` statement with the following:

   ```
   CGPROGRAM
   #pragma surface surf Lambert vertex:vert
   ```

3. As usual, if we have included properties in our `Properties` block, we must make sure to create a corresponding variable in our `CGPROGRAM` statement. Enter the following code just below the `#pragma target 3.0` statement, replacing the originally given parameters:

   ```
   float4 _MainTint;
   ```

4. We now turn our attention to the `Input` struct. Add a new variable so that our `surf()` function can access the data given to us by our `vert()` function:

   ```
   struct Input
   {
       float2 uv_MainTex;
       float4 vertColor;
   };
   ```

5. Now, start by writing a simple `vert()` function to gain access to the colors stored in each vertex of our mesh:

   ```
   void vert(inout appdata_full v, out Input o)
   {
       UNITY_INITIALIZE_OUTPUT(Input,o);
       o.vertColor = v.color;
   }
   ```

6. Finally, use the vertex color data from our `Input` struct to be assigned to the `o.Albedo` parameters in the built-in `SurfaceOutput` struct:

   ```
   void surf (Input IN, inout SurfaceOutput o)
   {
       o.Albedo = IN.vertColor.rgb * _MainTint.rgb;
   }
   ```

7. With our code completed, re-enter the Unity Editor and let the shader compile. If all goes well, you should see something similar to this:

Figure 7.2 – Completed shader result

How it works...

Unity provides us with a way to access the vertex information of the model to which a shader is attached. This gives us the power to modify things such as the vertices' position and color. With this recipe, we have imported a mesh from Maya (although just about any 3D software application can be used), where vertex colors were added to Verts. You'll notice that by importing the model, the default material will not display the vertex colors. We actually have to write a shader to extract the vertex color and display it on the surface of the model. Unity provides us with a lot of built-in functionality when using Surface Shaders, which makes the process of extracting this vertex information quick and efficient.

Our first task is to tell Unity that we will be using a vertex function when creating our shader. We do this by adding the vertex:vert parameter to the #pragma statement of CGPROGRAM. This automatically makes Unity look for a vertex function named vert() when it goes to compile the shader. If it doesn't find one, Unity will throw a compiling error and ask you to add a vert() function to your shader.

This brings us to our next step. We have to actually code the vert() function, as seen in *Step 5* of this recipe. We first use a built-in macro to make sure that the o variable is initialized to 0. If it doesn't have anything that is a requirement if you are targeting DirectX 11 or above.

> **Note**
>
> For more information on the macro, as well as all of the other macros that ShaderLab has to offer, check out https://docs.unity3d.com/Manual/SL-BuiltinMacros.html.

By having this function, we can access the appdata_full built-in data struct. This built-in struct is where the vertex information is stored. So, we then extract the vertex color information by passing it to our Input struct by adding the code, o.vertColor = v.color.

The `o` variable represents our `Input` struct and the `v` variable is our `appdata_full` vertex data. In this case, we are simply taking the color information from the `appdata_full` struct and putting it in our `Input` struct. Once the vertex color is in our `Input` struct, we can use it in our `surf()` function. In the case of this recipe, we simply apply the color of the `o.Albedo` parameter to the built-in `SurfaceOutput` struct.

There's more...

You can also access the fourth component from the `vert` color data. If you notice, the `vertColor` variable we declared in the `Input` struct is of the `float4` type. This means that we are also passing the alpha value of the vertex colors. Knowing this, you can use it to your advantage to store a fourth vertex channel that can perform effects such as transparency or to give yourself one more mask to blend two textures. It's really up to you and your production to determine if you really need to use the fourth component, but it is worth mentioning here.

Animating vertices in a Surface Shader

Now we know how to access data on a per-vertex basis, let's expand our knowledge set to include other types of data and the position of a vertex.

Using a vertex function, we can access the position of each vertex in a mesh. This allows us to actually modify each individual vertex while the shader does the processing.

In this recipe, we will create a shader that will allow us to modify the positions of each vertex on a mesh with a sine wave. This technique can be used to create animations for objects such as flags or waves on an ocean.

Getting ready

Let's gather our assets together so that we can create the code for our Vertex Shader. Follow these steps:

1. Create a new scene and place a plane mesh in the center of the scene (**GameObject | 3D Object | Plane**).

    The `Plane` object created may seem to be a single quad but, in fact, has 121 verts that we are going to be moving. Using a quad would provide unexpected results. To check for yourself, select the circle to the right of the `Plane` object from the **Inspector** tab on the **Mesh Filter** component and note the properties displayed when selected in the **Select Mesh** menu.

Figure 7.3 – The Plane mesh's properties

2. Create a new shader (`VertexAnimation`) and material (`VertexAnimationMat`).
3. Finally, assign the shader to the material and the material to the plane mesh.

Your scene should look similar to this:

Figure 7.4 – Recipe setup

How to do it...

With our scene ready to go, let's double-click on our newly created shader to open it in the code editor. Proceed as follows:

1. Let's start with our shader and populate the `Properties` block:

```
Properties
{
    _MainTex ("Base (RGB)", 2D) = "white" {}
    _tintAmount ("Tint Amount", Range(0,1)) = 0.5
    _ColorA ("Color A", Color) = (1,1,1,1)
    _ColorB ("Color B", Color) = (1,1,1,1)
    _Speed ("Wave Speed", Range(0.1, 80)) = 5
    _Frequency ("Wave Frequency", Range(0, 5)) = 3.16
    _Amplitude ("Wave Amplitude", Range(-1, 1)) = 1
}
```

2. Add the following code to the `#pragma` statement to inform Unity that we are going to use a vertex function::

```
CGPROGRAM
#pragma surface surf Lambert vertex:vert
```

3. In order to access the values that have been given to us by our properties, declare a corresponding variable in our `CGPROGRAM` block:

```
sampler2D _MainTex;
float4 _ColorA;
float4 _ColorB;
float _tintAmount;
float _Speed;
float _Frequency;
float _Amplitude;
float _OffsetVal;
```

4. Use the vertex position modification as a `vert` color as well. This will allow us to tint our object:

```
struct Input
{
    float2 uv_MainTex;
    float3 vertColor;
};
```

5. At this point, perform vertex modification using a sine wave and vertex function. Enter the following code after the `Input` struct:

```
void vert(inout appdata_full v, out Input o)
{
    UNITY_INITIALIZE_OUTPUT(Input, o);

    float time = _Time * _Speed;
```

```
            float waveValueA = sin(time + v.vertex.x *
                            _Frequency) * _Amplitude;

            v.vertex.xyz = float3(v.vertex.x, v.vertex.y +
                            waveValueA, v.vertex.z);

            v.normal = normalize(float3(v.normal.x +
                        waveValueA, v.normal.y, v.normal.z));

            o.vertColor = float3(waveValueA, waveValueA,
                            waveValueA);
        }
```

6. Finally, complete our shader by performing a `lerp()` function between two colors so that we can tint the peaks and valleys of our new mesh, modified by our vertex function:

```
    void surf (Input IN, inout SurfaceOutput o)
    {
        half4 c = tex2D (_MainTex, IN.uv_MainTex);
        float3 tintColor = lerp(_ColorA, _ColorB,
                            IN.vertColor).rgb;
        o.Albedo = c.rgb * (tintColor * _tintAmount);
        o.Alpha = c.a;
    }
```

7. After completing the code for your shader, switch back to Unity and let the shader compile. Once compiled, select **Material** and set the **Base (RGB) Texture** property to the `UV Checker` material that is included in the `Chapter 07 | Textures` folder of this book's example code.

208   Vertex Functions

8. From there, assign **Color A** and **Color B** to different colors. After the changes, you should see something similar to this:

Figure 7.5 – Final version of the shader

Play the game, and you should notice how over time the shader will affect the vertices of the given plane object! You can see how this looks here:

Figure 7.6 – The vertices being adjusted over time

How it works...

This particular shader uses the same concept from the last recipe, except that this time, we are modifying the positions of the vertices in the mesh. This is really useful if you don't want to rig up simple objects such as a flag, and then animate them using a skeleton structure or hierarchy of transforms.

We simply create a sine wave value using the `sin()` function that is built into the Cg language. After calculating this value, we add it to the *y* value of each vertex position, creating a wave-like effect.

We also modified the normal on the mesh just to give it more realistic shading based on the sine wave value.

You will see how easy it is to perform more complex vertex effects by utilizing the built-in vertex parameters that Surface Shaders give us.

Extruding your models

One of the biggest problems in games is repetition. Creating new content is a time-consuming task, and when you have to face thousands of enemies, chances are that they will all look the same. A relatively cheap technique to add variation to your models is using a shader that alters their basic geometry. This recipe will show you a technique called **normal extrusion**, which can be used to create a chubbier or skinnier version of a model, as shown in the following screenshot of a soldier from the Unity camp demo:

Figure 7.7 – Using normal extrusion to adjust a model's visuals

For ease of use, I have provided a prefab of the soldier in the example code for this book under the `Chapter 07 | Prefabs` folder.

Getting ready

For this recipe, you need to have access to the shader used by the model that you want to alter. Once you have it, we duplicate it so that we can edit it safely. This is how it can be done:

1. Find the shader your model is using and, once selected, duplicate it by pressing *Ctrl* + *D*. If it is just using the Standard Shader, as in this example, it is also possible to just create a new Standard Material shader. Either way, rename this new shader `NormalExtrusion`.
2. Duplicate the original material of the model and assign the cloned shader to it.
3. Assign the new material to your model (`NormalExtrusionMat`) and start editing it.

In order for this effect to work, your model should have **normals**.

How to do it...

To create this effect, start by modifying the duplicated shader, as follows:

1. Let's start by adding a property to our shader, which will be used to modulate its extrusion. The range presented here goes from `-0.0001` to `0.0001`, but you might have to adjust this according to your own needs:

   ```
   _Amount ("Extrusion Amount", Range(-0.0001, 0.0001)) = 0
   ```

2. Couple the property with its respective variable:

   ```
   float _Amount;
   ```

3. Change the `#pragma` directive so that it now uses a vertex modifier. You can do this by adding `vertex:function_name` at the end of it. In our case, we have called the `vert` function:

   ```
   #pragma surface surf Standard vertex:vert
   ```

4. Add the following vertex modifier:

   ```
   void vert (inout appdata_full v)
   {
       v.vertex.xyz += v.normal * _Amount;
   }
   ```

5. The shader is now ready; you can use the **Extrusion Amount** slider in the material's **Inspector** tab to make your model skinnier or chubbier. Also, feel free to create a clone of the material in order to have different extrusion amounts for each character:

Figure 7.8 – The results of modifying the Extrusion Amount parameter

How it works...

Surface Shaders work in two steps. In all the previous chapters, we only explored their last one: the surface function. There is another function that can be used: the vertex modifier. This takes the data structure of a vertex (which is usually called appdata_full) and applies a transformation to it. This gives us the freedom to do virtually anything with the geometry of our model. We signal to the **graphics processing unit** (**GPU**) that such a function exists by adding vertex:vert to the #pragma directive of the Surface Shader. You can refer to *Chapter 8*, *Fragment Shaders and Grab Passes* to learn how vertex modifiers can be defined in a Vertex and Fragment Shader instead.

One of the simplest yet effective techniques that can be used to alter the geometry of a model is that of normal extrusion. This works by projecting a vertex along its normal direction and is done with the following line of code:

```
v.vertex.xyz += v.normal * _Amount;
```

The position of a vertex is displaced by _Amount units toward the vertex normal. If _Amount gets too high, the results can be quite unpleasant. With smaller values, however, you can add a lot of variation to your models.

There's more...

If you have multiple enemies and want each one to have its own weight, you have to create a different material for each one of them. This is necessary as materials are normally shared between models, and changing one will change all of them. There are several ways in which you can do this; the quickest one is to create a script that automatically does it for you. The following script, once attached to an object with a `Renderer`, will duplicate its first material and set the `_Amount` property automatically:

```
using UnityEngine;
public class NormalExtruder : MonoBehaviour
{
    [Range(-0.0001f, 0.0001f)]
    public float amount = 0;
    // Use this for initialization
    void Start()
    {
        Material =
            GetComponent<Renderer>().sharedMaterial;
        Material newMaterial = new Material(material);
        newMaterial.SetFloat("_Amount", amount);
        GetComponent<Renderer>().material = newMaterial;
    }
}
```

Adding extrusion maps

This technique can actually be improved even further. We can add an extra texture (or use the alpha channel of the main one) to indicate the amount of extrusion. This allows for much better control over which parts are raised or lowered. The following code snippet shows you how it is possible to achieve such an effect (the main difference from what we've done before is shown in bold):

```
Shader "CookbookShaders/Chapter 07/Normal Extrusion Map"
{
    Properties
    {
        _MainTex ("Texture", 2D) = "white" {}
        _ExtrusionTex ("Extrusion map", 2D) = "white" {}
```

```
    _Amount("Extrusion Amount", Range(-0.0001, 0.0001)) = 0
}
SubShader
{
  Tags{ "RenderType" = "Opaque" }

  CGPROGRAM
  #pragma surface surf Standard vertex:vert
  struct Input
  {
    float2 uv_MainTex;
  };

  float _Amount;

  sampler2D _ExtrusionTex;

  void vert(inout appdata_full v)
  {
      float4 tex = tex2Dlod (_ExtrusionTex,
                  float4(v.texcoord.xy,0,0));
      float extrusion = tex.r * 2 - 1;
      v.vertex.xyz += v.normal * _Amount * extrusion;
  }

  sampler2D _MainTex;
  void surf(Input IN, inout SurfaceOutputStandard o)
  {
      float4 tex = tex2D(_ExtrusionTex, IN.uv_MainTex);
      float extrusion = abs(tex.r * 2 - 1);

      o.Albedo = tex2D(_MainTex, IN.uv_MainTex).rgb;
      o.Albedo = lerp(o.Albedo.rgb, float3(0, 0, 0),
                  extrusion * _Amount / 0.0001 * 1.1);
  }
```

```
    ENDCG
    }

    Fallback "Diffuse"
}
```

The red channel of `_ExtrusionTex` is used as a multiplying coefficient for normal extrusion. A value of `0.5` leaves the model unaffected; darker or lighter shades are used to extrude vertices inward or outward, respectively. You should note that in order to sample a texture within a vertex modifier, `tex2Dlod` should be used instead of `tex2D`.

> **Note**
>
> In shaders, color channels go from `0` to `1`, although sometimes you need to represent negative values as well (such as inward extrusion). When this is the case, treat `0.5` as `0`; consider having smaller values as negative and higher values as positive. This is exactly what happens with normals, which are usually encoded in **Red-Green-Blue** (**RGB**) textures. The `UnpackNormal()` function is used to map a value in the range (`0,1`) on the range (`-1,+1`). Mathematically speaking, this is equivalent to `tex.r * 2 -1`.

Extrusion maps are perfect for zombifying characters by shrinking the skin to highlight the shape of the bones underneath. The following screenshot shows you how a healthy soldier can be transformed into a corpse using just a shader and extrusion map. Compared to the previous example, you may notice how the clothing is unaffected. The shader used in the following screenshot also darkens the extruded regions to give an even more emaciated look to the soldier:

Figure 7.9 – The zombified character

Implementing a snow shader

The simulation of snow has always been a challenge in games. The vast majority of games simply include snow directly in the model's texture so that their tops look white. However, what if one of these objects starts rotating? Snow is not just a lick of paint on a surface; it is a proper accumulation of material and should be treated as such. This recipe shows you how to give a snowy look to your models using just a shader.

This effect is achieved in two steps. First, white is used for all the triangles facing the sky. Second, their vertices are extruded to simulate the effect of snow accumulation. You can see the result in the following screenshot:

Figure 7.10 – Result of the recipe

> **Important Note**
> Keep in mind that this recipe does not aim to create a photorealistic snow effect. It provides a good starting point, but it is up to you to create the right textures and find the right parameters to make it fit your game.

Getting ready

This effect is purely based on shaders. We will need to do the following:

1. Create a new shader for the snow effect (`SnowShader`).
2. Create a new material for the shader (`SnowMat`).

216   Vertex Functions

3. Assign the newly created material to the object that you want to be snowy and assign a color so that it's easier to tell where the snow is:

Figure 7.11 – Recipe setup

How to do it...

To create a snowy effect, open your shader and make the following changes:

1. Replace the properties of the shader with the following ones:

```
_Color("Main Color", Color) = (1.0,1.0,1.0,1.0)
_MainTex("Base (RGB)", 2D) = "white" {}
_Bump("Bump", 2D) = "bump" {}
_Snow("Level of snow", Range(-1.0, 1.0)) = 0.5
_SnowColor("Color of snow", Color) = (1.0,1.0,1.0,1.0)
_SnowDirection("Direction of snow", Vector) = (0,1,0)
_SnowDepth("Depth of snow", Range(0,1)) = 0
```

2. Complete them with their relative variables:

```
sampler2D _MainTex;
sampler2D _Bump;
float _Snow;
float4 _SnowColor;
float4 _Color;
```

Implementing a snow shader

```
float4 _SnowDirection;
float _SnowDepth;
```

3. Replace the Input structure with the following one:

```
struct Input
{
    float2 uv_MainTex;
    float2 uv_Bump;
    float3 worldNormal;
    INTERNAL_DATA
};
```

4. Replace the surface function with the following one. It will color the snowy parts of the model white:

```
void surf(Input IN, inout SurfaceOutputStandard o)
{
    half4 c = tex2D(_MainTex, IN.uv_MainTex);

    o.Normal = UnpackNormal(tex2D(_Bump, IN.uv_Bump));

    if (dot(WorldNormalVector(IN, o.Normal),
        _SnowDirection.xyz) >= _Snow)
    {
        o.Albedo = _SnowColor.rgb;
    }
    else
    {
        o.Albedo = c.rgb * _Color;
    }

    o.Alpha = 1;
}
```

5. Configure the #pragma directive so that it uses vertex modifiers:

```
#pragma surface surf Standard vertex:vert
```

6. Add the following vertex modifiers, which extrude the vertices covered in snow:

```
void vert(inout appdata_full v)
{
   float4 sn = mul(UNITY_MATRIX_IT_MV, _SnowDirection);

   if (dot(v.normal, sn.xyz) >= _Snow)
   {
      v.vertex.xyz += (sn.xyz + v.normal) * _SnowDepth *
         _Snow;
   }
}
```

7. You can now use the material's **Inspector** tab to select how much of your model is going to be covered and how thick the snow should be:

Figure 7.12 – Adjusting the Level of Snow and Depth of Snow properties

How it works...

This shader works in two steps:

- Coloring the surface
- Altering the geometry

Coloring the surface

The first step alters the color of the triangles that are facing the sky. It affects all the triangles with a normal direction similar to `_SnowDirection`. As seen before in *Chapter 5*, *Understanding Lighting Models*, comparing unit vectors can be done using the **dot product**. When two vectors are orthogonal, their dot product is 0; it is 1 (or -1) when they are parallel to each other. The `_Snow` property is used to decide how aligned they should be in order to be considered as facing the sky.

If you look closely at the surface function, you can see that we are not dotting the normal and snow direction directly. This is because they are usually defined in a different space. The snow direction is expressed in world coordinates, while the object normals are usually relative to the model itself. If we rotate the model, its normals will not change, which is not what we want. To fix this, we need to convert the normals from their object coordinates to world coordinates. This is done with the `WorldNormalVector()` function, as seen in the following code snippet:

```
if (dot(WorldNormalVector(IN, o.Normal),
    _SnowDirection.xyz) >= _Snow)
{
   o.Albedo = _SnowColor.rgb;
}
else
{
   o.Albedo = c.rgb * _Color;
}
```

This shader simply colors the model white; a more advanced one should initialize the `SurfaceOutputStandard` structure with textures and parameters from a realistic snow material.

Altering the geometry

The second effect of this shader alters the geometry to simulate the accumulation of snow. Firstly, we identify which triangles have been colored white by testing the same condition used in the surface function. This time, unfortunately, we cannot rely on `WorldNormalVector()` as the `SurfaceOutputStandard` structure is not yet initialized in the vertex modifier. We use this other method instead, which converts `_SnowDirection` to object coordinates:

```
float4 sn = mul(UNITY_MATRIX_IT_MV, _SnowDirection);
```

Then, we can extrude the geometry to simulate the accumulation of snow:

```
if (dot(v.normal, sn.xyz) >= _Snow)
{
    v.vertex.xyz += (sn.xyz + v.normal) * _SnowDepth * _Snow;
}
```

Once again, this is a very basic effect. You could use a texture map to control the accumulation of snow more precisely or give a peculiar, uneven look.

See also

If you need high-quality snow effects and props for your game, you can also check these resources on the Unity Asset Store:

- **Winter Suite (US Dollars (USD) $30)**: A much more sophisticated version of the snow shader presented in this recipe can be found at `https://assetstore.unity.com/packages/vfx/shaders/winter-suite-13927`.
- **Winter Pack ($60)**: A very realistic set of props and materials for snowy environments can be found at `https://assetstore.unity.com/packages/3d/environments/winter-pack-13316`.

Implementing a volumetric explosion

The art of game development is a clever trade-off between realism and efficiency. This is particularly true for explosions; they are at the heart of many games, yet the physics behind them is often beyond the computational power of modern machines. Explosions are, essentially, nothing more than very hot balls of gas; hence, the only way to correctly simulate them is by integrating a fluid simulation into your game. As you can imagine, this is unfeasible for a runtime application, and many games simulate them simply with particles. When an object explodes, it is common to simply instantiate fire, smoke, and debris particles so that together they can achieve believable results. This approach, unfortunately, is not very realistic and is easy to spot. There is an intermediate technique that can be used to achieve a much more realistic effect: volumetric explosions. The idea behind this concept is that explosions are not treated like a bunch of particles; they are evolving 3D objects, not just flat **two-dimensional** (2D) textures.

Getting ready

Complete this recipe with the following steps:

1. Create a new shader for this effect (`VolumetricExplosion`).
2. Create a new material to host the shader (`VolumetricExplosionMat`).
3. Attach the material to a sphere. You can create one directly from the editor, navigating to **GameObject** | **3D Object** | **Sphere**:

Figure 7.13 – Recipe setup

> **Tip**
> This recipe works well with the standard Unity Sphere, but if you need big explosions, you might need to use a high-poly sphere. In fact, a vertex function can only modify the vertices of a mesh. All the other points will be interpolated using the positions of the nearby vertices. Fewer vertices mean a lower resolution for your explosions.

4. For this recipe, you will also need a ramp texture that has, in a gradient, all the colors your explosions will have. You can create a texture such as this one using **GNU Image Manipulation Program** (**GIMP**) or Photoshop:

Figure 7.14 – The example ramp texture used in this recipe

222 Vertex Functions

> **Note**
> You can find this image (`explosionRamp`) in the `Chapter 07 | Textures` folder in the example code provided with this book.

5. Once you have the picture, import it to Unity. Then, from its **Inspector** tab, make sure that **Filter Mode** is set to **Bilinear** and that **Wrap Mode** is set to **Clamp**. These two settings make sure that the ramp texture is sampled smoothly:

Figure 7.15 – Setting the Wrap Mode and Filter Mode properties

6. Lastly, you will need a noisy texture. You can search on the internet for freely available noise textures. The most commonly used ones are generated using Perlin noise. I have included an example in the `Chapter 07 | Textures` folder for your use:

Figure 7.16 – Example of the noise texture

How to do it...

This effect works in two steps: a vertex function to change the geometry, and a surface function to give it the right color. The steps are listed here:

1. Remove the current properties and add the following properties to the shader:

```
Properties
{
    _RampTex("Color Ramp", 2D) = "white" {}
    _RampOffset("Ramp offset", Range(-0.5,0.5))= 0

    _NoiseTex("Noise Texture", 2D) = "gray" {}
    _Period("Period", Range(0,1)) = 0.5

    _Amount("_Amount", Range(0, 1.0)) = 0.1
    _ClipRange("ClipRange", Range(0,1)) = 1
}
```

2. Add their relative variables so that the Cg code of the shader can actually access them:

```
sampler2D _RampTex;
half _RampOffset;

sampler2D _NoiseTex;
float _Period;

half _Amount;
half _ClipRange;
```

3. Change the Input structure so that it receives the UV data of the ramp texture:

```
struct Input
{
    float2 uv_NoiseTex;
};
```

4. Add the following vertex function:

```
void vert(inout appdata_full v)
{
    float disp = tex2Dlod(_NoiseTex,
                    float4(v.texcoord.xy, 0, 0)).r;
    float time = sin(_Time[3] * _Period + disp * 10);
    v.vertex.xyz += v.normal * disp * _Amount * time;
}
```

5. Add the following surface function:

```
void surf(Input IN, inout SurfaceOutput o)
{
    float3 noise = tex2D(_NoiseTex, IN.uv_NoiseTex);

    float n = saturate(noise.r + _RampOffset);
```

```
        clip(_ClipRange - n);

        half4 c = tex2D(_RampTex, float2(n,0.5));

        o.Albedo = c.rgb;
        o.Emission = c.rgb*c.a;
    }
```

6. We specify the vertex function in the #pragma directive, adding the nolightmap parameter to prevent Unity from adding realistic lighting to our explosion:

    ```
    #pragma surface surf Lambert vertex:vert nolightmap
    ```

7. The last step is to select the material and, from its **Inspector** tab, attach the two textures in the relative slots:

Figure 7.17 – Attaching the Color Ramp and Noise Texture files

8. This is animated material, meaning that it evolves over time. You can watch the material changing in the editor by clicking on **Always Refresh** from the **Scene** window:

Figure 7.18 – Enabling the Always Refresh option

How it works...

If you are reading this recipe, you should already be familiar with how Surface Shaders and vertex modifiers work. The main idea behind this effect is to alter the geometry of the sphere in a seemingly chaotic way, exactly as it happens in a real explosion. The following screenshot shows you what such an explosion will look like inside the editor. You can see that the original mesh has been heavily deformed:

Figure 7.19 – The mesh deformation

The vertex function is a variant of a technique called normal extrusion introduced in the *Extruding your models* recipe of this chapter. The difference here is that the amount of extrusion is determined by both the time and noise texture.

> **Tip**
>
> When you need a random number in Unity, you can rely on the Random. Range() function. There is no standard way to get random numbers in a shader, so the easiest way is to sample a noise texture.

There is no standard way to do this, so take this as an example only:

```
float time = sin(_Time[3] *_Period + disp.r*10);
```

The built-in _Time[3] variable is used to get the current time from within the shader, and the red channel of the disp.r noise texture is used to make sure that each vertex moves independently. The sin() function makes the vertices go up and down, simulating the chaotic behavior of an explosion. Then, the normal extrusion takes place:

```
v.vertex.xyz += v.normal * disp.r * _Amount * time;
```

You should play with these numbers and variables until you find a pattern of movement that you are happy with.

The last part of the effect is achieved by the surface function. Here, the noise texture is used to sample a random color from the ramp texture. However, two more aspects are worth noting. The first one is the introduction of `_RampOffset`. Its usage forces the explosion to sample colors from the left or right side of the texture. With positive values, the surface of the explosion tends to show more gray tones—exactly what happens when it is dissolving. You can use `_RampOffset` to determine how much fire or smoke there should be in your explosion. The second aspect introduced in the surface function is the usage of `clip()`. What `clip()` does is it clips (removes) pixels from the rendering pipeline. When invoked with a negative value, the current pixel is not drawn. This effect is controlled by `_ClipRange`, which determines which pixels of the volumetric explosions are going to be transparent.

By controlling both `_RampOffset` and `_ClipRange`, you have full control and can determine how the explosion behaves and dissolves.

There's more...

The shader presented in this recipe makes a sphere look like an explosion. If you really want to use it, you should couple it with some scripts to get the most out of it. The best thing to do is to create an explosion object and make it into a prefab so that you can reuse it every time you need to. You can do this by dragging the sphere back into the **Project** window. Once this is done, you can create as many explosions as you want using the `Instantiate()` function.

It is worth noticing, however, that all the objects with the same material share the same look. If you have multiple explosions at the same time, they should not use the same material. When you are instantiating a new explosion, you should also duplicate its material. You can do this easily with this piece of code:

```
GameObject explosion = Instantiate(explosionPrefab) as GameObject;
Renderer = explosion.GetComponent<Renderer>();
Material = new Material(renderer.sharedMaterial);
renderer.material = material;
```

Lastly, if you are going to use this shader in a realistic way, you should attach a script to it that changes its size, `_RampOffset`, and `_ClipRange` according to the type of explosion that you want to recreate.

See also

- Much more can be done to make explosions realistic. The approach presented in this recipe only creates an empty shell; inside it, the explosion is actually empty. An easy trick to improve this is to create particles inside it. However, you can only go so far with this. The short movie *The Butterfly Effect* (http://unity3d.com/pages/butterfly), created by Unity Technologies in collaboration with Passion Pictures and Nvidia, is the perfect example. It is based on the same concept of altering the geometry of a sphere, but it renders it with a technique called **volume ray casting**. In a nutshell, it renders the geometry as if it's full. You can see an example in the following screenshot:

Figure 7.20 – An explosion example

- If you are looking for high-quality explosions, check out Pyro Technix (https://assetstore.unity.com/packages/vfx/shaders/pyro-technix-16925) in the Asset Store. It includes volumetric explosions and couples them with realistic shockwaves.

8
Fragment Shaders and Grab Passes

So far, we have relied on Surface Shaders. They have been designed to simplify the way shader coding works, providing meaningful tools for artists. If we want to push our knowledge of shaders further, we need to venture into the territory of Vertex and Fragment Shaders.

Compared to Surface Shaders, Vertex and Fragment Shaders come with little to no information about the physical properties that determine how light reflects on surfaces. What they lack in expressivity, they compensate for with power. Vertex and Fragment Shaders are not limited by physical constraints and are perfect for non-photorealistic effects. This chapter will focus on a technique called the **grab pass**, which allows these shaders to simulate deformations.

In this chapter, we will cover the following recipes:

- Understanding Vertex and Fragment Shaders
- Using grab passes to draw behind objects
- Implementing a Glass Shader
- Implementing a Water Shader for 2D games

Technical requirements

You can find the code samples present in this chapter on GitHub at `https://github.com/PacktPublishing/Unity-2021-Shaders-and-Effects-Cookbook-Fourth-Edition/tree/main/Shaders-and-Effects-Cookbook-2021/Assets/Chapter%2008`.

Understanding Vertex and Fragment Shaders

The best way to understand how Vertex and Fragment Shaders work is by creating one yourself. This recipe will show you how to write one of these shaders, which will simply apply a texture to a model and multiply it by a given color, as shown in the following screenshot:

Figure 8.1 – Result of the following recipe

Notice how it works similarly to how the Multiply filter in Photoshop works. That's because we will be doing the same calculation that's done there!

The shader presented here is very simple, and it will be used as a starting base for all the other Vertex and Fragment Shaders.

Getting ready

For this recipe, we will need a new shader. Follow these steps:

1. Create a new shader (`Multiply`).
2. Create a new material (`MultiplyMat`) and assign the shader to it.

3. Bring the soldier prefab from the `Chapter 07 | Prefabs` folder into the scene and attach the new material to the prefab's head. To do this, from the **Hierarchy** window, select the **Soldier** child of the **Soldier** object.

4. From there, in the **Inspector** tab, scroll down to the **Skinned Mesh Renderer** component and, under **Materials**, set **Element 0** to the new materials:

Figure 8.2 – Replacing the Material property used for the soldier's head

5. Lastly, in the **Albedo (RGB)** property, drag and drop the **Unity_soldier_Head_DIF_01** texture. The following screenshot demonstrates what we are looking for:

Figure 8.3 – Adding the texture to the Albedo (RGB) property

How to do it...

In all the previous chapters, we have always been able to refit Surface Shaders. This is not the case anymore since Surface and Fragment Shaders are structurally different. We will need to implement the following changes:

1. Delete all the properties of the shader, replacing them with the following:

```
Properties
{
    _Color ("Color", Color) = (1,0,0,1)
    _MainTex ("Albedo (RGB)", 2D) = "white" {}
}
```

2. Delete all the code in the `SubShader` block and replace it with this:

```
SubShader
{
    Pass
    {
        CGPROGRAM

        #pragma vertex vert
        #pragma fragment frag

        half4 _Color;
        sampler2D _MainTex;

        struct vertInput
        {
            float4 pos : POSITION;
            float2 texcoord : TEXCOORD0;
        };
```

```
            struct vertOutput
            {
                float4 pos : SV_POSITION;
                float2 texcoord : TEXCOORD0;
            };

            vertOutput vert(vertInput input)
            {
                vertOutput o;
                o.pos = UnityObjectToClipPos(input.pos);
                o.texcoord = input.texcoord;
                return o;
            }

            half4 frag(vertOutput output) : COLOR
            {
                half4 mainColour = tex2D(_MainTex,
                    output.texcoord);
                return mainColour * _Color;
            }

            ENDCG
        }
    }

    FallBack "Diffuse"
```

3. Save your shader script and return to the Unity Editor. Once you've finished, modify the **Color** property of the **MultiplyMat** material. You will see that we get the result we are looking for:

Figure 8.4 – Changing the Color property of Multiply Mat (Material)

This will also be the base for all future Vertex and Fragment Shaders.

How it works...

As the name suggests, Vertex and Fragment Shaders work in two steps. The model is first passed through a `vertex` function; the result is then inputted to a `fragment` function. Both these functions are assigned using `#pragma` directives:

```
#pragma vertex vert
#pragma fragment frag
```

In this case, they are simply called `vert` and `frag`.

Conceptually speaking, fragments are closely related to pixels; the term fragment is often used to refer to collecting the necessary data to draw a pixel. This is also why Vertex and Fragment Shaders are often called **Pixel Shaders**.

The `vertex` function takes the input data in a structure that is defined as `vertInput` in the shader:

```
struct vertInput
{
    float4 pos : POSITION;
```

```
        float2 texcoord : TEXCOORD0;
};
```

Its name is arbitrary, but its content is not. Each field of `struct` must be decorated with a **binding semantic**. This is a feature of Cg that allows us to mark variables so that they will be initialized with certain data, such as normal vectors and the vertex position. The binding semantic, `POSITION`, indicates that when `vertInput` is inputted into the `vertex` function, `pos` will contain the position of the current vertex. This is similar to the `vertex` field of the `appdata_full` structure in a Surface Shader. The main difference is that `pos` is represented in model coordinates (relative to the 3D object), which we need to convert into view coordinates manually (relative to the position on the screen).

> **Note**
> The `vertex` function in a Surface Shader is only used to alter the geometry of the model. However, in a Vertex or Fragment Shader, the `vertex` function is necessary to project the coordinates of the model on the screen.

The mathematics behind this conversion is beyond the scope of this chapter. However, this transformation can be achieved by using the `UnityObjectToClipPos` function, which will take a point from the object's space to the camera's clip space in homogeneous coordinates. This is done by multiplying by the **model-view-projection matrix**, and it is essential to find the position of a Vertex on the screen:

```
vertOutput o;
o.pos = UnityObjectToClipPos(input.pos);
```

> **Note**
> For more information about this and other helper functions that ShaderLab has built into it, check out `https://docs.unity3d.com/Manual/SL-BuiltinFunctions.html`.

The other piece of information that's initialized is `texcoord`, which uses the `TEXCOORD0` binding semantics to get the UV data of the first texture. No further processing is required, and this value can be passed directly to the fragment function (`frag`):

```
o.texcoord = input.texcoord;
```

While Unity will initialize `vertInput` for us, we are responsible for initializing `vertOutput`. Despite this, its fields still need to be decorated with binding semantics:

```
struct vertOutput
{
    float4 pos : SV_POSITION;
    float2 texcoord : TEXCOORD0;
};
```

Once the `vertex` function has initialized `vertOutput`, the structure is passed to the fragment function (`frag`). This samples the main texture of the model and multiplies it by the color provided.

As you can see, the Vertex and Fragment Shaders do not know the physical properties of the material. This means that the material does not have the same effect as light sources, and it does not have data regarding how light reflects to create bumped surfaces compared to a Surface Shader; it works closer to the architecture of the graphics GPU.

There's more...

One of the most confusing aspects of Vertex and Fragment Shaders is binding semantics. There are many others that you can use, and their meanings depend on the context.

Input semantics

The binding semantics shown in the following table can be used in `vertInput`, which is the structure that Unity provides to the `vertex` function. The fields that are decorated with these semantics will be initialized automatically:

Binding Semantics	Description
POSITION, SV_POSITION	The position of a vertex in world coordinates (this is also often in object space, but can technically be in whatever space the programmer wants, such as screen space).
NORMAL	The normal of a vertex, relative to the object (not to the camera).
COLOR, COLOR0, DIFFUSE, SV_TARGET	The color information that's stored in the vertex.
COLOR1, SPECULAR	The secondary color information that's stored in the vertex (usually the specular).
TEXCOORD0, TEXCOORD1, ...,TEXCOORDi	The i-th UV data that's stored in the vertex.

Output semantics

When binding, semantics are used in `vertOutput`; they do not automatically guarantee that fields will be initialized. This is quite the opposite; it's our responsibility to do this. The compiler will do its best to ensure that the fields are initialized with the right data:

Binding Semantics	Description
`POSITION, SV_POSITION, HPOS`	The position of a vertex in camera coordinates (can also be clip space or from zero to one for each dimension).
`COLOR, COLOR0, COL0, COL, SV_TARGET`	The front primary color.
`COLOR1, COL1`	The front secondary color.
`TEXCOORD0, TEXCOORD1, ..., TEXCOORDi, TEXi`	The i-th UV data that's stored in the vertex.
`WPOS`	The position, in pixels, in the window (origin in the lower-left corner).

> **Note**
>
> For more information about clip space and what that means and how it is different between DirectX and OpenGL, check out `https://answers.unity.com/questions/1443941/shaders-what-is-clip-space.html`.

If, for any reason, you need a field that will contain a different type of data, you can decorate it with one of the many `TEXCOORD` data that's available. The compiler will not allow fields to be left undecorated.

See also

You can refer to the NVIDIA Reference Manual to check out the other binding semantics that are available in Cg:

`http://developer.download.nvidia.com/cg/Cg_3.1/Cg-3.1_April2012_ReferenceManual.pdf`

Using grab passes to draw behind objects

In the *Adding transparency to PBR* recipe of *Chapter 6, Physically Based Rendering*, we learned how a material can be made transparent. Even if a transparent material can draw over a scene, it cannot change what has been drawn underneath it. This means that those Transparent Shaders cannot create distortions such as the ones typically seen in glass or water. To simulate them, we need to introduce another technique known as grab pass. This allows us to access what has been drawn on-screen so far so that a shader can use it (or alter it) with no restrictions. To learn how to use grab passes, we will create a material that grabs what's rendered behind it and draws it again on the screen. It's a shader that, paradoxically, performs several operations to show no changes at all.

Getting ready

For this recipe, you will need to do the following:

1. Create a shader (`GrabShader`) that we will initialize later.
2. Create a material (`GrabMat`) that will host the shader.
3. Attach the material to a flat piece of geometry, such as a quad. Place it in front of another object so that you cannot see through it. The quad will appear transparent as soon as the shader is complete:

Figure 8.5 – Quad

How to do it...

To use a grab pass, follow these steps:

1. Remove the `Properties` section as this shader will not use it.

2. In the `SubShader` section, remove everything so that you're left with the following code for the shader:

```
Shader "CookbookShaders/Chapter 08/GrabShader"
{
    SubShader
    {

    }
    FallBack "Diffuse"
}
```

3. Next, add the following to the `SubShader` section to ensure that the object is treated as `Transparent`:

```
Tags{ "Queue" = "Transparent" }
```

4. Then, below that, add a grab pass:

```
GrabPass{ }
```

5. After `GrabPass`, we will need to add the following extra pass:

```
Pass
{
    CGPROGRAM
    #pragma vertex vert
    #pragma fragment frag

    #include "UnityCG.cginc"
    sampler2D _GrabTexture;

    struct vertInput
    {
        float4 vertex : POSITION;
    };

    struct vertOutput
    {
        float4 vertex : POSITION;
```

```
            float4 uvgrab : TEXCOORD1;
        };

        // Vertex function
        vertOutput vert(vertInput v)
        {
            vertOutput o;
            o.vertex = UnityObjectToClipPos(v.vertex);
            o.uvgrab = ComputeGrabScreenPos(o.vertex);
            return o;
        }
        // Fragment function
        half4 frag(vertOutput i) : COLOR
        {
            fixed4 col = tex2Dproj(_GrabTexture,
                UNITY_PROJ_COORD(i.uvgrab));
            return col + half4(0.5,0,0,0);
        }
        ENDCG
}
```

6. Save your script and return to the Unity Editor. At this point, you should see your material now works the way you intend it to:

Figure 8.6 – The result of the created shader

How it works...

So far, our code has always been placed directly in the `SubShader` section. This is because our previous shaders required only a single pass. This time, two passes are required. The first one is `GrabPass{}`, which is defined by `GrabPass{}`. The rest of the code is placed in the second pass, which is contained in a `Pass` block.

The second pass is not structurally different from the shader shown in the first recipe of this chapter; we use the `vertex` function, `vert`, to get the position of the vertex, and then we give it a color in the `Fragment` function. The difference is that `vert` calculates another important detail: the UV data for `GrabPass{}`. `GrabPass{}` automatically creates a texture that can be referred to as follows:

```
sampler2D _GrabTexture;
```

To sample this texture, we need its UV data. The `ComputeGrabScreenPos` function returns data that we can use later to sample the grab texture correctly. This is done in the Fragment Shader using the following code:

```
fixed4 col = tex2Dproj(_GrabTexture,
                      UNITY_PROJ_COORD(i.uvgrab));
```

This is the standard way in which a texture is grabbed and applied to the screen in its correct position. If everything has been done correctly, this shader will simply clone what has been rendered behind the geometry. In the following recipes, we will how this technique can be used to create materials such as water and glass.

There's more...

Every time you use a material with `GrabPass{}`, Unity will have to render the screen to a texture. This operation is very expensive and limits the number of `GrabPass` instances that you can use in a game. Cg offers a slightly different variation:

```
GrabPass {"TextureName"}
```

This line not only allows you to give a name to the texture but also shares the texture with all the materials that have a `GrabPass` called `TextureName`. This means that if you have 10 materials, Unity will only do a single `GrabPass` and share the texture with all of them. The main problem with this technique is that it doesn't allow effects that can be stacked. If you are creating a glass with this technique, you won't be able to have two glasses one after the other.

Implementing a Glass Shader

Glass is a very complicated material; it should not be a surprise that other recipes have already created shaders to simulate it, such as in the *Adding transparency to PBR* recipe of *Chapter 6, Physically Based Rendering*. We already know how to make our glasses semi-transparent to show the objects behind them perfectly, and this works for several applications. However, most glasses are not perfect. For instance, if you look through a stained glass window, you may notice distortions or deformations. This recipe will teach you how to achieve that effect. The idea behind this effect is to use a Vertex and Fragment Shader with a `GrabPass`, and then sample the grab texture by changing its UV data to create a distortion. You can see this effect in the following screenshot. Here, we used the glass-stained textures from Unity's Standard Assets:

Figure 8.7 – The effect that will be created in this recipe

Getting ready

The setup for this recipe is similar to the one presented in the previous recipe:

1. Create a new Vertex and Fragment Shader. You can start by copying the one that we used in the previous recipe, *Using grab passes to draw behind objects*, as a base by selecting it and hitting *Ctrl* + *D* to duplicate it. Once duplicated, change its name to `WindowShader`.
2. Create a material that will use the shader (`WindowMat`).
3. Assign the material to a quad or another flat geometry that will simulate your glass.
4. Place some objects behind it so that you can see the distortion effect:

Figure 8.8 – The setup for this recipe

How to do it...

Let's start by editing the Vertex and Fragment Shaders:

1. Above the `SubShader` section of your script, create a `Properties` block with the following items in it:

```
Shader "CookbookShaders/Chapter 08/WindowShader"
{
    Properties
    {
        _MainTex("Base (RGB) Trans (A)", 2D) = "white"
            {}
        _Colour("Colour", Color) = (1,1,1,1)
        _BumpMap("Noise text", 2D) = "bump" {}
        _Magnitude("Magnitude", Range(0,1)) = 0.05
    }

    SubShader
    {
        Tags{ "Queue" = "Transparent" }
        // Rest of WindowShader.shader
```

2. Add their variables in the second pass:

```
sampler2D _MainTex;
fixed4 _Colour;

sampler2D _BumpMap;
float _Magnitude;
```

3. Add the texture information to the vertInput and vertOutput structures:

```
float2 texcoord : TEXCOORD0;
```

4. Transfer the UV data from the input to the output structure:

```
// Vertex function
vertOutput vert(vertInput v)
{
    vertOutput o;
    o.vertex = UnityObjectToClipPos(v.vertex);
    o.uvgrab = ComputeGrabScreenPos(o.vertex);
    o.texcoord = v.texcoord;
    return o;
}
```

5. Use the following Fragment function:

```
half4 frag(vertOutput i) : COLOR
{
    half4 mainColour = tex2D(_MainTex, i.texcoord);
    half4 bump = tex2D(_BumpMap, i.texcoord);
    half2 distortion = UnpackNormal(bump).rg;

    i.uvgrab.xy += distortion * _Magnitude;

    fixed4 col = tex2Dproj(_GrabTexture,
                    UNITY_PROJ_COORD(i.uvgrab));
    return col * mainColour * _Colour;
}
```

6. This material is transparent, so we will need to change the `Tags` section of the `SubShader` block:

    ```
    Tags
    {
        "Queue" = "Transparent"
        "IgnoreProjector" = "True"
        "RenderType" = "Transparent"
    }
    ```

7. Save the script and return to the Unity Editor. You may not see anything in the **Scene** window at this point where the window was. All we need to do now is set the texture for the glass and use a normal map to displace the grab texture (you can find an example of this within the `Chapter 08 | Textures` folder of the example code for this book):

Figure 8.9 – Attaching the texture and normal map for the Window Mat (Material) shader

How it works...

This shader uses a grab pass to take what has already been rendered on the screen. The part where the distortion takes place is in the `Fragment` function. Here, a normal map is unpacked and used to offset the UV data of the grab texture:

```
half4 bump = tex2D(_BumpMap, i.texcoord);
half2 distortion = UnpackNormal(bump).rg;


i.uvgrab.xy += distortion * _Magnitude;
```

The `_Magnitude` slider is used to determine how strong the effect is:

Figure 8.10 – Increasing the magnitude of the effect

There's more...

This effect is very generic; it grabs the screen and creates a distortion based on a normal map. There is no reason why it shouldn't be used to simulate more interesting things. Many games use distortions around explosions or other sci-fi devices. This material can be applied to a sphere and, with a different normal map, it would simulate the heatwave of an explosion perfectly.

Implementing a Water Shader for 2D games

The Glass Shader that we introduced in the previous recipe is static; its distortion never changes. It takes just a few changes to convert it into an animated material, making it perfect for 2D games that feature water. This uses a similar technique to the one shown in *Chapter 7*, *Vertex Functions*, in the *Animating Vertices in a Surface Shader* recipe:

Figure 8.11 – The result of the following recipe

Getting ready

This recipe is based on the Vertex and Fragment Shaders described in the *Using grab passes to draw behind objects* recipe, as it will rely heavily on `GrabPass`. Let's get started:

1. Create a new Vertex and Fragment Shader. You can start by copying the one used in the previous recipe, *Using grab passes to draw behind objects*, as a base (`GrabShader`) by selecting it and hitting *Ctrl + D* to duplicate it. Once duplicated, change its name to `2DWaterShader`.

2. Create a material that will use the shader (`2DWaterMat`).

3. Assign the material to a flat geometry that will represent your 2D water. For this effect to work, you should have something rendered behind it so that you can see the water-like displacement:

Figure 8.12 – Setup for this recipe

4. This recipe requires a noise texture, which is used to get pseudo-random values. You must choose a seamless noise texture, such as the ones generated by tileable 2D Perlin noise, as shown in the following screenshot:

Figure 8.13 – Noise texture

This ensures that when the material is applied to a large object, you will not see any discontinuity. For this effect to work, the texture has to be imported and have its **Wrap Mode** property set to `Repeat`. If you want a smooth and continuous look for your water, you should also set **Filter Mode** to `Bilinear` from the **Inspector** window. These settings ensure that the texture is sampled correctly from the shader.

> **Note**
>
> You can find an example noise texture in the `Chapter 07 | Textures` folder of this book's example code.

How to do it...

To create this animated effect, you can start by refitting the shader. Follow these steps:

1. Add the following properties:

   ```
   Properties
   {
       _NoiseTex("Noise text", 2D) = "white" {}
       _Colour("Colour", Color) = (0.67, 1, 0.96, 1)
       _Period("Period", Range(0, 50)) = 1
       _Magnitude("Magnitude", Range(0, 0.5)) = 0.05
       _Scale("Scale", Range(0, 10)) = 1
   }
   ```

2. Add their respective variables to the second pass of the shader:

   ```
   #include "UnityCG.cginc"
   sampler2D _GrabTexture;
   sampler2D _NoiseTex;
   fixed4 _Colour;

   float _Period;
   float _Magnitude;
   float _Scale;
   ```

3. Define the following input and output structures for the `vertex` function:

```
struct vertInput
{
    float4 vertex : POSITION;
    fixed4 color : COLOR;
    float2 texcoord : TEXCOORD0;
};

struct vertOutput
{
    float4 vertex : POSITION;
    fixed4 color : COLOR;
    float2 texcoord : TEXCOORD0;
    float4 worldPos : TEXCOORD1;
    float4 uvgrab : TEXCOORD2;
};
```

4. This shader needs to know the exact position of the space of every fragment. To do this, update the `vertex` function to the following:

```
// Vertex function
vertOutput vert(vertInput v)
{
    vertOutput o;
    o.vertex = UnityObjectToClipPos(v.vertex);
    o.color = v.color;
    o.texcoord = v.texcoord;

    o.worldPos = mul(unity_ObjectToWorld, v.vertex);
    o.uvgrab = ComputeGrabScreenPos(o.vertex);

    return o;
}
```

5. Use the following `Fragment` function:

```
fixed4 frag(vertOutput i) : COLOR
{
    float sinT = sin(_Time.w / _Period);

    float2 xyOverScale = i.worldPos.xy / _Scale;
    float2 xCoords = xyOverScale + float2(sinT, 0);
    float2 yCoords = xyOverScale + float2(0, sinT);

    float distX = tex2D(_NoiseTex, xCoords).r - 0.5;
    float distY = tex2D(_NoiseTex, yCoords).r - 0.5;

    float2 distortion = float2(distX, distY);
    i.uvgrab.xy += distortion * _Magnitude;
    fixed4 col = tex2Dproj(_GrabTexture,
                    UNITY_PROJ_COORD(i.uvgrab));
    return col * _Colour;
}
```

6. Save your script and return to the Unity Editor. Afterward, select your water material (`WatMat`) and apply the noise texture. Then, tweak the properties in the water material and notice how it modifies the things behind it:

Figure 8.14 – Tweaking the properties of the 2D water shader

How it works...

This shader is very similar to the one that was introduced in the *Implementing a Glass Shader* recipe. The major difference is that this is an animated material; the displacement is not generated from a normal map but takes the current time into account to create a constant animation. The code that displaces the UV data of the grab texture seems quite complicated; let's try to understand how it has been generated. The idea behind it is that a sinusoid function is used to make the water oscillate. This effect needs to evolve over time; to achieve this effect, the distortion that's generated by the shader depends on the current time that is retrieved with the built-in _Time variable. The _Period variable determines the period of the sinusoid, which means how fast the waves appear:

```
float2 distortion = float2( sin(_Time.w/_Period),
    sin(_Time.w/_Period) ) - 0.5;
```

The problem with this code is that you have the same displacement on the *x* and *y* axes; as a result, the entire grab texture will rotate in a circular motion, which looks nothing like water. We need to add some randomness to this.

The most common way to add random behaviors to shaders is by including a noise texture. The problem now is finding a way to sample the texture at seemingly random positions. The best way to avoid seeing an obvious sinusoid pattern is to use the sine waves as an offset in the UV data of the _NoiseTex texture:

```
float sinT = sin(_Time.w / _Period);
float2 distortion = float2(
    tex2D(_NoiseTex, i.texcoord / _Scale + float2(sinT, 0)
        ).r - 0.5,
    tex2D(_NoiseTex, i.texcoord / _Scale + float2(0, sinT)
        ).r - 0.5
);
```

The _Scale variable determines the size of the waves. This solution is closer to the final version but has a severe issue – if the water quad moves, the UV data follows it and you can see the water waves following the material rather than them being anchored to the background. To solve this, we need to use the world position of the current fragment as the initial position for the UV data:

```
float sinT = sin(_Time.w / _Period);
float2 distortion = float2(
    tex2D(_NoiseTex, i.worldPos.xy / _Scale + float2(sinT,
        0) ).r - 0.5,
```

```
        tex2D( _NoiseTex, i.worldPos.xy / _Scale + float2(0,
            sinT) ).r - 0.5
);
i.uvgrab.xy += distortion * _Magnitude;
```

The result is a pleasant, seamless distortion that doesn't move in any clear direction.

We can also improve the readability of the code by breaking the distortion into smaller steps:

```
float sinT = sin(_Time.w / _Period);

float2 xyOverScale = i.worldPos.xy / _Scale;
float2 xCoords = xyOverScale + float2(sinT, 0);
float2 yCoords = xyOverScale + float2(0, sinT);

float distX = tex2D(_NoiseTex, xCoords).r - 0.5;
float distY = tex2D(_NoiseTex, yCoords).r - 0.5;

float2 distortion = float2(distX, distY);
i.uvgrab.xy += distortion * _Magnitude;
```

That is what you should see in the final result.

> **Note**
>
> As with all these special effects, there is no perfect solution. This recipe has shown a technique you can use to create water-like distortion, but you are encouraged to play with it until you find an effect that fits the aesthetics of your game.

9
Mobile Shader Adjustment

In the next two chapters, we are going to take a look at making the shaders that we write performance-friendly for different platforms. We won't be talking about one platform in particular, but we are going to break down the elements of shaders that we can adjust to make them more optimized for mobile and efficient on any platform in general. These techniques range from understanding what Unity offers in terms of built-in variables that reduce the overhead of the shader's memory to learning about the ways in which we can make our shader code more efficient.

Learning the art of optimizing your shaders will come up in just about any game project that you work on. There will always come a point in any production environment where a shader needs to be optimized, or maybe it needs to use fewer textures but produce the same effect. As a technical artist or shader programmer, you have to understand these core fundamentals to optimize your shaders so that you can increase the performance of your game while still achieving the same visual fidelity. Having this knowledge can also help with how you write your shader from the start. For instance, by knowing that the game that was built using your shader will be played on a mobile device, we can automatically set all our `Lighting` functions to use a half vector as the view direction, or we can even set all of our float variable types to fixed or half to reduce the amount of memory that's used. These, and many other techniques, all contribute to your shaders running efficiently on your target hardware. Let's begin our journey and start learning how to optimize our shaders.

This chapter will cover the following recipes:

- Techniques to make shaders more efficient
- Profiling your shaders
- Modifying our shaders for mobile

Technical requirements

This chapter was created with Unity 2021.1.9f1 but should work with future versions of Unity with minimal revisions.

You can find the code samples present in this chapter on GitHub at `https://github.com/PacktPublishing/Unity-2021-Shaders-and-Effects-Cookbook-Fourth-Edition/tree/main/Shaders-and-Effects-Cookbook-2021/Assets/Chapter%2009`.

Techniques to make shaders more efficient

What is a cheap shader? When you're asked the question for the first time, it might be a little tough to answer since many elements go into making a more efficient shader. It could be the amount of memory that's used up by your variables. It could be the number of textures the shader is using. It could also be that our shader is working fine, but we can produce the same visual effect with half the amount of data by reducing the amount of code we are using or the data we are creating. We are going to explore a few of these techniques in this recipe. We will show how they can be combined to make your shader fast and efficient while still producing the high-quality visuals everyone expects from games today, whether on a mobile or PC.

Getting ready

To get started, we need to gather a few resources. So, let's perform the following tasks:

1. Create a new scene and fill it with a simple sphere object and a single directional light.
2. Create a new shader (`OptimizedShader01`) and material (`OptimizedShader01Mat`) and assign the shader to the material.

3. Now, we need to assign the material we just created to the sphere object in our new scene:

Figure 9.1 – This recipe's setup

4. Finally, modify the shader so that it uses a diffuse texture and normal map and includes your custom `Lighting` function:

```
Properties
{
    _MainTex("Base (RGB)", 2D) = "white" {}
    _NormalMap("Normal Map", 2D) = "bump" {}
}

SubShader
{
    Tags { "RenderType" = "Opaque" }
    LOD 200

    CGPROGRAM
    #pragma surface surf SimpleLambert

    sampler2D _MainTex;
    sampler2D _NormalMap;
```

```
        struct Input
        {
            float2 uv_MainTex;
            float2 uv_NormalMap;
        };

        inline float4 LightingSimpleLambert(SurfaceOutput
                                            s, float3
                                            lightDir,
                                            float atten)
        {
            float diff = max(0, dot(s.Normal, lightDir));

            float4 c;
            c.rgb = s.Albedo * _LightColor0.rgb * (diff *
                atten * 2);
            c.a = s.Alpha;
            return c;
        }

        void surf(Input IN, inout SurfaceOutput o)
        {
            fixed4 c = tex2D(_MainTex, IN.uv_MainTex);

            o.Albedo = c.rgb;
            o.Alpha = c.a;
            o.Normal = UnpackNormal(tex2D(_NormalMap,
                            IN.uv_NormalMap));
        }
        ENDCG
}

FallBack "Diffuse"
```

5. Lastly, assign a base and normal map to your material (I used the `MudRocky` texture, which is included in the assets for *Chapter 1*, *Post Processing Stack*, in the `Assets\Chapter 01\Standard Assets\Environment\TerrainAssets\SurfaceTextures` folder). You should now have a setup similar to the following screenshot:

Figure 9.2 – Assigning a texture and normal map to the material

This setup will allow us to take a look at some of the basic concepts that go into optimizing shaders using Surface Shaders in Unity.

How to do it...

We are going to build a simple `DiffuseShader` to take a look at a few ways in which you can optimize your shaders in general.

First, we'll optimize our variable types so that they use less memory when they are processing data:

1. Let's begin with `struct Input` in our shader. Currently, our UVs are being stored in a variable of the `float2` type.

2. Remember that floats provide the highest form of precision at a full 32 bits of memory. This is needed for complex trigonometry or exponents, but if you can handle less precision, it's much better to use either a half or a fixed instead. The half type provides up to three digits of precision using half the size or 16 bits of memory. This means we can have half2 with the same amount of memory as a single float. We need to change this to use half2 instead:

```
struct Input
{
    half2 uv_MainTex;
    half2 uv_NormalMap;
};
```

3. We can then move to our Lighting function and reduce the variables' memory footprint by changing their types to the following:

```
inline fixed4 LightingSimpleLambert (SurfaceOutput s,
fixed3 lightDir, fixed atten)
{
    fixed diff = max (0, dot(s.Normal, lightDir));

    fixed4 c;
    c.rgb = s.Albedo * _LightColor0.rgb * (diff * atten
                                                   * 2);
    c.a = s.Alpha;
    return c;
}
```

4. In this case, we are using the lowest precision type of fixed, which is only 11 bits compared to the float type's 32. This is useful for simple calculations such as color or texture data, which is perfect for this particular case.

> **Tip**
> If you'd like a refresher on the fixed type, as well as all of the other types we are using, please check out *Chapter 2, Creating Your First Shader*, or look at https://docs.unity3d.com/Manual/SL-DataTypesAndPrecision.html.

5. Finally, we can complete this optimization pass by updating the variables in our `surf()` function. Since we're using texture data, it's fine for us to use `fixed4` here instead:

```
void surf(Input IN, inout SurfaceOutput o)
{
    fixed4 c = tex2D(_MainTex, IN.uv_MainTex);

    o.Albedo = c.rgb;
    o.Alpha = c.a;
    o.Normal = UnpackNormal(tex2D(_NormalMap,
                                  IN.uv_NormalMap));
}
```

6. Now that we have optimized our variables, we are going to take advantage of a built-in `Lighting` function variable so that we can control how lights are processed by this shader. By doing this, we can greatly reduce the number of lights the shader processes. Modify the `#pragma` statement in your shader with the following code:

```
CGPROGRAM
#pragma surface surf SimpleLambert noforwardadd
```

7. We can optimize this further by sharing UVs between the normal map and diffuse texture. To do this, we can simply change the UV lookup in our `UnpackNormal()` function so that it uses _MainTex UVs instead of the UVs of _NormalMap:

```
void surf(Input IN, inout SurfaceOutput o)
{
    fixed4 c = tex2D(_MainTex, IN.uv_MainTex);

    o.Albedo = c.rgb;
    o.Alpha = c.a;
    o.Normal = UnpackNormal(tex2D(_NormalMap,
                                  IN.uv_MainTex));
}
```

8. Now that we have removed the need for the normal map UVs, we need to make sure that we have removed the normal map UV code from `struct Input`:

```
struct Input
{
    half2 uv_MainTex;
};
```

9. Finally, we can further optimize this shader by telling the shader that it only works with certain renderers:

```
CGPROGRAM
#pragma surface surf SimpleLambert exclude_path:prepass noforwardadd
```

The result of our optimization passes shows us that we don't notice a difference in the visual quality, but we have reduced the amount of time it takes for this shader to be drawn to the screen. You will find out how much time it takes for a shader to render in the next recipe, but the idea to focus on here is that we can achieve the same result with fewer data. So, keep this in mind when you're creating your shaders.

> **Note**
> It's also important to note that when using fixed/half on PC, you won't notice any difference at all because it still uses full precision.

The following screenshot shows the final result of our shader:

Figure 9.3 – The result of our optimized textures

How it works...

Now that we have seen how we can optimize our shaders, let's dive in a bit deeper and understand how all of these techniques work, why we should use them, and look at a couple of other techniques that you can try for yourself in your shaders.

First, let's focus our attention on the size of the data each of our variables is storing when we declare them. If you are familiar with programming, then you will understand that you can declare values or variables with different types of sizes. This means that a float has a maximum size in memory. The following list describes these variable types in much more detail:

- **Float**: A float is a full 32-bit precision value and is the slowest of the three different types we will look at here. It also has corresponding values of `float2`, `float3`, and `float4`, which allow us to store multiple floats in one variable.
- **Half**: The half variable type is a reduced 16-bit floating-point value and is suitable for storing UV values and color values. It is much faster than using a float value. As with the float type, it has its corresponding values, which are `half2`, `half3`, and `half4`.
- **Fixed**: A fixed value is the smallest of the three types, but it can be used for lighting calculations and colors and has the corresponding values of `fixed2`, `fixed3`, and `fixed4`.

> **Note**
> For more information on working with array types for shaders, check out the *Accessing and modifying packed arrays* recipe from *Chapter 3, Working with Surface Shaders*.

The second phase of optimizing our simple shader was to declare the `noforwardadd` value to our `#pragma` statement. This is a switch that automatically tells Unity that any object with this particular shader receives only per-pixel light from a single directional light. Any other lights that are calculated by this shader will be forced to be processed as per-vertex lights using *spherical harmonic* values produced internally by Unity. This is especially obvious when we place another light in the scene to light our sphere object. This is because our shader is doing a per-pixel operation using the normal map.

This is great, but what if you wanted to have a bunch of directional lights in the scene and control over which of these lights is used for the main per-pixel light? Well, as you may have noticed, each light has a **Render Mode** dropdown. If you click on this dropdown, you will see a couple of flags that can be set. These are **Auto**, **Important**, and **Not Important**. By selecting a light, you can tell Unity that a light should be considered more as a per-pixel light than a per-vertex light, by setting its render mode to **Important** and vice versa. If you leave a light set to **Auto**, then you are letting Unity decide the best course of action:

Figure 9.4 – Setting Render Mode to Auto

Place another light in your scene and remove the texture that is currently in the main texture for our shader. You will notice that the second point light does not react with the normal map, only the directional light that we created first. The concept here is that you save on per-pixel operations by calculating all the extra lights as vertex lights, and save performance by just calculating the main directional light as a per-pixel light. The following diagram demonstrates this concept as the point light is not reacting to the normal map:

Figure 9.5 – Effect of using noforwardadd in a shader's #pragam statement

Finally, we did a bit of cleaning up and simply told the normal map texture to use the main texture's UV values, and we got rid of the line of code that pulled in a separate set of UV values specifically for the normal map. This is always a nice way to simplify your code and clean up any unwanted data.

We also declared `exclude_pass: prepass` in our `#pragma` statement so that this shader wouldn't accept any custom lighting from the deferred renderer. This means that we can only use this shader effectively in the forward renderer, which is set in the main camera's settings.

By spending a bit of time on this, you will be amazed at how much a shader can be optimized. So far, you have seen how we can pack grayscale textures into a single RGBA texture, as well as using lookup textures to fake lighting (the `lut` phrase that you may see refers to using a lookup texture).

> **Note**
>
> You can see an example of how to create and use a lookup texture with the Color Grading attribute from the Post Processing Stack shown in Chapter 1 here: `https://www.youtube.com/watch?v=hYhL0qK_NC0`.

There are many ways in which a shader can be optimized, which is why it is always an ambiguous question to ask in the first place, but by knowing about these different optimization techniques, you can cater your shaders to your game and target platform, ultimately resulting in very streamlined shaders and a nice, steady frame rate.

Another way of optimizing shaders is to look at the math. Sometimes, it can be simplified or rewritten using algebra so that it's more efficient. Also, sometimes, complicated equations can be approximated by a polynomial such as a Maclaurin series.

Profiling your shaders

Now that we know how we can reduce the overhead that our shaders might take, let's take a look at how to find problematic shaders in a scene where you might have a lot of shaders or a ton of objects, shaders, and scripts all running at the same time. Finding a single object or shader among a whole game can be quite daunting, but Unity provides us with its built-in **Profiler**. This allows us to see, on a frame-by-frame basis, what is happening in the game, and each item that is being used by the GPU and CPU.

Using **Profiler**, we can isolate items such as shaders, geometry, and general rendering items using its interface to create blocks of profiling jobs. We can filter out items until we are looking at the performance of just a single object. This lets us see the effects that the object has on the CPU and GPU while it is performing its functions at runtime.

Let's take a look through the different sections of **Profiler** and learn how to debug our scenes and, most importantly, our shaders.

Getting ready

Let's use our **Profiler** by getting a few assets ready and launching the **Profiler** window:

1. Let's use the scene from the previous recipe and launch the Unity **Profiler** from **Window | Analysis | Profiler** or by using *Ctrl + 7*. Feel free to drag and drop or move it so that you can see it well. I put it where the **Inspector** tab is.

2. In the **Scene** view, duplicate our sphere a couple more times to see how that affects our rendering.

3. From the **Profiler** tab, click on the **Deep Profile** option to get additional information about the project. Then, play your game!

You should see something similar to the following:

Figure 9.6 – Utilizing Profiler

How to do it...

To use **Profiler**, we will take a look at some of the UI elements of this window. Before we hit **Play**, let's take a look at how to get the information we need from **Profiler**:

1. First, click on the larger blocks in the **Profiler** window called **CPU Usage**, **Rendering**, and **Memory**. You will find these blocks on the left-hand side of the upper window:

Figure 9.7 – Profiler Blocks (Modules) within the Profiler window

Using these blocks, we can see different data that's specific to those major functions of our game. **CPU Usage** is showing us what most of our scripts are doing, as well as physics and overall rendering. The **Rendering** block is giving us information about the draw calls and the amount of geometry we have in our scene at any one frame. The **Memory** block shows the total memory being used, when allocations are happening, and when the garbage collector is being utilized. This panel is used to give us detailed information about the elements that are specific to our lighting, shadows, and render queues.

2. Go to the top left of the window to the **Profiler Modules** dropdown. From there, check the **GPU Usage** option if it isn't there already:

Figure 9.8 – Enabling the GPU Usage panel

The **GPU Usage** block is giving us detailed information about the elements that are specific to our lighting, shadows, and render queues. It is disabled by default because collecting the GPU Profiler data may cause overhead. However, since this is information directly related to shaders, we will want to have it running.

> **Important Note**
> The **GPU Usage** menu may not show up if your graphics card drivers are not up to date.

By clicking on each of these blocks, we can isolate the type of data we see during our profiling session.

3. Now, click on the tiny colored blocks in one of these **Profile** blocks and hit **Play**, or *Ctrl + P*, to run the scene.

272   Mobile Shader Adjustment

4. This lets us dive even deeper into our profiling session so that we can filter out what is being reported back to us. While the scene is running, uncheck all of the boxes, except for **Opaque** in the **GPU Usage** block. We can now see just how much time is being used to render the objects that are set to **Render Queue** of **Opaque**:

Figure 9.9 – The time required for Opaque objects by the GPU

5. Another great function of the **Profiler** window is the action of clicking and dragging in the graph view.

6. This will automatically pause your game so that you can analyze a certain spike in the graph. By doing this, you can find out exactly which item is causing the performance problem. Click and drag around in the graph view to pause the game and see the effect of using this functionality:

Figure 9.10 – The Graph view

7. Let's turn our attention to the lower half of the **Profiler** window. You will notice that there is a drop-down item available called **Timeline**, which lets us view the time spent in each part of the program, in percent. For a more detailed view, we can change the mode by clicking on the **Timeline** dropdown and selecting **Hierarchy**. From there, select **GPU Block**. At this point, you should be able to see a list of things detailing how the GPU is being used on a particular frame. We can expand this to get even more detailed information about the current active profiling session and, in this case, more information about what the camera is currently rendering and how much time it is taking up:

Figure 9.11 – Detailed Profile View

It is also possible to sort the options using the tops of the columns. For instance, we can use **GPU ms** to measure the amount of time it is taking to perform various actions:

Figure 9.12 – The total percentage and milliseconds used to do different operations

> **Note**
>
> If you click on the dropdown on the right-hand side of the view that says **No Details** and change the option to **Related Data**, you can see what objects are being used in the functions being called.

8. This gives us a complete look at the inner workings of what Unity is processing in this particular frame. In this case, we can see that our three spheres with our optimized shader are taking roughly **0.101** milliseconds to draw to the screen, they are taking up 15 draw calls, and that this process is taking **25.9%** of the GPU's time in every frame (the numbers will likely be different, depending on what hardware you have for your computer). We can use this information to diagnose and solve performance issues concerning shaders. Let's conduct a test to see the effects of adding one more texture to our shader and blending two diffuse textures using a `lerp` function. You will see these effects in **Profiler** pretty clearly.

9. Modify the `Properties` block of your shader with the following code so that we have another texture we can use:

```
Properties
{
    _MainTex("Base (RGB)", 2D) = "white" {}
    _NormalMap("Normal Map", 2D) = "bump" {}
    _BlendTex("Blend Texture", 2D) = "white" {}
}
```

10. Now, let's feed our texture to `CGPROGRAM`:

```
sampler2D _MainTex;
sampler2D _NormalMap;
sampler2D _BlendTex;
```

11. Now, it's time to update our `surf()` function accordingly so that we can blend our diffuse textures:

    ```
    void surf(Input IN, inout SurfaceOutput o)
    {
        fixed4 c = tex2D(_MainTex, IN.uv_MainTex);
        fixed4 blendTex = tex2D(_BlendTex, IN.uv_MainTex);

        c = lerp(c, blendTex, blendTex.r);

        o.Albedo = c.rgb;
        o.Alpha = c.a;
        o.Normal = UnpackNormal(tex2D(_NormalMap,
                                IN.uv_MainTex));
    }
    ```

    Once you've saved your modifications in your shader and returned to Unity's editor, you can run the game and see the new shader's increase in milliseconds.

12. Attach a new texture to `Blend Texture`:

Figure 9.13 – Adding Blend Texture to our Material

13. Press **Play** to start the game again with **Profiler** turned on. Press **Play** once you have returned to Unity. Now, let's take a look at the results in our **Profiler**:

Figure 9.14 – The results in the Profiler window

Here, you can see that the amount of time to render our **Opaque** Shaders in this scene is taking **0.116** milliseconds, up from **0.101** milliseconds. By adding another texture and using the `lerp()` function, we increased the render time for our spheres. While this was a small change, imagine having 20 shaders all working in different ways on different objects.

Using the information given here, you can pinpoint areas that are causing performance decreases more quickly and solve these issues using the techniques shown in the previous recipe.

How it works...

While it is completely outside the scope of this book to describe how this tool works internally, we can surmise that Unity has given us a way to view the computer's performance while our game is running. This window is tied very tightly to the CPU and GPU to give us real-time feedback on how much time is being taken for each of our scripts, objects, and render queues. Using this information, we have seen that we can track the efficiency of our shader writing to eliminate problem areas and code.

Note that games running with **Profiler** open, as well as from within the editor in general, will make the game slightly slower than it would be when compiled and running in a normal situation. You might even see **Editor** in the **Profilers** list of CPU expenses.

There's more...

It is also possible to profile specifically for mobile platforms. Unity provides us with a couple of extra features when the Android or iOS build target is set in **Build Settings**. We can get real-time information from our mobile devices while the game is running. This becomes very useful because you can profile directly on the device itself instead of profiling directly in your editor. To find out more about this process, refer to Unity's documentation at the following link:

http://docs.unity3d.com/Documentation/Manual/MobileProfiling.html

Profiling on a mobile device and PC may give completely different results, to the point where it may not be worth the time performing profiling on PC within the editor if you are making a mobile-only game. For example, there may be a situation where dynamic batching worked fine on a PC but was not working correctly on a mobile device. I recommend always profiling on the target device with a standalone build if possible.

Modifying our shaders for mobile

Now that we have looked at a broad set of techniques for making optimized shaders, let's take a look at writing a nice, high-quality shader targeted at a mobile device. It is quite easy to make a few adjustments to the shaders we have written so that they run faster on a mobile device. This includes elements such as using the `approxview` or `halfasview` `Lighting` function variables. We can also reduce the number of textures we need and even apply better compression to the textures we are using. By the end of this recipe, we will have a nicely optimized, normally mapped Specular Shader that we can use in our mobile games.

Getting ready

Before we begin, let's create a fresh new scene and fill it with some objects that we will apply to our `MobileShader`:

1. Create a new scene and fill it with a default sphere and a single directional light.
2. Create a new material (`MobileMat`) and shader (`MobileShader`), and assign the shader to the material.
3. Finally, assign the material to the sphere object in our scene.

Once you've done this, you should have a scene similar to the one shown in the following screenshot:

Figure 9.15 – Setup for this recipe

How to do it...

For this recipe, we will write a mobile-friendly shader from scratch and discuss the elements that make it more mobile-friendly:

1. First, let's populate our `Properties` block with the required textures. In this case, we are going to use a single `_Diffuse` texture with the gloss map in its alpha channel, `Normal Map`, and a slider for specular intensity:

```
Properties
{
    _Diffuse ("Base (RGB) Specular Amount (A)", 2D) =
        "white" {}
    _SpecIntensity ("Specular Width", Range(0.01, 1)) =
        0.5
    _NormalMap ("Normal Map", 2D) = "bump"{}
}
```

2. Next, we must set up our `#pragma` declarations. This will simply turn certain features of the Surface Shader on and off, ultimately making the shader cheaper or more expensive:

```
CGPROGRAM
#pragma surface surf MobileBlinnPhong exclude_path:prepass nolightmap noforwardadd halfasview
```

> **Note**
> The highlighted line should be on one line.

3. Next, remove the `#pragma target 3.0` line as we are not using any of its features.

4. Now, we need to make the connection between our `Properties` block and `CGPROGRAM`. This time, we are going to use the fixed variable type for our specular intensity slider to reduce its memory usage:

```
sampler2D _Diffuse;
sampler2D _NormalMap;
fixed _SpecIntensity;
```

5. For us to map our textures to the surface of our object, we need to get some UVs. In this case, we are going to get one set of UVs to keep the amount of data in our shader down to a minimum:

```
struct Input
{
    half2 uv_Diffuse;
};
```

6. The next step is to fill in our `Lighting` function using a few of the new input variables that are available to us when using the new `#pragma` declarations:

```
inline fixed4 LightingMobileBlinnPhong(SurfaceOutput
                                       s, fixed3
                                       lightDir,
                                       fixed3 halfDir,
                                       fixed atten)
```

```
{
    fixed diff = max(0, dot(s.Normal, lightDir));
    fixed nh = max(0, dot(s.Normal, halfDir));
    fixed spec = pow(nh, s.Specular * 128) * s.Gloss;

    fixed4 c;

    c.rgb = (s.Albedo * _LightColor0.rgb * diff +
            _LightColor0.rgb * spec) * (atten * 2);

    c.a = 0.0;

    return c;
}
```

7. Finally, we will complete the shader by creating the `surf()` function and processing the final color of our surface:

```
void surf (Input IN, inout SurfaceOutput o)
{
    fixed4 diffuseTex = tex2D (_Diffuse, IN.uv_Diffuse);
    o.Albedo = diffuseTex.rgb;
    o.Gloss = diffuseTex.a;
    o.Alpha = 0.0;
    o.Specular = _SpecIntensity;
    o.Normal = UnpackNormal(tex2D(_NormalMap,
        IN.uv_Diffuse));
}
```

8. Now, save your shader and return to the Unity Editor to let the shader compile. If no errors occurred, assign some properties to the **Base** and **Normal Map** properties:

Figure 9.16 – Assigning the textures to Mobile Mat (Material)

9. Add a few point lights and some copies of the new object. At this point, you should see a result similar to the following:

Figure 9.17 – The result of the created Mobile Shader

How it works...

So, let's explain what this shader does and doesn't do. First, it excludes the deferred lighting pass. This means that if you created a `Lighting` function that was connected to the deferred renderer's `prepass`, it wouldn't use that particular `Lighting` function and would look for the default `Lighting` function, similar to the ones that we have been creating thus far in this book.

This particular shader does not support *lightmapping* by Unity's internal lightmapping system. This just keeps the shader from trying to find lightmaps for the object that the shader is attached to, making the shader more performance-friendly because it is not having to perform a lightmapping check.

We included the `noforwardadd` declaration so that we only process per-pixel textures with a single directional light. All the other lights are forced to become per-vertex lights and will not be included in any per-pixel operations you might do in the `surf()` function.

Finally, we are using the `halfasview` declaration to tell Unity that we aren't going to use the main `viewDir` parameter that can be found in a normal `Lighting` function. Instead, we are going to use the half vector as the view direction and process our specular with this. This becomes much faster for the shader to process as it will be done on a per-vertex basis. It isn't completely accurate when it comes to simulating a specular in the real world, but visually, on a mobile device, it looks just fine and the shader is more optimized.

It is techniques like these that make a shader more efficient and cleaner code-wise. Always make sure that you are using only the data you need while weighing this against your target hardware and the visual quality that the game requires. In the end, a cocktail of these techniques is what ultimately makes up the shaders for your games.

10
Screen Effects with Unity Render Textures

One of the most impressive aspects of learning to write shaders is the process of creating your own screen effects, also known as post effects. With these screen effects, we can create stunning real-time images with **Bloom**, **Motion Blur**, **high-dynamic-range** (**HDR**) effects, and so on. Most modern games on the market today make heavy use of these screen effects for their depth-of-field effects, Bloom effects, and even color-correction effects.

In *Chapter 1*, *Post Processing Stack*, we discussed how to use this with Unity's built-in Post Processing Stack, but in this chapter, you will learn how to build up the script system yourself. This system will give you the control to create many kinds of screen effects. We will cover `RenderTexture`, what the depth buffer is, and how to create effects that give you Photoshop-like control over the final rendered image of your game. By utilizing screen effects for your games, you not only round out your shader writing knowledge, but you will also have the power to create your own incredible real-time renders with Unity from scratch.

In this chapter, you will learn the following recipes:

- Setting up a screen effects script system
- Using brightness, saturation, and contrast with screen effects
- Using basic Photoshop-like Blend Modes with screen effects
- Using the overlay Blend Mode with screen effects

Technical requirements

This chapter was created with Unity 2021.1.9f1 but should work in future versions of Unity with minimal revisions.

You can find the code samples present in this chapter on GitHub at `https://github.com/PacktPublishing/Unity-2021-Shaders-and-Effects-Cookbook-Fourth-Edition/tree/main/Shaders-and-Effects-Cookbook-2021/Assets/Chapter%2010`.

Setting up a screen effects script system

The process of creating screen effects is one in which we grab a fullscreen image (or texture), use a shader to process its pixels on the **graphics processing unit** (**GPU**), and then send it back to Unity's renderer to apply it to the whole rendered image of the game. This allows us to perform per-pixel operations on the rendered image of the game in real time, giving us a more global artistic control.

Imagine if you had to go through and adjust each material on each object in your game to just adjust the contrast of the final look of your game. While not impossible, this would take a bit of labor to perform. By utilizing a screen effect, we can adjust the screen's final look as a whole, thereby giving us more Photoshop-like control over our game's final appearance.

To get a screen effects system up and running, we have to set up a single script to act as the courier of the game's current rendered image, or what Unity calls the `RenderTexture`. By utilizing this script to pass the `RenderTexture` to a shader, we can create a flexible system for establishing screen effects. For our first screen effect, we are going to create a very simple grayscale effect and make our game look black and white. Let's take a look at how this is done.

Getting ready

To get our screen effects system up and running, we need to create a few assets for our current Unity project. By doing this, we will set ourselves up for the steps in the following sections.

1. In the current project, create a new scene to work in.
2. Create a simple sphere in the scene and assign it a new material (I called mine `RedMat`). This new material can be anything, but for our example, we will make a simple red material using the Standard Shader.
3. Finally, create a new directional light if one isn't there already and save the scene.
4. We need to create a new C# script and call it `TestRenderImage.cs`. For organization purposes, create a folder called `Scripts` from the **Project** tab to put the script in.

With all of our assets ready, you should have a simple scene set up that looks similar to this:

Figure 10.1 – The setup for this recipe

How to do it...

In order to make our grayscale screen effect work, we need a script and a shader. So, we will complete these two new items here and fill them in with the appropriate code to produce our first screen effect. Our first task is to complete the C# script. This will get the whole system running. After this, we will complete the shader and see the results of our screen effect. Let's complete our script and shader with the following steps:

1. Open the `TestRenderImage.cs` C# script and begin by entering a few variables that we will need to store important objects and data. Enter the following code at the very top of the `TestRenderImage` class:

   ```
   #region Variables
   public Shader curShader;
   public float greyscaleAmount = 1.0f;
   private Material screenMat;
   #endregion
   ```

2. In order for us to edit the screen effect in real time, when the Unity Editor isn't playing, we need to enter the following line of code just above the declaration of the `TestRenderImage` class:

   ```
   using UnityEngine;


   [ExecuteInEditMode]
   public class TestRenderImage : MonoBehaviour {
   ```

3. As our screen effect is using a shader to perform the pixel operations on our screen image, we have to create a material to run the shader. Without this, we can't access the properties of the shader. For this, we will create a C# property to check for materials and create one if it doesn't find one. Enter the following code just after the declaration of the variables from *Step 1*:

   ```
   #region Properties
   Material ScreenMat
   {
       get
       {
           if (screenMat == null)
           {
               screenMat = new Material(curShader);
   ```

```
                screenMat.hideFlags =
                    HideFlags.HideAndDontSave;
        }
        return screenMat;
    }
}
#endregion
```

4. We now want to set up some checks in our script so that if our properties are not set before the start of this script, the script will then disable itself:

```
void Start()
{

    if (!curShader && !curShader.isSupported)
    {
        enabled = false;
    }
}
```

5. To actually grab the rendered image from the Unity renderer, we need to make use of the following built-in function that Unity provides us, called OnRenderImage(). Enter the following code so that we can have access to the current RenderTexture:

```
void OnRenderImage(RenderTexture sourceTexture,
                    RenderTexture destTexture)
{
    if (curShader != null)
    {
        ScreenMat.SetFloat("_Luminosity",
                            greyscaleAmount);

        Graphics.Blit(sourceTexture, destTexture,
                        ScreenMat);
    }
    else
    {
```

```
            Graphics.Blit(sourceTexture, destTexture);
        }
    }
```

6. Our screen effect has a variable called `grayScaleAmount` with which we can control how much grayscale we want for our final screen effect. So, in this case, we need to make the value go from 0 to 1, where 0 is no grayscale effect and 1 is a full grayscale effect. We will perform this operation in the `Update()` function, which will be called every frame while the game is running:

```
void Update ()
{
    greyscaleAmount = Mathf.Clamp(greyscaleAmount,
                                    0.0f, 1.0f);
}
```

7. Finally, we complete our script by doing a little bit of cleanup of objects we created when the script started:

```
void OnDisable()
{
    if(screenMat)
    {
        DestroyImmediate(screenMat);
    }
}
```

8. At this point, we can now apply this script to the camera (if it compiled without errors) in Unity. Let's apply the `TestRenderImage.cs` script to our main camera in our scene. You should see the `grayScaleAmount` value and a field for a shader, but the script throws an error to the console window. It says that it is missing an instance of an object and so won't process appropriately. If you recall from *Step 4*, we are doing some checks to see whether we have a shader and if the current platform supports the shader. As we haven't given the screen effects script a shader to work with, then the `curShader` variable is just `null`, which throws an error. Let's continue with our screen effects system by completing the shader.

9. Create a new shader called `ScreenGrayscale`. To begin our shader, we will populate our `Properties` block with some variables so that we can send data to this shader:

```
Properties
{
    _MainTex ("Base (RGB)", 2D) = "white" {}
    _Luminosity("Luminosity", Range(0.0, 1)) = 1.0
}
```

10. Our shader is now going to utilize pure **C for Graphics** (**Cg**) shader code instead of utilizing Unity's built-in Surface Shader code. This will make our screen effect more optimized as we need to work only with the pixels of the `RenderTexture`. So, we will delete everything inside of the `SubShader` that was there before, create a new `Pass` block in our shader, and fill it with some new `#pragma` statements that we haven't seen before:

```
SubShader
{
    Pass
    {
        CGPROGRAM
        #pragma vertex vert_img
        #pragma fragment frag
        #pragma fragmentoption ARB_precision_hint_fastest
        #include "UnityCG.cginc"
```

11. In order to access the data being sent to the shader from the Unity Editor, we need to create corresponding variables in our `CGPROGRAM` block:

```
uniform sampler2D _MainTex;
fixed _Luminosity;
```

12. Finally, all we need to do is set up our pixel function—in this case, called `frag()`. This is where the meat of the screen effect is. This function will process each pixel of the `RenderTexture` and return a new image to our `TestRenderImage.cs` script:

```
fixed4 frag(v2f_img i) : COLOR
{
    //Get the colors from the RenderTexture and the uv's
```

```
    //from the v2f_img struct
    fixed4 renderTex = tex2D(_MainTex, i.uv);

    //Apply the Luminosity values to our render texture
    float luminosity = 0.299 * renderTex.r +
                       0.587 * renderTex.g +
                       0.114 * renderTex.b;
    fixed4 finalColor = lerp(renderTex, luminosity,
                        _Luminosity);

    renderTex.rgb = finalColor;

    return renderTex;
}
```

13. At the end of the `Pass` block, add an `ENDCG` statement.
14. Lastly, change the `FallBack` line to the following:

```
FallBack Off
```

15. The final shader should look like this:

```
Shader "CookbookShaders/Chapter 10/ScreenGrayscale"
{
    Properties
    {
        _MainTex ("Base (RGB)", 2D) = "white" {}
        _Luminosity("Luminosity", Range(0.0, 1)) = 1.0
    }

    SubShader
    {
        Pass
        {
            CGPROGRAM
            #pragma vertex vert_img
            #pragma fragment frag
```

```
            #pragma fragmentoption
                ARB_precision_hint_fastest
            #include "UnityCG.cginc"

            uniform sampler2D _MainTex;
            fixed _Luminosity;

            fixed4 frag(v2f_img i) : COLOR
            {
                // Get the colors from the
                // RenderTexture and the
                // uv's from the v2f_img struct
                fixed4 renderTex = tex2D(_MainTex,
                                            i.uv);

                // Apply the Luminosity values to our
                // render texture
                float luminosity = 0.299 * renderTex.r
                    + 0.587 * renderTex.g + 0.114 *
                    renderTex.b;

                fixed4 finalColor = lerp(renderTex,
                                            luminosity,
                                            _Luminosity);

                renderTex.rgb = finalColor;

                return renderTex;
            }

            ENDCG
        }
    }
    FallBack Off
}
```

Once the shader is complete, return to Unity and let it compile to see whether any errors occurred. If not, assign the new shader to the `TestRenderImage.cs` script and change the value of the grayscale amount variable. You should see the **Game** view go from a colored version of the game to a grayscale version of the game:

Figure 10.2 – The result of our newly created shader

The following screenshot demonstrates this screen effect:

Figure 10.3 – The screen effect created

With this complete, we now have an easy way to test out new screen effects shaders without having to write our whole screen effects system over and over again. Let's dive in a little deeper and learn about what's going on with `RenderTexture` and how it is processed throughout its existence.

How it works...

To get a screen effect up and running inside of Unity, we need to create a script and shader. The script drives the real-time update in the editor and is also responsible for capturing the `RenderTexture` from the main camera and passing it to the shader. Once the `RenderTexture` gets to the shader, we can use the shader to perform per-pixel operations.

At the start of the script, we perform a few checks to make sure that the currently selected build platform actually supports screen effects and the shader itself. There are instances where a current platform will not support screen effects or the shader that we are using. So, the checks that we do in the `Start()` function ensure we don't get any errors if the platform doesn't support the screen system.

Once the script passes these checks, we initiate the screen effects system by calling the built-in `OnRenderImage()` function. This function is responsible for grabbing the `RenderTexture`, giving it to the shader using the `Graphics.Blit()` function, and returning the processed image to the Unity renderer. You can find more information on these two functions at the following links:

- `OnRenderImage`: http://docs.unity3d.com/Documentation/ScriptReference/MonoBehaviour.OnRenderImage.html
- `Graphics.Blit`: http://docs.unity3d.com/Documentation/ScriptReference/Graphics.Blit.html

Once the current `RenderTexture` reaches the shader, the shader takes it, processes it through the `frag()` function, and returns the final color for each pixel.

You can see how powerful this becomes as it gives us Photoshop-like control over the final rendered image of our game. These screen effects work sequentially like Photoshop layers, on top of what the camera sees. When you place these screen effects one after the other, they will be processed in that order. These are just the bare-bones steps to get a screen effect working, but it is the core of how a screen effects system works.

There's more...

Now that we have our simple screen effects system up and running, let's take a look at some of the other useful information we can obtain from Unity's renderer:

Figure 10.4 – Scene depth

We can actually get the depth of everything in our current game by turning on Unity's built-in **Depth** mode. Once this is turned on, we can use the depth information for a ton of different effects. Let's take a look at how this is done.

1. Duplicate the sphere we created twice and create a plane underneath:

Figure 10.5 – The scene setup

2. Create a new shader by duplicating the `ScreenGrayscale` code by selecting it and pressing *Ctrl + D*. Once duplicated, rename the script `SceneDepth`, then double-click on this shader to open it in your script editor.

3. We will create a main texture (`_MainTex`) property and a property to control the power of the scene-depth effect. Enter the following code in your shader:

```
Properties
{
    _MainTex ("Base (RGB)", 2D) = "white" {}
    _DepthPower("Depth Power", Range(0, 1)) = 1
}
```

4. Now, we need to create the corresponding variables in our `CGPROGRAM` block. We are going to add one more variable called `_CameraDepthTexture`. This is a built-in variable that Unity has provided us with through the use of the `UnityCG.cginclude` file. It gives us the depth information from the camera:

```
Pass
{
    CGPROGRAM
    #pragma vertex vert_img
    #pragma fragment frag
    #pragma fragmentoption ARB_precision_hint_fastest
    #include "UnityCG.cginc"

    uniform sampler2D _MainTex;
    fixed _DepthPower;
    sampler2D _CameraDepthTexture;
```

5. We will complete our depth shader by utilizing a couple of built-in functions that Unity provides us with, the `UNITY_SAMPLE_DEPTH()` and `linear01Depth()` functions. The first function actually gets the depth information from our `_CameraDepthTexture` variable and produces a single float value for each pixel. The `Linear01Depth()` function then makes sure that the values are within the 0-1 range by taking this final depth value to a power we can control, where the mid-value in the 0-1 range sits in the scene based off of the camera position:

```
fixed4 frag(v2f_img i) : COLOR
{
    // Get the colors from the RenderTexture and the
    // uv's from the v2f_img struct
    float depth = UNITY_SAMPLE_DEPTH(tex2D(
        _CameraDepthTexture, i.uv.xy));
```

```
            depth = pow(Linear01Depth(depth), _DepthPower);

            return depth;
}
```

6. With our shader complete, let's turn our attention to the Unity Editor and create a new script to work with. Select our `TestRenderImage` script and duplicate it. Name this new script `RenderDepth` and open it up in your script editor.

7. Update the script to have the same class name as what we renamed it to in the previous step (`RenderDepth`):

```
using UnityEngine;

[ExecuteInEditMode]
public class RenderDepth : MonoBehaviour {
```

8. We need to add a `depthPower` variable to the script so that we can let users change the value in the editor:

```
#region Variables
public Shader curShader;
public float depthPower = 0.2f;
private Material screenMat;
#endregion
```

9. Our `OnRenderImage()` function then needs to be updated so that it is passing the right value to our shader:

```
void OnRenderImage(RenderTexture sourceTexture,
RenderTexture destTexture)
{
    if (curShader != null)
    {
        ScreenMat.SetFloat("_DepthPower", depthPower);

        Graphics.Blit(sourceTexture, destTexture,
                      ScreenMat);
    }
```

```
        else
        {
            Graphics.Blit(sourceTexture, destTexture);
        }
    }
}
```

10. To complete our depth screen effect, we need to tell Unity to turn on the depth rendering in the current camera. This is done by simply setting the main camera's `depthTextureMode`:

```
void Update ()
{
    Camera.main.depthTextureMode =
        DepthTextureMode.Depth;
    depthPower = Mathf.Clamp(depthPower, 0, 1);
}
```

With all the code set up, save your script and shader and return to Unity to let them both compile. Afterward, select **Main Camera**, right-click on the `TextRenderImage` component, and select **Remove Component**. Afterward, attach this new component to the object, and drag and drop our new shader inside. If no errors are encountered, you should see a result similar to this:

Figure 10.6 – The result of the render depth shader

Here's an example of what we can get if we tweak the values even more:

Figure 10.7 – The result with different Depth Power values

Using brightness, saturation, and contrast with screen effects

Now that we have our screen effects system up and running, we can explore how to create more involved pixel operations to perform some of the more common screen effects found in games today.

Using brightness, saturation, and contrast with screen effects

Using a screen effect to adjust the overall final colors of your game is crucial in giving artists global control over the final look of the game. Techniques such as color-adjustment sliders allow users to adjust the intensity of the reds, blues, and greens of the final rendered game. This concept is also used with techniques such as putting a certain tone of color over the whole screen, as seen in something such as a sepia film effect.

For this particular recipe, we are going to cover some of the more core color-adjustment operations we can perform on an image. These are brightness, saturation, and contrast. Learning how to code these color adjustments gives us a nice base from which we can learn the art of screen effects.

Getting ready

We will need to create a couple of new assets. We can utilize the same scene as our test scene, but we will need a new script and a shader.

1. Create a new scene by going to **File | New Scene** and use the **Basic (Built-in)** template.
2. Add a couple of new objects to the scene, set up some different colored diffuse materials, and randomly assign them to the new objects in the scene. This will give us a good range of colors to test with our new screen effect:

Figure 10.8 – Setup for this recipe

How to do it...

Now that we have completed our scene setup and created our new script and shader, we can begin to fill in the code necessary to achieve the brightness, saturation, and contrast screen effects. We will be focusing on just the pixel operation and variable setup for our script and shader, since getting a screen effects system up and running is described in the *Setting up a screen effects script system* recipe in this chapter.

1. Create a new shader by duplicating the `ScreenGrayscale` code by selecting it from the **Project** tab under the `Chapter 10 | Shaders` folder and pressing *Ctrl + D*. Once duplicated, rename the script `ScreenBSC`, then double-click on this shader to open it in your script editor.

2. Editing the shader first makes more sense so that we know what kind of variables we will need for our C# script. Let's begin by entering the appropriate properties for our brightness, saturation, and contrast effects. Remember that we need to keep the `_MainTex` property in our shader as this is the property that `RenderTexture` targets when creating screen effects:

    ```
    Properties
    {
        _MainTex ("Base (RGB)", 2D) = "white" {}
        _Brightness("Brightness", Range(0.0, 1)) = 1.0
        _Saturation("Saturation", Range(0.0, 1)) = 1.0
        _Contrast("Contrast", Range(0.0, 1)) = 1.0
    }
    ```

3. As usual, in order for us to access the data coming in from our properties in our `CGPROGRAM` block, we need to create corresponding variables in the `CGPROGRAM` block, replacing the previous ones:

    ```
    Pass
    {
        CGPROGRAM
        #pragma vertex vert_img
        #pragma fragment frag
        #pragma fragmentoption ARB_precision_hint_fastest
        #include "UnityCG.cginc"

        uniform sampler2D _MainTex;
        fixed _Brightness;
    ```

Using brightness, saturation, and contrast with screen effects   301

```
        fixed _Saturation;
        fixed _Contrast;
```

4. Now, we need to create operations that will perform the brightness, saturation, and contrast effects. Enter the following new function in our shader, just above the `frag()` function:

```
float3 ContrastSaturationBrightness(float3 color, float
brt, float sat, float con)
{
    // Increase or decrease these values to
    //adjust r, g and b color channels separately
    float AvgLumR = 0.5;
    float AvgLumG = 0.5;
    float AvgLumB = 0.5;

    //Luminance coefficients for getting luminance
    //from the image
    float3 LuminanceCoeff = float3(0.2125, 0.7154,
                                        0.0721);

    //Operation for brightness
    float3 AvgLumin = float3(AvgLumR, AvgLumG,
                                AvgLumB);
    float3 brtColor = color * brt;
    float intensityf = dot(brtColor, LuminanceCoeff);
    float3 intensity = float3(intensityf, intensityf,
                                intensityf);

    //Operation for Saturation
    float3 satColor = lerp(intensity, brtColor, sat);

    //Operation for Contrast
    float3 conColor = lerp(AvgLumin, satColor, con);
    return conColor;
}
```

> **Note**
> Don't worry if the code doesn't make sense just yet; all the code will be explained in the *How it works...* section of this recipe.

5. Finally, we just need to update our `frag()` function to actually use the `ContrastSaturationBrightness()` function. This will process all the pixels of our `RenderTexture` and pass it back to our script:

```
fixed4 frag(v2f_img i) : COLOR
{
    // Get the colors from the RenderTexture and the
    // uv's from the v2f_img struct
    fixed4 renderTex = tex2D(_MainTex, i.uv);

    // Apply the Brightness, saturation, contrast
    // operations
    renderTex.rgb =
        ContrastSaturationBrightness(renderTex.rgb,
                                     _Brightness,
                                     _Saturation,
                                     _Contrast);

    return renderTex;
}
```

With the code entered in the shader, return to the Unity Editor to let the new shader compile. If there are no errors, we can return to our code editor to work on our script. Let's begin by creating a couple of new lines of code that will send the proper data to our shade:.

1. Now that the shader is finished, let's work on the script needed to make the effect show up. From the **Project** tab, go to the `Chapter 10 | Scripts` folder. Once there, select the `TestRenderImage` script and duplicate it by pressing *Ctrl + D*. Rename the newly created script `RenderBSC`. Once renamed, double-click on it to enter your **integrated development environment** (**IDE**) of choice.

2. To modify our script, we need to rename the class to match our filename, `RenderBSC`:

```
[ExecuteInEditMode]
public class RenderBSC : MonoBehaviour {
```

3. Afterward, we need to add the proper variables that will drive the values of our screen effect. In this case, we will need a slider for brightness, a slider for saturation, and a slider for contrast:

```
#region Variables
public Shader curShader;
public float brightness = 1.0f;
public float saturation = 1.0f;
public float contrast = 1.0f;
private Material screenMat;
#endregion
```

4. With our variables set up, we now need to tell the script to send the values of the variables we created to the shader. We do this in the `OnRenderImage()` function:

```
void OnRenderImage(RenderTexture sourceTexture,
RenderTexture destTexture)
{
    if (curShader != null)
    {
        ScreenMat.SetFloat("_Brightness", brightness);
        ScreenMat.SetFloat("_Saturation", saturation);
        ScreenMat.SetFloat("_Contrast", contrast);

        Graphics.Blit(sourceTexture, destTexture,
                    ScreenMat);
    }
    else
    {
        Graphics.Blit(sourceTexture, destTexture);
    }
}
```

5. Finally, all we need to do is clamp the values of the variables within a range that is reasonable. These clamp values are entirely preferential, so you can use whichever values you see fit:

```
void Update()
{
```

```
        brightness = Mathf.Clamp(brightness, 0.0f, 2.0f);
        saturation = Mathf.Clamp(saturation, 0.0f, 2.0f);
        contrast = Mathf.Clamp(contrast, 0.0f, 3.0f);
    }
```

With the script completed and shader finished, we simply assign our script to **Main Camera** and our shader to the script, and you should see the effects of brightness, saturation, and contrast by manipulating the property values:

Figure 10.9 – The result of the newly created shader

The following screenshot shows what you can achieve with this screen effect:

Figure 10.10 – Result of the brightness, saturation, and contrast effects

The following screenshot shows another example of what can be done by adjusting the colors of the rendered image:

Figure 10.11 – Result of adjusting the image

How it works...

Since we now know how a basic screen effects system works, let's just cover the per-pixel operations we created in the ContrastSaturationBrightness() function.

The function starts by taking a few arguments. The first and most important is the current RenderTexture. The other arguments simply adjust the overall effect of the screen effect and are represented by sliders in the screen effect's **Inspector** tab. Once the function receives the RenderTexture and the adjustment values, it declares a few constant values that we use to modify and compare against the original RenderTexture.

The luminanceCoeff variable stores the values that will give us the overall brightness of the current image. These coefficients are based on the **International Commission on Illumination** (**CIE**) color-matching functions and are pretty standard throughout the industry. We can find the overall brightness of the image by getting the dot product of the current image dotted with these luminance coefficients. Once we have the brightness, we simply use a couple of lerp functions to blend the grayscale version of the brightness operation and the original image, multiplied by the brightness value being passed into the function.

Screen effects such as this are crucial to achieving high-quality graphics for your games as they let you tweak the final look of your game without you having to edit each material in your current game scene.

Using basic Photoshop-like Blend Modes with screen effects

The screen effects aren't just limited to adjusting the colors of a rendered image from our game. We can also use them to combine other images with our RenderTexture. This technique is no different than creating a new layer in Photoshop and choosing a **Blend** mode to blend two images together—or, in our case, a texture with a RenderTexture. This becomes a very powerful technique as it gives the artists in a production environment a way to simulate their blending modes in the game rather than just in Photoshop.

For this particular recipe, we are going to take a look at some of the more common Blend Modes, such as **Multiply**, **Add**, and **Overlay**. You will see how simple it is to have the power of Photoshop **Blend** modes in your game.

Getting ready

To begin, we have to get our assets ready. So, let's follow the next few steps to get our screen effects system up and running for our new **Blend** mode screen effect:

1. We will need another texture to perform our **Blend** mode effect. In this recipe, we will use a grunge-type texture. This will make the effect very obvious when we are testing it out.

2. The following screenshot shows the grunge map used in the making of this effect. Finding a texture with enough detail and a nice range of grayscale values will make for a nice texture to test our new effect:

Figure 10.12 – The grunge map used in this recipe

> **Note**
> The preceding texture is available in the example code for this book in the `Chapter 10 | Textures` folder.

How to do it...

The first **Blend** mode that we will implement is the **Multiply** Blend Mode, as seen in Photoshop. Let's begin by modifying the code in our shader first.

1. Create a new shader by duplicating the `ScreenGrayscale` code by selecting it from the **Project** tab under the `Chapter 10 | Shaders` folder and pressing *Ctrl + D*. Once duplicated, rename the script `ScreenBlendMode`, then double-click on this shader to open it in your script editor.

2. We need to add some new properties so that we have a texture to blend with and a slider for an opacity value. Enter the following code in your new shader:

```
Properties
{
    _MainTex ("Base (RGB)", 2D) = "white" {}
    _BlendTex ("Blend Texture", 2D) = "white"{}
    _Opacity ("Blend Opacity", Range(0,1)) = 1
}
```

3. Enter the corresponding variables in our `CGPROGRAM` block so that we can access the data from our `Properties` block, replacing the previously created variables:

```
Pass
{
    CGPROGRAM
    #pragma vertex vert_img
    #pragma fragment frag
    #pragma fragmentoption ARB_precision_hint_fastest
    #include "UnityCG.cginc"

    uniform sampler2D _MainTex;
    uniform sampler2D _BlendTex;
    fixed _Opacity;
```

4. We modify our `frag()` function so that it performs a multiply operation on our two textures:

```
fixed4 frag(v2f_img i) : COLOR
{
    // Get the colors from the RenderTexture and the
    // uv's from the v2f_img struct
    fixed4 renderTex = tex2D(_MainTex, i.uv);
    fixed4 blendTex = tex2D(_BlendTex, i.uv);

    // Perform a Multiply Blend Mode
    fixed4 blendedMultiply = renderTex * blendTex;

    // Adjust amount of Blend Mode with a lerp
    renderTex = lerp(renderTex, blendedMultiply,
                     _Opacity);

    return renderTex;
}
```

5. Save the shader and return to the Unity Editor to let the new shader code compile and check for errors. If no errors occurred, then we can move on to creating our script file.

6. Now the shader is finished, let's work on the script needed to make the effect show up. From the **Project** tab, go to the `Chapter 10 | Scripts` folder. Once there, select the `TestRenderImage` script and duplicate it by pressing *Ctrl + D*. Rename the newly created script to `RenderBlendMode`. Once renamed, double-click on it to enter your IDE of choice.

7. Our first step in modifying our script is to rename the class to match our filename, `RenderBlendMode`:

```
[ExecuteInEditMode]
public class RenderBlendMode : MonoBehaviour {
```

8. In our script file, we need to create the corresponding variables. We will need a texture so that we can assign one to the shader and a slider to adjust the final amount of the Blend Mode we want to use:

```
#region Variables
public Shader curShader;
public Texture2D blendTexture;
public float blendOpacity = 1.0f;
private Material screenMat;
#endregion
```

9. We then need to send our variable data to the shader through the `OnRenderImage()` function:

```
void OnRenderImage(RenderTexture sourceTexture,
RenderTexture destTexture)
{
    if (curShader != null)
    {
        ScreenMat.SetTexture("_BlendTex",
                            blendTexture);
        ScreenMat.SetFloat("_Opacity", blendOpacity);

        Graphics.Blit(sourceTexture, destTexture,
                      ScreenMat);
    }
    else
    {
        Graphics.Blit(sourceTexture, destTexture);
    }
}
```

310   Screen Effects with Unity Render Textures

10. To complete the script, we simply fill in our `Update()` function so that we can clamp the value of the `blendOpacity` variable between a value of `0.0` and `1.0`:

```
void Update()
{
    blendOpacity = Mathf.Clamp(blendOpacity, 0.0f,
                                             1.0f);
}
```

11. With this complete, we assign the screen effects script to **Main Camera** (remove the previous `Render BSC` script if it is attached) and add our screen effects shader to our script so that it has a shader to use for the per-pixel operations. For the effect to be fully functional, the script and shader look for a texture. You can assign any texture to the **Texture** field in the **Inspector** tab for the screen effects script. Once this texture is in place, you will see the effect of multiplying this texture over the game's rendered screenshot:

Figure 10.13 – Texture effect

12. The following screenshot demonstrates the screen effect with a smaller **Blend Opacity** option:

Figure 10.14 – Texture with blend effect

With our first Blend Mode set up, we can begin to add a couple of simpler Blend Modes to get a better understanding of how easy it is to add more effects and really fine-tune the final result in your game. However, let's first break down what is happening here.

How it works...

We are now starting to gain a ton of power and flexibility in our screen effects programming. I am sure that you are now starting to understand how much you can do with this simple system in Unity. We can literally replicate the effects of Photoshop layer-blending modes in our game to give artists the flexibility they need to achieve high-quality graphics in a short amount of time.

With this particular recipe, we look at how to multiply two images together, add two images together, and perform a screen-blending mode, using just a little bit of mathematics. When working with Blend Modes, you have to think on a per-pixel level. For instance, when we are using the Multiply Blend Mode, we literally take each pixel from the original `RenderTexture` and multiply it by each pixel of the Blend texture. The same goes for the Add Blend Mode. It is just a simple mathematical operation of adding each pixel from the source texture, or `RenderTexture`, to the Blend texture.

The Screen Blend Mode is definitely a bit more involved, but it is actually doing the same thing. It takes each image, `RenderTexture`, and Blend texture, inverts them, multiplies them together, and inverts them again to achieve the final look. Just as Photoshop blends its textures together using Blend Modes, we can do the same with screen effects.

There's more...

Let's continue this recipe by adding a couple more Blend Modes to our screen effect:

1. In the screen effects shader (`ScreenBlendMode`), let's add the following code to our `frag()` function and change the value we are returning to our script. We will also need to comment out the Multiply Blend so that we don't return that as well:

   ```
   fixed4 frag(v2f_img i) : COLOR
   {
       //Get the colors from the RenderTexture and the
       // uv's from the v2f_img struct
       fixed4 renderTex = tex2D(_MainTex, i.uv);
       fixed4 blendTex = tex2D(_BlendTex, i.uv);

       //Perform a Multiply Blend Mode
       //fixed4 blendedMultiply = renderTex * blendTex;

       //Perform an additive Blend Mode
       fixed4 blendedAdd = renderTex + blendTex;

       //Adjust amount of Blend Mode with a lerp
       renderTex = lerp(renderTex, blendedAdd, _Opacity);

       return renderTex;
   }
   ```

2. Save the shader file in your IDE of choice and return to the Unity Editor to let the shader compile. If no errors occurred, you should see a result similar to this:

Figure 10.15 – The result of using an additive Blend Mode

3. This is a simple add blending mode with a figure of 0.5 set for **Blend Opacity**:

Figure 10.16 – Add blending mode

> **Note**
> As you can see, this has the opposite effect of multiplying because we are adding the two images together.

4. Finally, let's add one more Blend Mode called a Screen Blend. This one is a little bit more involved from a mathematical standpoint but is still simple to implement. Enter the following code in the `frag()` function of our shader:

```
fixed4 frag(v2f_img i) : COLOR
{
    // Get the colors from the RenderTexture and the
    // uv's from the v2f_img struct
    fixed4 renderTex = tex2D(_MainTex, i.uv);
    fixed4 blendTex = tex2D(_BlendTex, i.uv);

    // Perform a multiply Blend Mode
    //fixed4 blendedMultiply = renderTex * blendTex;

    // Perform an additive Blend Mode
    //fixed4 blendedAdd = renderTex + blendTex;

    //Perform Screen Blending mode
    fixed4 blendedScreen = (1.0 - ((1.0 - renderTex) *
                                    (1.0 - blendTex)));

    //Adjust amount of Blend Mode with a lerp
    renderTex = lerp(renderTex, blendedScreen,
                    _Opacity);

    return renderTex;
}
```

The following screenshot demonstrates the results of using a screen-type Blend Mode to blend two images together in a screen effect:

Figure 10.17 – The result of the screen-blending effect

Here's a screenshot displaying the effect:

Figure 10.18 – Screen Blend Mode

Using the Overlay Blend Mode with screen effects

For our final recipe, we are going to take a look at another type of Blend Mode, the Overlay Blend Mode. This Blend Mode actually makes use of some conditional statements that determine the final color of each pixel in each channel, so the process of using this type of Blend Mode requires a bit more coding to work. Let's take a look at how this is done.

How to do it...

To begin our Overlay Screen effect, we will need to get the code of our shader up and running without errors. We can then modify our script file to feed the correct data to the shade:.

1. Create a new shader by duplicating the `ScreenGrayscale` code and selecting it from the **Project** tab under the `Chapter 10 | Shaders` folder and pressing *Ctrl* + *D*. Once duplicated, rename the script `ScreenOverlay`, then double-click on this shader to open it in your script editor.

2. We first need to set up properties in our `Properties` block. We will use the same properties from the previous few recipes in this chapter:

   ```
   Properties
   {
       _MainTex ("Base (RGB)", 2D) = "white" {}
       _BlendTex ("Blend Texture", 2D) = "white"{}
       _Opacity ("Blend Opacity", Range(0,1)) = 1
   }
   ```

3. We then need to create corresponding variables in our `CGPROGRAM` block, removing the previously created ones:

   ```
   Pass
   {
       CGPROGRAM
       #pragma vertex vert_img
       #pragma fragment frag
       #pragma fragmentoption ARB_precision_hint_fastest
       #include "UnityCG.cginc"
   ```

```
uniform sampler2D _MainTex;
uniform sampler2D _BlendTex;
fixed _Opacity;
```

4. In order for the Overlay Blend effect to work, we will have to process each pixel from each channel individually. To do this in a shader, we have to write a custom function that will take in a single channel (for instance, the red channel) and perform the overlay operation. Enter the following code in the shader just below the variable declarations:

```
fixed OverlayBlendMode(fixed basePixel, fixed blendPixel)
{
    If (basePixel < 0.5)
    {
        return (2.0 * basePixel * blendPixel);
    }
    else
    {
        return (1.0 - 2.0 * (1.0 - basePixel) * (1.0 -
            blendPixel));
    }
}
```

5. We need to update our `frag()` function to process each channel of our textures in order to perform the blending:

```
fixed4 frag(v2f_img i) : COLOR
{
    // Get the colors from the RenderTexture and the
    // uv's from the v2f_img struct
    fixed4 renderTex = tex2D(_MainTex, i.uv);
    fixed4 blendTex = tex2D(_BlendTex, i.uv);

    fixed4 blendedImage = renderTex;

    blendedImage.r = OverlayBlendMode(renderTex.r,
                                      blendTex.r);
    blendedImage.g = OverlayBlendMode(renderTex.g,
                                      blendTex.g);
```

```
    blendedImage.b = OverlayBlendMode(renderTex.b,
                                      blendTex.b);

    // Adjust amount of Blend Mode with a lerp
    renderTex = lerp(renderTex, blendedImage,
                     _Opacity);

    return renderTex;
}
```

6. With the code completed in the shader, our effect should be working. Save the shader and return to the Unity Editor to let the shader compile. Our script is already set up; select the **Main Camera** object. From the **Project** tab, drag and drop the **ScreenOverlay** shader onto the **curShader** property from the **Render Blend Mode** component in the **Inspector** tab. After that, assign the **Blend Texture** property with a texture file, such as the one in the Chapter 10 | Textures folder. Once the shader compiles, you should see a result similar to this:

Figure 10.19 – An example of the Screen Overlay shader

Here's a screenshot using a **Blend Opacity** setting of 0.5:

Figure 10.20 – Overlay Blend Mode

How it works...

Our Overlay Blend Mode is definitely a lot more involved, but if you really break down the function, you will notice that it is simply a Multiply Blend Mode and Screen Blend Mode. In this case, we are doing a conditional check to apply one or the other Blend Mode to a pixel.

With this particular screen effect, when the overlay function receives a pixel, it checks to see whether it is less than 0.5. If it is, we then apply a modified Multiply Blend Mode to that pixel; if it's not, we apply a modified Screen Blend Mode to the pixel. We do this for each pixel for each channel, giving us the final **Red-Green-Blue** (**RGB**) pixel values for our screen effect.

As you can see, many things can be done with screen effects. It really just depends on the platform and the amount of memory you have allocated for screen effects. Usually, this is determined throughout the course of a game project, so have fun and get creative with your screen effects!

11
Gameplay and Screen Effects

When it comes to creating believable and immersive games, material design is not the only aspect we need to take into account. The overall feeling can be altered using screen effects. This is very common in movies, for instance, when colors are corrected in the post-production phase. You can implement these techniques in your games too, using the knowledge from *Chapter 10, Screen Effects with Unity Render Textures*. Two interesting effects are presented in this chapter; you can, however, adapt them to fit your needs and create your very own screen effect.

If you are reading this book, you are most likely a person who has played a game or two in your time. One of the aspects of real-time games is the effect of immersing a player in a world to make it feel as if they were actually playing in the real world. More modern games make heavy use of screen effects to achieve this immersion.

With screen effects, we can turn the mood of a certain environment from calm to scary, just by changing the look of the screen. Imagine walking into a room that is contained within a level, then the game takes over and goes into a cinematic moment. Many modern games will turn on different screen effects to change the mood of the current moment. Understanding how to create effects triggered by gameplay is next in our journey through shader writing.

In this chapter, we are going to take a look at some of the more common gameplay screen effects. You are going to learn how to change the look of a game from normal to an old movie effect, and we are going to take a look at how many **first-person shooter** (**FPS**) games apply their night-vision effects to the screen. With each of these recipes, we are going to look at how to hook these up to game events so that they are turned on and off as the game's current presentation requires.

In this chapter, you will learn the following recipes:

- Creating an old movie screen effect
- Creating a night-vision screen effect

Technical requirements

This chapter was created with Unity 2021.1.9f1 but should work in future versions of Unity with minimal revisions.

You can find the code files present in this chapter on GitHub at `https://github.com/PacktPublishing/Unity-2021-Shaders-and-Effects-Cookbook-Fourth-Edition/tree/main/Shaders-and-Effects-Cookbook-2021/Assets/Chapter%2011`.

Creating an old movie screen effect

Many games are set in different times. Some take place in fantasy worlds or future sci-fi worlds, and some even take place in the Old West, where film cameras were just being developed and the movies that people watched were black and white or sometimes tinted with what is called a **sepia effect**. The look is very distinct, and we are going to replicate this look using a screen effect in Unity.

There are a few steps to achieving this look; just to make the whole screen black and white or grayscale, we need to break down this effect into its component parts. If we analyze some reference footage of an old movie, we can begin to do this. Let's take a look at the following screenshot and break down the elements that make up the old movie look:

Figure 11.1 – A demonstration of an old movie look

We constructed this screenshot using a few reference images found online. It is always a good idea to try and utilize Photoshop to construct images such as this to aid you in creating a plan for your new screen effect. Performing this process not only tells us the elements we will have to code in but also gives us a quick way to see which blending modes work and how we will construct the layers of our screen effect.

Getting ready

Now we know what we have to make, let's take a look at how each of the layers is combined to create the final effect and gather some resources for our shader and screen-effects script:

- **Sepia tone**: This is a relatively simple effect to achieve, as we just need to bring all the pixel colors of the original render texture to a single color range. This is easily achieved using the luminance of the original image and adding a constant color. Our first layer will look like this:

Figure 11.2 – Original image with added color

- **Vignette effect**: We can always see some sort of soft border around old films when they are being projected using an old movie projector. This is caused because the bulb that is used for the movie projector has more brightness in the middle than it does at the edges of the film. This effect is generally called a vignette effect and is the second layer in our screen effect. We can achieve this with an overlaid texture over the whole screen. The following screenshot demonstrates what this layer looks like, isolated as a texture:

Figure 11.3 – Vignette texture

- **Dust and scratches**: The third and final layer in our old movie screen effect is dust and scratches. This layer will utilize two different tiled textures, one for scratches and one for dust. The reason is that we will want to animate these two textures over time at different tiling rates. This will give the effect that the film is moving along and there are small scratches and dust on each frame of the old film. The following screenshot demonstrates this effect isolated to its own texture:

Figure 11.4 – Dust and scratches texture

Let's get our screen-effects system ready with the preceding textures. Perform the following steps:

1. Gather a vignette texture and a dust and scratches texture, like the ones we just saw.
2. We will also need a scene for which we want to emulate the effect we're trying to build. I have created a sample scene that you can use in the `Chapter 11` folder of the example code, called `11.1 Starting Point`:

Figure 11.5 – Opening the starter-scene file

3. Create a new shader by duplicating the `ScreenGrayscale` code; select it from the **Project** tab under the `Chapter 10 | Shaders` folder and press *Ctrl + D*. Once duplicated, rename the script `ScreenOldFilm`. Then, drag and drop the script into the `Chapter 11 | Shaders` folder, creating it if needed.
4. Next, go to the `Chapter 10 | Scripts` folder and duplicate the `TestRenderImage` script. Rename the new file `RenderOldFilm` and then drag and drop it into the `Chapter 11 | Scripts` folder, creating it if needed.

Finally, with our screen-effects system up and running and our textures gathered, we can begin the process of recreating this old movie effect.

How to do it...

Our individual layers for our old movie screen effect are quite simple, but when combined, we get some very stunning visual effects. Let's run through how to construct the code for our script and shader, and we can then step through each line of code and learn why things are working the way they are. At this point, you should have the screen-effects system up and running, as we will not be covering how to set this up in this recipe.

1. We will begin by entering the code in our script. Our first step in modifying our script is to rename the class to match our filename, `RenderOldFilm`:

   ```
   [ExecuteInEditMode]
   public class RenderOldFilm : MonoBehaviour
   ```

2. The first block of code that we will enter will define the variable that we want to expose to the **Inspector** tab, in order to let the user of this effect adjust it as they see fit. We can also use our mocked-up Photoshop file as a reference when deciding what we will need to expose to the **Inspector** tab of this effect. Enter the following code in your effect script:

   ```
   #region Variables
   public Shader curShader; // old film shader

   public float OldFilmEffectAmount = 1.0f;

   public Color sepiaColor = Color.white;
   public Texture2D vignetteTexture;
   public float vignetteAmount = 1.0f;

   public Texture2D scratchesTexture;
   public float scratchesYSpeed = 10.0f;
   public float scratchesXSpeed = 10.0f;

   public Texture2D dustTexture;
   public float dustYSpeed = 10.0f;
   public float dustXSpeed = 10.0f;

   private Material screenMat;
   private float randomValue;
   #endregion
   ```

3. Next, we need to fill in the contents of our `OnRenderImage()` function. Here, we will be passing the data from our variables to our shader so that the shader can then use this data in the processing of the render texture:

```
void OnRenderImage(RenderTexture sourceTexture,
                  RenderTexture destTexture)
{
    if (curShader != null)
    {
        ScreenMat.SetColor("_SepiaColor", sepiaColor);
        ScreenMat.SetFloat("_VignetteAmount",
                            vignetteAmount);
        ScreenMat.SetFloat("_EffectAmount",
                            OldFilmEffectAmount);

        if (vignetteTexture)
        {
            ScreenMat.SetTexture("_VignetteTex",
                                  vignetteTexture);
        }

        if (scratchesTexture)
        {
            ScreenMat.SetTexture("_ScratchesTex",
                                  scratchesTexture);
            ScreenMat.SetFloat("_ScratchesYSpeed",
                                scratchesYSpeed);
            ScreenMat.SetFloat("_ScratchesXSpeed",
                                scratchesXSpeed);
        }

        if (dustTexture)
        {
            ScreenMat.SetTexture("_DustTex",
                                  dustTexture);
            ScreenMat.SetFloat("_dustYSpeed",
                                dustYSpeed);
```

328 Gameplay and Screen Effects

```
            ScreenMat.SetFloat("_dustXSpeed",
                              dustXSpeed);
            ScreenMat.SetFloat("_RandomValue",
                              randomValue);
        }

        Graphics.Blit(sourceTexture, destTexture,
                      ScreenMat);
    }
    else
    {
        Graphics.Blit(sourceTexture, destTexture);
    }
}
```

4. To complete the script portion of this effect, we simply need to make sure that we clamp the values of the variables that need to have a clamped range instead of being any value:

```
void Update()
{
    vignetteAmount = Mathf.Clamp01(vignetteAmount);
    OldFilmEffectAmount =
        Mathf.Clamp(OldFilmEffectAmount, 0f, 1.5f);
    randomValue = Random.Range(-1f, 1f);
}
```

5. With our script complete, let's turn our attention to our shader file. We need to create corresponding variables to what we created in our script in our shader. This will allow the script and shader to communicate with one another. Enter the following code in the Properties block of the shader:

```
Properties
{
    _MainTex ("Base (RGB)", 2D) = "white" {}
    _VignetteTex ("Vignette Texture", 2D) = "white"{}
    _ScratchesTex ("Scratches Texture", 2D) =
        "white"{}
    _DustTex ("Dust Texture", 2D) = "white"{}
```

```
        _SepiaColor ("Sepia Color", Color) = (1,1,1,1)
        _EffectAmount ("Old Film Effect Amount",
            Range(0,1)) = 1.0
        _VignetteAmount ("Vignette Opacity", Range(0,1)) =
            1.0
        _ScratchesYSpeed ("Scratches Y Speed", Float) =
            10.0
        _ScratchesXSpeed ("Scratches X Speed", Float) =
            10.0
        _dustXSpeed ("Dust X Speed", Float) = 10.0
        _dustYSpeed ("Dust Y Speed", Float) = 10.0
        _RandomValue ("Random Value", Float) = 1.0
        _Contrast ("Contrast", Float) = 3.0
    }
```

6. Then, as usual, we need to add these same variable names to our CGPROGRAM block so that the Properties block can communicate with the CGPROGRAM block:

```
Pass
{
    CGPROGRAM
    #pragma vertex vert_img
    #pragma fragment frag
    #pragma fragmentoption ARB_precision_hint_fastest
    #include "UnityCG.cginc"

    uniform sampler2D _MainTex;
    uniform sampler2D _VignetteTex;
    uniform sampler2D _ScratchesTex;
    uniform sampler2D _DustTex;
    fixed4 _SepiaColor;
    fixed _VignetteAmount;
    fixed _ScratchesYSpeed;
    fixed _ScratchesXSpeed;
    fixed _dustXSpeed;
    fixed _dustYSpeed;
```

```
        fixed _EffectAmount;
        fixed _RandomValue;
        fixed _Contrast;
```

7. Now, we simply fill in the guts of our `frag()` function so that we can process the pixels for our screen effect. To start with, let's get the render texture and vignette texture passed to us by the script:

```
fixed4 frag(v2f_img i) : COLOR
{
        // Get the colors from the RenderTexture and the
        // uv's from the v2f_img struct
        fixed4 renderTex = tex2D(_MainTex, i.uv);

        // Get the pixels from the Vignette Texture
        fixed4 vignetteTex = tex2D(_VignetteTex, i.uv);
```

8. We then need to add the process for the dust and scratches by entering the following code:

```
        // Process the Scratches UV and pixels
        half2 scratchesUV = half2(i.uv.x + (_RandomValue *
           _SinTime.z * _ScratchesXSpeed), i.uv.y + (_Time.x
           * _ScratchesYSpeed));
        fixed4 scratchesTex = tex2D(_ScratchesTex,
                                    scratchesUV);

        // Process the Dust UV and pixels
        half2 dustUV = half2(i.uv.x + (_RandomValue *
           (_SinTime.z * _dustXSpeed)), i.uv.y + (_RandomValue
           * (_SinTime.z * _dustYSpeed)));
        fixed4 dustTex = tex2D(_DustTex, dustUV);
```

9. The sepia-tone process is next on our list:

```
// Get the luminosity values from the render texture
// using the YIQ values.
fixed lum = dot (fixed3(0.299, 0.587, 0.114),
                renderTex.rgb);

// Add the constant color to the lum values
fixed4 finalColor = lum + lerp(_SepiaColor,_SepiaColor
    + fixed4(0.1f,0.1f,0.1f,1.0f), _RandomValue);
finalColor = pow(finalColor, _Contrast);
```

10. Finally, we combine all of our layers and colors and return the final screen-effect texture:

```
// Create a constant white color we can use to
// adjust opacity of effects
fixed3 constantWhite = fixed3(1,1,1);

// Composite together the different layers to create //
final Screen Effect
  finalColor = lerp(finalColor, finalColor *
                    vignetteTex, _VignetteAmount);
  finalColor.rgb *= lerp(scratchesTex, constantWhite,
                    (_RandomValue));
  finalColor.rgb *= lerp(dustTex.rgb, constantWhite,
                    (_RandomValue * _SinTime.z));
  finalColor = lerp(renderTex, finalColor,
                    _EffectAmount);

  return finalColor;
}
```

332   Gameplay and Screen Effects

11. With all of our code entered and no errors, return to the Unity editor and add the `RenderOldFilm` component to **Main Camera** in our example scene. From there, drag and drop our shader into the **Cur Shader** property. Afterward, under **Sepia Color**, assign a brown color like the one shown here:

Figure 11.6 – Color for the Sepia Color field

12. Afterward, assign each of the textures given to the appropriate property:

Figure 11.7 – Textures assigned to the Render Old Film (Script)

13. After applying the images, you should then see something similar to this:

Figure 11.8 – The result of our new shader

14. Also, make sure to hit **Play** in the Unity editor to see the full extent of the effects of the dust and scratches and the slight image shift that we gave the screen effect.

How it works...

Now, let's walk through each of the layers in this screen effect, break down why each of the lines of code is working the way it is, and get more insight about how we can add more to this screen effect.

Now that our old film screen effect is working, let's step through the lines of code in our `frag()` function, as all the other code should be pretty self-explanatory at this point in the book.

Just as with our Photoshop layers, our shader is processing each layer and then compositing them together, so while we go through each layer, try to imagine how the layers in Photoshop work. Keeping this concept in mind always helps when developing new screen effects.

Here, we have the first set of lines of code in our `frag()` function:

```
fixed4 frag(v2f_img i) : COLOR
{
    //Get the colors from the RenderTexture and the uv's
    //from the v2f_img struct
    fixed4 renderTex = tex2D(_MainTex, i.uv);

    //Get the pixels from the Vignette Texture
    fixed4 vignetteTex = tex2D(_VignetteTex, i.uv);
```

The first line of code, just after the `frag()` function declaration, is the definition of how the UVs should work for our main render texture or the actual rendered frame of our game.

As we are looking to fake the effect of an old film style, we want to adjust the UVs of our render texture in every frame, such that they flicker. This flickering simulates how the winding of the film's projector is just a bit off. This tells us that we need to animate the UVs, and this first line of code gives us the ability to do just that.

We used the built-in `_SinTime` variable, which Unity provides, to get a value between -1 and 1. We then multiply this by a very small number—in this case, 0.005—to reduce the intensity of the effect. The final value is then multiplied again by the `_RandomValue` variable, which we generated in the effect script. This value bounces back and forth between -1 and 1 to basically flip the direction of the motion back and forth.

Once our UVs are built and stored in the `renderTexUV` variable, we can sample the render texture using a `tex2D()` function. This operation then gives us our final render texture, which we can use to process further in the rest of the shader.

Moving on to the last line in the previous code snippet, we simply do a straight sample of the vignette texture using the `tex2D()` function. We don't need to use the animated UVs we already created, as the vignette texture will be tied to the motion of the camera itself and not to the flickering of the camera film.

The following code snippet illustrates the second set of lines of code in our `frag()` function:

```
//Process the Scratches UV and pixels
half2 scratchesUV = half2(i.uv.x + (_RandomValue *
    _SinTime.z * _ScratchesXSpeed), i.uv.y + (_Time.x *
    _ScratchesYSpeed));
fixed4 scratchesTex = tex2D(_ScratchesTex, scratchesUV);

//Process the Dust UV and pixels
half2 dustUV = half2(i.uv.x + (_RandomValue * (_SinTime.z *
    _dustXSpeed)), i.uv.y + (_RandomValue * (_SinTime.z *
    _dustYSpeed)));
fixed4 dustTex = tex2D(_DustTex, dustUV);
```

These lines of code are almost exactly like the previous lines of code, in which we need to generate unique animated UV values to modify the position of our screen-effect layers. We simply use the built-in `_SinTime` value to get a value between -1 and 1, multiply it by our random value, and then by another multiplier to adjust the overall speed of the animation. Once these UV values are generated, we can then sample our dust and scratches texture using these new animated values.

Our next set of code handles the creation of a colorizing effect for our old film screen effect. The following code snippet demonstrates these lines:

```
// get the luminosity values from the render texture using
// the YIQ values
fixed lum = dot (fixed3(0.299, 0.587, 0.114),
                 renderTex.rgb);

//Add the constant color to the lum values
fixed4 finalColor = lum + lerp(_SepiaColor, _SepiaColor +
    fixed4(0.1f,0.1f,0.1f,1.0f), _RandomValue);
```

With this set of code, we are creating the actual color tinting of the entire render texture. To accomplish this, we first need to turn the render texture into the grayscale version of itself. To do this, we can use the luminosity values given to us by the YIQ values. YIQ values are the color space used by the **National Television System Committee (NTSC)** color TV system. Each letter in YIQ actually stores color constants that are used by TVs to adjust the color for readability.

While it is not necessary to actually know the reasons for this color scale, it should be known that the Y value in YIQ is the constant luminance value for any image. So, we can generate a grayscale image of our render texture by taking each pixel of the render texture and dotting it with our luminance values. This is what the first line in this set of code is doing.

Once we have the luminance values, we can simply add the color we want to tint the image with. This color is passed from our script to our shader, then to our CGPROGRAM block, where we can add it to our grayscale render to texture. Once completed, we will have a perfectly tinted image.

Finally, we create a blending between each of our layers in our screen effect. The following code snippet shows the set of code we are looking at:

```
//Create a constant white color we can use to adjust
//opacity of effects
fixed3 constantWhite = fixed3(1,1,1);

//Composite together the different layers to create final
//Screen Effect
finalColor = lerp(finalColor, finalColor * vignetteTex,
                _VignetteAmount);
finalColor.rgb *= lerp(scratchesTex, constantWhite,
                (_RandomValue));
finalColor.rgb *= lerp(dustTex.rgb, constantWhite,
                (_RandomValue * _SinTime.z));
finalColor = lerp(renderTex, finalColor, _EffectAmount);

return finalColor
```

Our last set of code is relatively simple and doesn't really need a lot of explanation. In short, it is simply multiplying all the layers together to reach our final result. Just as we multiplied our layers together in Photoshop, we multiply them together in our shader. Each layer is processed through a `lerp()` function so that we can adjust the opacity of each layer, which gives more artistic control over the final effect. The more tweaks we can offer, the better it is when it comes to screen effects.

See also

For more information on `YIQ` values, refer to the following links:

- `http://en.wikipedia.org/wiki/YIQ`
- `http://www.blackice.com/colorspaceYIQ.htm`

Creating a night-vision screen effect

Our next screen effect is definitely a more popular one. A night-vision screen effect is seen in *Call of Duty*, *Halo*, and just about any FPS out in the market today. It is the effect of brightening the whole image using that very distinct lime-green color.

In order to achieve our night-vision effect, we need to break down our effect using Photoshop. This is a simple process of finding some reference images online and composing a layered image to see what kinds of blending modes you will need or in which order we will need to combine our layers. The following screenshot shows the result of just performing this process in Photoshop:

Figure 11.9 – The result we are trying to achieve in this recipe

Let's begin to break down our rough Photoshop composite image into its component parts so that we can better understand the assets we will have to gather. In this recipe, we will cover the process of doing this.

Getting ready

Let's begin this screen effect by again breaking down our effect into its component layers. Using Photoshop, we can construct a layered image to better illustrate how we can go about capturing the effect of night vision:

- **Tinted green**: Our first layer in our screen effect is the iconic green color, found in just about every night-vision image. This will give our effect that signature night-vision look, as shown in the following screenshot:

Figure 11.10 – A tinted green visual

- **Scan lines**: To increase the effect of this being a new type of display for the player, we include scan lines over the top of our tinted layer. For this, we will use a texture created in Photoshop and let the user tile it so that the scan lines can be bigger or smaller.

> **Note**
> Scan lines can also be created without a texture with various methods such as those found at `https://github.com/vanruesc/postprocessing/blob/main/src/effects/glsl/scanlines/shader.frag` or `https://gist.github.com/code-disaster/869c1c47d8b708dc2458538907445952`.

- **Noise**: Our next layer is a simple noise texture that we tile over the tinted image and scan lines to break up the image and add even more detail to our effect. This layer simply emphasizes that digital readout look:

Figure 11.11 – A noise texture

- **Vignette**: The last layer in our night-vision effect is the vignette. If you look at the night-vision effect in *Call of Duty*, you will notice that it uses a vignette that fakes the effect of looking down a scope. We will do that for this screen effect:

Figure 11.12 – A vignette texture

Let's create a screen-effects system by gathering our textures. Perform the following steps:

1. Gather up a vignette texture, noise texture, and scan-line texture, like the ones we just saw. As before, I have these textures available in the book's example code under the `Chapter 11 | Textures` folder.

2. Find a sample scene to make it easy to see the effect of the shader. I will be using the same scene as in the previous recipe, so feel free to use the `11.1 Starting Point` sample scene again.

3. Create a new shader by duplicating the `ScreenGrayscale` code by selecting it from the **Project** tab under the `Chapter 10 | Shaders` folder and then pressing *Ctrl + D*. Once duplicated, rename the script `ScreenNightVision` and then drag and drop the script into the `Chapter 11 | Shaders` folder, creating it if needed.

4. Next, go to the `Chapter 10 | Scripts` folder and duplicate the `TestRenderImage` script. Rename the new file `RenderNightVision` and then drag and drop it into the `Chapter 11 | Scripts` folder, creating it if needed.

Finally, with our screen-effects system up and running and our textures gathered, we can begin the process of recreating this night-vision effect.

How to do it...

With all of our assets gathered and the screen-effects system running smoothly, let's begin to add the code necessary to both the script and shader. We will begin our coding with the `RenderNightVision.cs` script, so double-click on this file now to open it in your code editor of choice.

1. We will begin by entering the code in our script. Our first step in modifying our script is to rename the class to match our filename, `RenderNightVision`:

    ```
    [ExecuteInEditMode]
    public class RenderNightVision : MonoBehaviour
    ```

2. We need to create a few variables that will allow the user of this effect to adjust it in the script's **Inspector** tab. Enter the following code into the `NightVisionEffect.cs` script:

    ```
    #region Variables
        public Shader curShader;

        public float contrast = 3.0f;
        public float brightness = 0.1f;
    ```

```
    public Color nightVisionColor = Color.green;

    public Texture2D vignetteTexture;

    public Texture2D scanLineTexture;
    public float scanLineTileAmount = 4.0f;

    public Texture2D nightVisionNoise;
    public float noiseXSpeed = 100.0f;
    public float noiseYSpeed = 100.0f;

    public float distortion = 0.2f;
    public float scale = 0.8f;

    private float randomValue = 0.0f;
    private Material screenMat;
    #endregion
```

3. Next, we need to complete our OnRenderImage() function so that we are passing the right data to the shader for the shader to process the screen effect properly. Complete the OnRenderImage() function with the following code:

```
void OnRenderImage(RenderTexture sourceTexture,
                   RenderTexture destTexture)
{
    if (curShader != null)
    {
        ScreenMat.SetFloat("_Contrast", contrast);
        ScreenMat.SetFloat("_Brightness", brightness);
        ScreenMat.SetColor("_NightVisionColor",
                           nightVisionColor);
        ScreenMat.SetFloat("_RandomValue",
                           randomValue);
        ScreenMat.SetFloat("_distortion", distortion);
        ScreenMat.SetFloat("_scale", scale);
```

```csharp
            if (vignetteTexture)
            {
                ScreenMat.SetTexture("_VignetteTex",
                                vignetteTexture);
            }
            
            if (scanLineTexture)
            {
                ScreenMat.SetTexture("_ScanLineTex",
                                scanLineTexture);
                ScreenMat.SetFloat("_ScanLineTileAmount",
                                scanLineTileAmount);
            }
            
            if (nightVisionNoise)
            {
                ScreenMat.SetTexture("_NoiseTex",
                                nightVisionNoise);
                ScreenMat.SetFloat("_NoiseXSpeed",
                                noiseXSpeed);
                ScreenMat.SetFloat("_NoiseYSpeed",
                                noiseYSpeed);
            }
            
        Graphics.Blit(sourceTexture, destTexture,
                ScreenMat);
    }
    else
    {
        Graphics.Blit(sourceTexture, destTexture);
    }
}
```

4. To complete the `NightVisionEffect.cs` script, we simply need to make sure that we clamp certain variables so that they stay within a range. These ranges are arbitrary and can be changed at a later time. These are just values that worked well:

```
void Update()
{
    contrast = Mathf.Clamp(contrast, 0f, 4f);
    brightness = Mathf.Clamp(brightness, 0f, 2f);
    randomValue = Random.Range(-1f, 1f);
    distortion = Mathf.Clamp(distortion, -1f, 1f);
    scale = Mathf.Clamp(scale, 0f, 3f);
}
```

5. We can now turn our attention over to the shader portion of this screen effect. Open the shader, if you haven't already, and begin by entering the following properties into the `Properties` block:

```
Properties
{
    _MainTex ("Base (RGB)", 2D) = "white" {}
    _VignetteTex ("Vignette Texture", 2D) = "white"{}
    _ScanLineTex ("Scan Line Texture", 2D) = "white"{}
    _NoiseTex ("Noise Texture", 2D) = "white"{}
    _NoiseXSpeed ("Noise X Speed", Float) = 100.0
    _NoiseYSpeed ("Noise Y Speed", Float) = 100.0
    _ScanLineTileAmount ("Scan Line Tile Amount",
                    Float) = 4.0
    _NightVisionColor ("Night Vision Color", Color) =
        (1,1,1,1)
    _Contrast ("Contrast", Range(0,4)) = 2
    _Brightness ("Brightness", Range(0,2)) = 1
    _RandomValue ("Random Value", Float) = 0
    _distortion ("Distortion", Float) = 0.2
    _scale ("Scale (Zoom)", Float) = 0.8
}
```

344 Gameplay and Screen Effects

6. To make sure that we are passing the data from our Properties block to our CGPROGRAM block, we need to make sure to declare them with the same name in the CGPROGRAM block:

```
Pass
{
    CGPROGRAM
    #pragma vertex vert_img
    #pragma fragment frag
    #pragma fragmentoption ARB_precision_hint_fastest
    #include "UnityCG.cginc"

    uniform sampler2D _MainTex;
    uniform sampler2D _VignetteTex;
    uniform sampler2D _ScanLineTex;
    uniform sampler2D _NoiseTex;
    fixed4 _NightVisionColor;
    fixed _Contrast;
    fixed _ScanLineTileAmount;
    fixed _Brightness;
    fixed _RandomValue;
    fixed _NoiseXSpeed;
    fixed _NoiseYSpeed;
    fixed _distortion;
    fixed _scale;
```

7. Our effect is also going to include a lens distortion to further convey the effect that we are looking through a lens and the edges of the image are being distorted by the angle of the lens. Enter the following function just after the variable declarations in the CGPROGRAM block:

```
    float2 barrelDistortion(float2 coord)
    {
        // lens distortion algorithm see
        // http://www.ssontech.com/content/lensalg.htm

        float2 h = coord.xy - float2(0.5, 0.5);
```

```
        float r2 = h.x * h.x + h.y * h.y;
        float f = 1.0 + r2 * (_distortion * sqrt(r2));

        return f * _scale * h + 0.5;
}
```

8. We can now concentrate on the meat of our `NightVisionEffect` shader. Let's start this by entering the code necessary to get the render texture and vignette texture. Enter the following code in the `frag()` function of our shader:

```
fixed4 frag(v2f_img i) : COLOR
{
        // Get the colors from the RenderTexture and
        // the uv's from the v2f_img struct
        half2 distortedUV = barrelDistortion(i.uv);
        fixed4 renderTex = tex2D(_MainTex,
                                        distortedUV);
        fixed4 vignetteTex = tex2D(_VignetteTex,
                                        i.uv);
```

9. The next step in our `frag()` function is to process the scan lines and `Noise` textures and apply the proper animated UVs to them:

```
// Process scan lines and noise
half2 scanLinesUV = half2(i.uv.x *
    _ScanLineTileAmount, i.uv.y * _ScanLineTileAmount);
fixed4 scanLineTex = tex2D(_ScanLineTex, scanLinesUV);

half2 noiseUV = half2(i.uv.x + (_RandomValue *
    _SinTime.z * _NoiseXSpeed), i.uv.y + (_Time.x *
    _NoiseYSpeed));
fixed4 noiseTex = tex2D(_NoiseTex, noiseUV);
```

10. To complete all of our layers in the screen effect, we simply need to process the luminance value of our render texture, and then apply the night-vision color to it to achieve that iconic night-vision look:

    ```
    // get the luminosity values from the render texture
    // using the YIQ values.
    fixed lum = dot (fixed3(0.299, 0.587, 0.114),
                    renderTex.rgb);
    lum += _Brightness;
    fixed4 finalColor = (lum *2) + _NightVisionColor;
    ```

11. Lastly, we will combine all the layers together and return the final color of our night-vision effect:

    ```
                // Final output
                finalColor = pow(finalColor,
                                _Contrast);
                finalColor *= vignetteTex;
                finalColor *= scanLineTex * noiseTex;

                return finalColor;
            }
            ENDCG
        }
    }
    FallBack Off
    }
    ```

12. When you have finished entering the code, return to the Unity editor to let the script and shader compile. If there are no errors, select **Main Camera** in your scene. Remove the **Render Old Film** component, if it is there already, and add the `RenderNightVision` component. Once there, drag and drop the `ScreenNightVision` shader into the **Cur Shader** property of the component and then assign the **Night Vision Color** property to a green color, like the one shown here:

Figure 11.13 – The night-vision color

13. Afterward, assign the textures to their proper spot:

Figure 11.14 – The settings for the night-vision script

14. Afterward, make sure to play in the editor to see the full, final version of the effect:

Figure 11.15 – The final result of our night-vision screen effect

How it works...

The night-vision effect is actually very similar to the old film screen effect, which shows us just how modular we can make these components. Just by simply swapping the textures that we are using for overlays and changing the speed at which our tiling rates are being calculated, we can achieve very different results using the same code.

The only difference with this effect is the fact that we are including a lens distortion in our screen effect, so let's break this down so that we can get a better understanding of how it works.

The following code snippet illustrates the code used in processing our lens distortion. It is a snippet of code provided to us by the makers of **SynthEyes**, and the code is freely available to use in your own effects:

```
float2 barrelDistortion(float2 coord)
{
    // Lens distortion algorithm
    // See http://www.ssontech.com/content/lensalg.htm
    float2 h = coord.xy - float2(0.5, 0.5);
    float r2 = h.x * h.x + h.y * h.y;
    float f = 1.0 + r2 * (_distortion * sqrt(r2));

    return f * _scale * h + 0.5;
}
```

There's more...

It is not uncommon in video games to need to highlight certain objects—for instance, a thermal visor should only apply a postprocessing effect to people and other sources of heat. Doing this is already possible with the knowledge gathered so far in this book; you can, in fact, change the shader or material of an object in code. However, this is often laborious and has to be replicated on every object.

A more effective way is to use replaced shaders. Each shader has a tag called `RenderType` that has never been used so far. This property can be used to force a camera to apply a shader only to certain objects. You can do this by attaching the following script to the camera:

```
using UnityEngine;

public class ReplacedShader : MonoBehaviour {

    public Shader shader;
    void Start () {
        GetComponent<Camera>().SetReplacementShader(shader,
            "Heat");
    }
}
```

After entering the **Play** mode, the camera will query all the objects that it has to render. If they don't have a shader decorated with `RenderType = "Heat"`, they will not be rendered. Objects with such a tag will be rendered with the shader attached to the script.

12
Advanced Shading Techniques

This chapter covers some advanced shader techniques that you can use for your game. You should remember that many of the most eye-catching effects that you see in games are made by testing the limits of what shaders can do. This book provides you with the technical foundations to modify and create shaders, but you are strongly encouraged to play and experiment with them as much as you can. Making a good game is not a quest for photorealism; you should not approach shaders with the intention of replicating reality because this is unlikely to happen. Instead, you should try to use shaders as a tool to make your game truly unique. With the knowledge of this chapter, you will be able to create the materials that you want.

In this chapter, you will learn about the following:

- Using Unity's built-in `CgInclude` files
- Making your shader work in a modular way with `CgInclude`
- Implementing a Fur Shader
- Implementing Heatmaps with arrays

Technical requirements

This chapter was created with Unity 2021.1.9f1 but should work in future versions of Unity with minimal revisions.

You can find the code files present in this chapter on GitHub at https://github.com/PacktPublishing/Unity-2021-Shaders-and-Effects-Cookbook-Fourth-Edition/tree/main/Shaders-and-Effects-Cookbook-2021/Assets/Chapter%2012.

Using Unity's built-in CgInclude files

Our first step in writing our own `CgInclude` files is to understand what Unity already provides us with for shaders. When writing Surface Shaders, there is a lot happening under the hood, which makes the process of writing them so efficient. We can see this code in the included `CgInclude` files found in the directory that you installed Unity in at **Editor | Data | CGIncludes**. All the files contained within this folder do their part to render our objects with our shaders on the screen. Some of these files take care of shadows and lighting, some take care of helper functions, and some manage platform dependencies. Without them, our shader-writing experience would be much more laborious.

> **Note**
> You can find a list of the information on built-in files that Unity has provided us with at the following link: http://docs.unity3d.com/Documentation/Components/SL-BuiltinIncludes.html.

Let's begin the process of understanding these built-in `CgInclude` files, using some of the built-in helper functions from the `UnityCG.cginc` file:

Using Unity's built-in CgInclude files   353

Figure 12.1 – The location of the UnityCG.cginc file

Getting ready

Before we start diving into the meat of writing the shader, we need to get a few items set up in our scene. Let's do the following and then open the shader in your IDE of choice:

1. Create a new scene with the **Basic (Built-in)** template and fill it with a simple sphere model.

2. Create a new Standard Surface shader (`Desaturate`) and material (`DesaturateMat`).

3. Attach the new shader to the new material and assign the material to the sphere.

4. Create a directional light and position it above your sphere.

5. Finally, open the `UnityCG.cginc` file from Unity's `CgInclude` folder located in Unity's `Install` directory. This will let us analyze some of the helper functions' code so that we can understand what is happening when we use them.

6. You should now have a simple scene set up to work on the shader. Refer to the following screenshot, which is an example:

Figure 12.2 – The setup for this recipe

How to do it...

With the scene prepared, we can now begin the process of experimenting with some of the built-in helper functions included with the `UnityCG.cginc` file. Double-click on the shader that was created for this scene in order to open it in your IDE of choice and insert the code given in the following steps:

1. Add the following code to the `Properties` block of the new shader file. We will need a single texture and slide for our example shader:

```
Properties
{
    _MainTex ("Base (RGB)", 2D) = "white" {}
    _DesatValue ("Desaturate", Range(0,1)) = 0.5
}
```

We then need to make sure that we create the data connection between our `Properties` and `CGPROGRAM` blocks.

2. Use the following code, placed after the `CGPROGRAM` declaration and `#pragma` directives, removing the other default properties:

```
sampler2D _MainTex;
fixed _DesatValue;
```

3. Next, we just have to update our `surf()` function to include the following code. We introduce a new function that we haven't seen yet, which is built into Unity's `UnityCG.cginc` file:

```
void surf (Input IN, inout SurfaceOutputStandard o)
{
    half4 c = tex2D (_MainTex, IN.uv_MainTex);
    c.rgb = lerp(c.rgb, Luminance(c.rgb), _DesatValue);

    o.Albedo = c.rgb;
    o.Alpha = c.a;
}
```

4. Save your script and return to the Unity Editor. From there, you should be able to assign a texture to the **Base (RGB)** value of **DesaturateMat** (I used the `TerrainBlend` texture from the `Chapter 3 | Textures` folder):

Figure 12.3 – Applying the texture to the material

5. With the shader code modified, you should see something similar to the preceding screenshot. We have simply used a helper function, built into Unity's `CgInclude` file, to give us an effect of desaturating the main texture of our shader. Notice that if we change the value to 1, all of the color leaves, giving us a grayscale effect:

Figure 12.4 – Desaturating the main texture

How it works...

Using the built-in helper function named `Luminance()`, we are able to quickly get a desaturation or grayscale effect on our shaders. This is all possible because the `UnityCG.cginc` file is brought automatically to our shader as we are using a Surface Shader.

If you search through the `UnityCG.cginc` file when opened in a script editor, you will find the implementation of this function at line *473*. The following snippet is taken from the file:

```
// Converts color to luminance (grayscale)
inline half Luminance(half3 rgb)
{
    return dot(rgb, unity_ColorSpaceLuminance.rgb);
}
```

As this function is included in the file and Unity automatically compiles with this file, we can use the function in our code as well, thereby reducing the amount of code that we have to write over and over again.

Notice there is also a `Lighting.cginc` file, which Unity comes with. This file houses all the lighting models that we use when we declare something such as `#pragma Surface surf Lambert`. Sifting through this file reveals that all the built-in lighting models are defined here for reuse and modularity.

There's more...

You'll notice that the `Luminance` function we are using will return the dot product between the color passed in and a property called `unity_ColorSpaceLuminance`. To see what that is, you can use the **Find** menu in your text editor (*Ctrl + F*) and type it in. After searching for it, you should be able to see the following on line *28*:

```
#ifdef UNITY_COLORSPACE_GAMMA
#define unity_ColorSpaceGrey fixed4(0.5, 0.5, 0.5, 0.5)
#define unity_ColorSpaceDouble fixed4(2.0, 2.0, 2.0, 2.0)
#define unity_ColorSpaceDielectricSpec half4(0.220916301, 0.220916301, 0.220916301, 1.0 - 0.220916301)
#define unity_ColorSpaceLuminance half4(0.22, 0.707, 0.071, 0.0) // Legacy: alpha is set to 0.0 to specify gamma mode
#else // Linear values
#define unity_ColorSpaceGrey fixed4(0.214041144, 0.214041144, 0.214041144, 0.5)
#define unity_ColorSpaceDouble fixed4(4.59479380, 4.59479380, 4.59479380, 2.0)
#define unity_ColorSpaceDielectricSpec half4(0.04, 0.04, 0.04, 1.0 - 0.04) // standard dielectric reflectivity coef at incident angle (= 4%)
#define unity_ColorSpaceLuminance half4(0.0396819152, 0.458021790, 0.00609653955, 1.0) // Legacy: alpha is set to 1.0 to specify linear mode
#endif
```

This means that, depending on the color space being used, the values given will change. By default, Unity uses a gamma color space as only certain platforms support linear. To check what color space you are using in your project, you can go to **Edit | Project Settings | Player | Other Settings** and look at the **Color Space** property:

Figure 12.5 – Location of the Color Space property

> **Note**
> For more information on color spaces, check out http://www.kinematicsoup.com/news/2016/6/15/gamma-and-linear-space-what-they-are-how-they-differ.

Making your shader work in a modular way with CgInclude

Knowing about the built-in CgInclude files is great, but what if we want to build our own CgInclude files to store our own lighting models and helper functions? We can, in fact, create our own CgInclude files, but we need to learn a little more code syntax before we can start using them efficiently in our shader-writing pipelines. Let's take a look at the process of creating a new CgInclude file from scratch.

Getting ready

Let's walk through the process of generating a new item for this recipe:

1. From the **Project** tab, right-click on the `Assets` folder and select **Show in Explorer**. You should see your project folder. Open the `Assets` folder by double-clicking on it and then create a text file by right-clicking and selecting **New | Text Document**:

Figure 12.6 – Creating a new text document

2. Rename the file to `MyCGInclude` and replace the `.txt` file extension with `.cginc`:

Figure 12.7 – Renaming the text file

3. Windows will give you a warning message saying **File may become unusable**, but it will still work, so go ahead and accept the change.

4. Import this new `.cginc` file into your Unity project and let it compile. If all goes well, you will see that Unity knew to compile it into a `CgInclude` file:

Figure 12.8 – The newly created file is now a part of our Unity project

We are now ready to begin creating our own custom `CgInclude` code. Simply double-click on the `CgInclude` file that you created in order to open it in your IDE of choice.

How to do it...

With our `CgInclude` file open, we can begin to enter the code that will get it working with our Surface Shaders. The following steps will get our `CgInclude` file ready for use within our Surface Shaders and allow us to continually add more code to it as we develop more shaders:

1. We begin our `CgInclude` file with what is called a preprocessor directive. These are statements such as `#pragma` and `#include`. In this case, we want to define a new set of code that will be executed if our shader includes this file in its compiler directives. Enter the following code at the top of your `CgInclude` file:

```
#ifndef MY_CG_INCLUDE
#define MY_CG_INCLUDE
```

2. We always need to make sure that we close `#ifndef` or `#ifdef` with `#endif` to close the definition check, just like an `if` statement needs to be closed with two brackets in C#. Enter the following code just after the `#define` directive:

```
#endif
```

3. At this point, we just need to implement the contents of the CgInclude file. So, we finish off our CgInclude file by entering the following code after `#define` and before `#endif`:

```
fixed4 _MyColor;

inline fixed4 LightingHalfLambert(SurfaceOutput s, fixed3 lightDir, fixed atten)
{
    fixed diff = max(0, dot(s.Normal, lightDir));
    diff = (diff + 0.5)*0.5;

    fixed4 c;
    c.rgb = s.Albedo * _LightColor0.rgb * ((diff *
        _MyColor.rgb) * atten);
    c.a = s.Alpha;
    return c;
}
```

4. With this completed, you now have your very first CgInclude file. With just this little bit of code, we can greatly reduce the amount of code that we have to rewrite, and we can begin to store the lighting models that we use all the time here so that we never lose them. Your CgInclude file should look similar to the following code:

```
#ifndef MY_CG_INCLUDE
#define MY_CG_INCLUDE

fixed4 _MyColor;

inline fixed4 LightingHalfLambert(SurfaceOutput s, fixed3 lightDir, fixed atten)
{
    fixed diff = max(0, dot(s.Normal, lightDir));
```

```
        diff = (diff + 0.5)*0.5;

    fixed4 c;
    c.rgb = s.Albedo * _LightColor0.rgb * ((diff *
        _MyColor.rgb) * atten);
    c.a = s.Alpha;
    return c;
}
#endif
```

There are a couple more steps that we need to complete before we can fully utilize this `CgInclude` file. We simply need to tell the current shader that we are working with to use this file and its code. To complete the process of creating and using `CgInclude` files, let's complete the next set of steps:

1. We have to have our `CgInclude` file in the same directory as our shader, so drag and drop it into the `Chapter 12 | Shaders` folder from the **Project** tab.

   > **Note**
   >
   > If *step 1* is not completed, you will get a compilation error.

2. Now that we are in the folder, select the **Desaturate** shader created in the previous recipe and duplicate it (*Ctrl + D*). Name the duplicate `Colorize`, and double-click on it to open it up.

3. From there, update the shader name. If you're following the same format as the example code, it would look something like the following:

   ```
   Shader "CookbookShaders/Chapter12/Colorize"
   ```

4. If you turn your attention to our shader, you will see that we need to tell our `CGPROGRAM` block to include our new `CgInclude` file, so that we can access the code it contains. Modify the directives of our `CGPROGRAM` block to include the following code:

   ```
   CGPROGRAM
   #include "MyCGInclude.cginc"
   // Physically based Standard lighting model, and
   // enable shadows on all light types
   #pragma surface surf Standard fullforwardshadows
   ```

5. Our current shader is currently using the built-in standard lighting model, but we want to use the `HalfLambert` lighting model that we created in `CgInclude`. As we have included the code from our `CgInclude` file, we can use the `HalfLambert` lighting model with the following code:

```
CGPROGRAM
#include "MyCGInclude.cginc"
#pragma surface surf HalfLambert
```

6. Finally, we have also declared a custom variable in our `CgInclude` file to show that we can set up default variables for our shaders to use. To see this in action, enter the following code in the `Properties` block of your shader:

```
Properties
{
    _MainTex ("Base (RGB)", 2D) = "white" {}
    _DesatValue ("Desaturate", Range(0,1)) = 0.5
    _MyColor ("My Color", Color) = (1,1,1,1)
}
```

7. Lastly, we need to update our `surf` function header since we use `SurfaceOutput` in our `LightingHalfLambert` function:

```
void surf (Input IN, inout SurfaceOutput o)
```

8. Back in Unity, create a new material that will use the newly created `Colorize` shader (`ColorizeMat`) and assign it to the sphere we created in the last recipe. Assign the material as normal and modify the **MyColor** value from the **Inspector** window to see how it modifies the object. The following screenshot shows the result of using our `CgInclude` file:

Figure 12.9 – The result of using our CgInclude file

How it works...

When using shaders, we can include other sets of code using the #include preprocessor directive. This tells Unity that we want to let the current shader use the code from within the included file in the shader; this is the reason why these files are called CgInclude files. We are including snippets of Cg code using the #include directive.

Once we have declared the #include directive and Unity is able to find the file in the project, Unity will then look for code snippets that have been defined. This is where we start to use the #ifndef and #endif directives. When we declare the #ifndef directive, we are simply saying "if not defined, define something with a name." In this recipe's case, we said we wanted to #define MY_CG_INCLUDE. So, if Unity doesn't find a definition called MY_CG_INCLUDE, it goes and creates it when the CgInclude file is compiled, thereby giving us access to the code that follows. The #endif method simply says that this is the end of this definition, so stop looking for more code.

You can now see how powerful this is. We can now store all of our lighting models and custom variables in one file and greatly reduce the amount of code that we have to write. The real power is when you can begin to give your shaders flexibility by defining multiple states of functions in the CgInclude files.

Implementing a Fur Shader

The look of a material depends on its physical structure. The shaders attempt to simulate them, but, in doing so, they oversimplify the way light behaves. Materials with a complex macroscopic structure are particularly hard to render. This is the case for many fabrics and animal furs. This recipe will show you how it is possible to simulate fur and other materials (such as grass) that are more than just a flat surface. In order to do this, the same material is drawn multiple times over and over, increasing in size every time. This creates the illusion of fur.

The shader presented here is based on the work of Jonathan Czeck and Aras Pranckevičius:

Figure 12.10 – An example of the finalized shader

Getting ready

In order for this recipe to work, you will need a texture that shows how you wish to have your fur displayed:

Figure 12.11 – The fur texture

I have provided two examples in the `Chapter 12 | Textures` folder with the book's example code (`Faux Fur` and `panda`).

Like all the other shaders before, you will need to create a new **Standard** Surface Shader (`Fur`) and a material (`FurMat`) to host it, and attach it to a sphere for demonstration purposes:

Figure 12.12 – Setup for this recipe

How to do it...

In this recipe, we can start modifying a **Standard** Surface Shader:

1. Double-click on the `Fur` Shader to open it up in your IDE of choice. Once opened, add the following bolded properties:

```
Properties
{
    _Color ("Color", Color) = (1,1,1,1)
    _MainTex ("Albedo (RGB)", 2D) = "white" {}
    _Glossiness ("Smoothness", Range(0,1)) = 0.5
    _Metallic ("Metallic", Range(0,1)) = 0.0

    _FurLength ("Fur Length", Range (.0002, 1)) = .25
    _Cutoff ("Alpha Cutoff", Range(0,1)) = 0.5
        // how "thick"
    _CutoffEnd ("Alpha Cutoff end", Range(0,1)) = 0.5
        // how thick they are at the end
```

368 Advanced Shading Techniques

```
    _EdgeFade ("Edge Fade", Range(0,1)) = 0.4

    _Gravity ("Gravity Direction", Vector) = (0,0,1,0)
    _GravityStrength ("Gravity Strength", Range(0,1))
        = 0.25
}
```

2. This shader requires you to repeat the same pass several times. We will use the technique introduced in the *Making your shader work in a modular way with CgInclude* recipe to group all the code necessary from a single pass in an external file. Let's start creating a new `CgInclude` file called `FurPass.cginc` with the following code:

```
#pragma target 3.0

fixed4 _Color;
sampler2D _MainTex;
half _Glossiness;
half _Metallic;

uniform float _FurLength;
uniform float _Cutoff;
uniform float _CutoffEnd;
uniform float _EdgeFade;

uniform fixed3 _Gravity;
uniform fixed _GravityStrength;

void vert (inout appdata_full v)
{
    fixed3 direction = lerp(v.normal, _Gravity *
        _GravityStrength + v.normal * (1-
        _GravityStrength), FUR_MULTIPLIER);
    v.vertex.xyz += direction * _FurLength *
        FUR_MULTIPLIER * v.color.a;
    /* v.vertex.xyz += v.normal * _FurLength *
```

```
              FUR_MULTIPLIER * v.color.a; */
}

struct Input {
  float2 uv_MainTex;
  float3 viewDir;
};

void surf (Input IN, inout SurfaceOutputStandard o) {
  fixed4 c = tex2D (_MainTex, IN.uv_MainTex) * _Color;
  o.Albedo = c.rgb;
  o.Metallic = _Metallic;
  o.Smoothness = _Glossiness;

  //o.Alpha = step(_Cutoff, c.a);
  o.Alpha = step(lerp(_Cutoff,_CutoffEnd,
              FUR_MULTIPLIER), c.a);

  float alpha = 1 - (FUR_MULTIPLIER * FUR_MULTIPLIER);
  alpha += dot(IN.viewDir, o.Normal) - _EdgeFade;

  o.Alpha *= alpha;
}
```

3. Got back to your original shader and add this extra pass after the ENDCG section:

```
void surf (Input IN, inout SurfaceOutputStandard o) {
  // Albedo comes from a texture tinted by color
  fixed4 c = tex2D (_MainTex, IN.uv_MainTex) * _Color;
  o.Albedo = c.rgb;
  // Metallic and smoothness come from slider
  // variables
  o.Metallic = _Metallic;
  o.Smoothness = _Glossiness;
  o.Alpha = c.a;
}
```

370 Advanced Shading Techniques

```
ENDCG

CGPROGRAM
#pragma surface surf Standard fullforwardshadows
alpha:blend vertex:vert
#define FUR_MULTIPLIER 0.05
#include "FurPass.cginc"
ENDCG
```

4. Go back into Unity and assign the FauxFur texture in the **Albedo (RGB)** property. You should notice little dots along the shader:

Figure 12.13 – The result after one pass

5. Add more passes, progressively increasing FUR_MULTIPLIER. You can get decent results with 20 passes, from 0.05 to 0.95:

```
CGPROGRAM
#pragma surface surf Standard fullforwardshadows
    alpha:blend vertex:vert
#define FUR_MULTIPLIER 0.05
#include "FurPass.cginc"
ENDCG
```

```
CGPROGRAM
#pragma surface surf Standard fullforwardshadows
    alpha:blend vertex:vert
#define FUR_MULTIPLIER 0.1
#include "FurPass.cginc"
ENDCG

CGPROGRAM
#pragma surface surf Standard fullforwardshadows
    alpha:blend vertex:vert
#define FUR_MULTIPLIER 0.15
#include "FurPass.cginc"
ENDCG

// ... 0.2 - 0.85 here

CGPROGRAM
#pragma surface surf Standard fullforwardshadows
    alpha:blend vertex:vert
#define FUR_MULTIPLIER 0.90
#include "FurPass.cginc"
ENDCG

CGPROGRAM
#pragma surface surf Standard fullforwardshadows
    alpha:blend vertex:vert
#define FUR_MULTIPLIER 0.95
#include "FurPass.cginc"
ENDCG
}

Fallback "Diffuse"
}
```

6. Once the shader has been compiled and attached to a material, you can change its appearance from the Inspector.

372 Advanced Shading Techniques

The **Fur Length** property determines the space between the fur shells, which will alter the length of the fur. Longer fur might require more passes to look realistic.

Alpha Cutoff and **Alpha Cutoff end** are used to control the density of the fur and how it gets progressively thinner.

Edge Fade determines the final transparency of the fur and how fuzzy it looks. Softer materials should have a high **Edge Fade** value.

Finally, **Gravity Direction** and **Gravity Strength** curve the fur shells to simulate the effect of gravity:

Figure 12.14 – Adjusting the properties on the fur shader

How it works...

The technique presented in this recipe is known as Lengyel's concentric fur shell technique or simply the shell technique. It works by creating progressively bigger copies of the geometry that needs to be rendered. With the right transparency, it gives the illusion of a continuous thread of hair:

Figure 12.15 – Real fur versus shell fur

The shell technique is extremely versatile and relatively easy to implement. Realistic fur requires not only extruding the geometry of the model but also altering its vertices. This is possible with tessellation shaders, which are much more advanced and not covered in this book.

Each pass in this `Fur Shader` is contained in `FurPass.cginc`. The vertex function creates a slightly bigger version of the model, which is based on the principle of normal extrusion. Additionally, the effect of gravity is taken into account, so that it gets more intense the further we are from the center:

```
void vert (inout appdata_full v)
{
    fixed3 direction = lerp(v.normal, _Gravity *
        _GravityStrength + v.normal * (1-_GravityStrength),
        FUR_MULTIPLIER);
    v.vertex.xyz += direction * _FurLength * FUR_MULTIPLIER
        * v.color.a;
}
```

In this example, the alpha channel is used to determine the final length of the fur. This allows for more precise control.

Finally, the surface function reads the control mask from the alpha channel. It uses the cutoff value to determine which pixels to show and which ones to hide. This value changes from the first to the final fur shell to match **Alpha Cutoff** and **Alpha Cutoff end**:

```
o.Alpha = step(lerp(_Cutoff,_CutoffEnd,FUR_MULTIPLIER),
          c.a);

float alpha = 1 - (FUR_MULTIPLIER * FUR_MULTIPLIER);
alpha += dot(IN.viewDir, o.Normal) - _EdgeFade;

o.Alpha *= alpha;
```

The final alpha value of the fur also depends on its angle from the camera, giving it a softer look.

There's more...

The Fur shader has been used to simulate fur. However, it can be used for a variety of other materials. It works very well for materials that are naturally made of multiple layers, such as forest canopies, fuzzy clouds, human hair, and even grass.

Some additional examples of the same shader being used by just tweaking the parameters can be seen in the book's example code:

Figure 12.16 – Additional examples using this shader

There are many other improvements that can dramatically increase its realism. You can add a very simple wind animation by changing the direction of the gravity based on the current time. If calibrated correctly, this can give the impression that the fur is moving because of the wind.

Additionally, you can make your fur move when the character is moving. All these little tweaks contribute to the believability of your fur, giving the illusion that it is not just a static material drawn on the surface. Unfortunately, this shader comes at a price: 20 passes are very heavy to compute. The number of passes determines roughly how believable the material is. You should play with the fur length and passes in order to get the effect that works best for you. Given the performance impact of this shader, it is advisable to have several materials with different numbers of passes; you can use them at different distances and save a lot of computation.

Implementing Heatmaps with arrays

One characteristic that makes shaders hard to master is the lack of proper documentation. Most developers learn how to use shaders by messing around with the code, without having a deep knowledge of what's going on. The problem is amplified by the fact that Cg/HLSL makes a lot of assumptions, some of which are not properly advertised. Unity3D allows C# scripts to communicate with shaders using methods such as SetFloat, SetInt, and SetVector. Unfortunately, Unity3D doesn't have a SetArray method, which leads many developers to believe that Cg/HLSL doesn't support arrays either. This is not true. This recipe will show you how it's possible to pass arrays to shaders. Just remember that GPUs are highly optimized for parallel computations, and using for loops in a shader will dramatically decrease its performance.

376   Advanced Shading Techniques

For this recipe, we will implement a heatmap, as shown in the following screenshot:

Figure 12.17 – Heatmap

Getting ready

The effect in this recipe creates a heatmap from a set of points. This heatmap can be overlaid on top of another picture, like in the preceding screenshot.

The following steps are necessary:

1. Create a quad with the texture that you want to use for the Heatmap (**GameObject | 3D Object | Quad**). In this example, a map of London has been used. In order to put the texture on the quad, create a new material (`Map`) using the **Unlit/Texture** shader, and assign the image to the **Base (RGB)** property. Once created, drag and drop that material onto the quad. The position of the quad object must be set to (**0, 0, 0**).

2. Create another quad and place it on top of the previous one. Our `Heatmap` will appear on this quad.

3. Attach a new shader (`Heatmap`) and material (`HeatmapMat`) to the second quad:

Figure 12.18 – The setup for this recipe

4. For ease of visualization, select the **MainCamera** and change the object's position to (**0, 0, -10**), and under the **Camera** component, change the **Projection** property to **Orthographic** and the **Size** property to 0.5.

In the **Game** view, you'll now only see a white box due to the second quad covering the map; but we will be changing that shortly.

How to do it...

This shader is quite different from the ones created before, yet it is relatively short. For this reason, the entire code is provided in the following steps:

1. Copy this code to the newly created shader:

```
Shader "CookbookShaders/Chapter 12/Heatmap"
{
    Properties
    {
        _HeatTex ("Texture", 2D) = "white" {}
    }
}
```

```
Subshader
{
    Tags {"Queue" = "Transparent"}
    Blend SrcAlpha OneMinusSrcAlpha // Alpha blend

    Pass
    {
        CGPROGRAM
        #pragma vertex vert
        #pragma fragment frag

        struct vertInput
        {
            float4 pos : POSITION;
        };

        struct vertOutput
        {
            float4 pos : POSITION;
            fixed3 worldPos : TEXCOORD1;
        };

        vertOutput vert(vertInput input)
        {
            vertOutput o;
            o.pos = UnityObjectToClipPos(
                input.pos);
            o.worldPos = mul(unity_ObjectToWorld,
                    input.pos).xyz;
            return o;
        }

        uniform int _Points_Length = 0;
        uniform float3 _Points[20];
            // (x, y, z) = position
        uniform float2 _Properties[20];
```

```
            // x = radius, y = intensity

        sampler2D _HeatTex;

        half4 frag(vertOutput output) : COLOR
        {
            // Loops over all the points
            half h = 0;

            for (int i = 0; i < _Points_Length;
                i++)
            {
                // Calculates the contribution of
                // each point
                half di = distance(
                output.worldPos, _Points[i].xyz);

                half ri = _Properties[i].x;
                half hi = 1 - saturate(di / ri);

                h += hi * _Properties[i].y;
            }

            // Converts (0-1) according to the
            // heat texture
            h = saturate(h);
            half4 color = tex2D(_HeatTex,
                                fixed2(h, 0.5));
            return color;
        }
        ENDCG
    }
  }

    Fallback "Diffuse"
}
```

2. Once you have attached this script to your material, you should provide a ramp texture for the heatmap. It is important to configure it so that **Wrap Mode** is set to **Clamp**:

Figure 12.19 – Setting Wrap Mode to Clamp

> **Note**
> If your heatmap is going to be used as an overlay, then make sure that the ramp texture has an alpha channel and the texture is imported with the **Alpha Is Transparency** option.

3. Afterward, assign the **Texture** property of the Heatmap material to the **heatramp** texture and you should notice the white box is now gone:

Implementing Heatmaps with arrays | 381

Figure 12.20 – Setting the heatramp texture

To have points show up, we will now create a new script to display the points we want to draw.

4. Create a new script called `HeatmapDrawer` using the following code:

```
using UnityEngine;

public class HeatmapDrawer : MonoBehaviour
{

    public Vector4[] positions;
    public float[] radiuses;
    public float[] intensities;
    public Material material;

    void Start()
    {
        material.SetInt("_Points_Length",
                        positions.Length);

        material.SetVectorArray("_Points", positions);
```

```
            Vector4[] properties =
                new Vector4[positions.Length];

            for (int i = 0; i < positions.Length; i++)
            {
                properties[i] = new Vector2(radiuses[i],
                    intensities[i]);
            }

            material.SetVectorArray("_Properties",
                                    properties);

        }
    }
```

5. Attach the script to an object in your scene, preferably to the quad. Then, drag the material created for this effect to the Material slot of the script. By doing this, the script will be able to access the Material and initialize it.

6. Lastly, expand the **Positions**, **Radiuses**, and **Intensities** fields of your script and fill them with the values of your heatmap. **Positions** indicates the points (in world coordinates) of your heatmap:

Figure 12.21 – Example values for Heatmap Drawer

7. **Radiuses** indicates their size, and **Intensities** indicates how strongly they affect the surrounding area:

Figure 12.22 – Radiuses and Intensities settings for Heatmap Drawer

8. If all went well, once you play the game, you should notice something similar to the following screenshot:

Figure 12.23 – The result of our shader

If you do not see this, make sure that the heatmap is placed in front of the map quad and that both objects are in front of the camera. Also, be sure that you are playing the game; the effect does not show up when in Edit Mode.

> **Note**
> If you get a warning saying the number of points has changed, go into your shader, modify the script by adding a space, and then save it again.

How it works...

This shader relies on things that have not been introduced before in this book; the first one is arrays. Cg allows arrays to be created with the following syntax:

```
uniform float3 _Points [20];
```

Cg doesn't support arrays with an unknown size: you must preallocate all the space that you need beforehand. The preceding line of code creates an array of 20 elements.

Unity allows us to set arrays using a number of methods, including `SetVectorArray`, `SetColorArray`, `SetFloatArray`, and `GetMatrixArray`.

> **Important Note**
> The `SetVectorArray` function only works with the `Vector4` class at present. That will not cause us any issues, though, as you can automatically assign `Vector3` to `Vector4`, and Unity will automatically include a zero for the last element. Also, it is possible to instead use our `Start` code in an `Update` loop to be able to see the values change as we're modifying them, but it would be computationally expensive.

In the fragment function of the shader, there is a similar `for` loop, which, for each pixel of the material, queries all the points to find their contribution to the heatmap:

```
half h = 0;
for (int i = 0; i < _Points_Length; i ++)
{
    // Calculates the contribution of each point
    half di = distance(output.worldPos, _Points[i].xyz);
```

```
        half ri = _Properties[i].x;
        half hi = 1 - saturate(di / ri);

        h += hi * _Properties[i].y;
}
```

The h variable stores the heat from all the points, given their radii and intensities. It is then used to look up which color to use from the ramp texture.

The shaders and arrays are a winning combination, especially as very few games are using them at their full potential. However, they introduce a significant bottleneck, as, for each pixel, the shader has to loop through all the points.

13
Shader Graph – 2D

First released in Unity 2018.1, Shader Graph allows you to create shaders using a visual interface by connecting nodes instead of having to dive into the code. This will allow developers, including artists, to create shaders in a similar manner to material editors in 3D modeling programs such as Autodesk Maya and Blender, or the material editor in the Unreal Engine. At the time of writing, Shader Graph is only supported for certain kinds of projects and doesn't allow the same flexibility as writing shaders from scratch.

In this chapter, you will learn the following recipes:

- Creating a URP-based Shader Graph project
- Implementing a simple Shader Graph
- Exposing properties to the Inspector via Shader Graph
- Implementing a Sprite Outline Shader

> **Note**
> Shader Graph is a node-based visual scripting language and as such we use images to illustrate the code written. If you have difficulty looking at any of the images in the chapter, please refer to the graphic bundle for this book; the link is available in the *Preface* or the example code for this book on GitHub.

Technical requirement

This chapter was created with Unity 2021.1.9f1 but should work for future versions of Unity with minimal revisions.

You can find the code files for this chapter on GitHub at `https://github.com/PacktPublishing/Unity-2021-Shaders-and-Effects-Cookbook-Fourth-Edition/tree/main/ShaderGraph-URP`.

Creating a URP-based Shader Graph project

Unlike all the previous shaders we have written, the Shader Graph tool requires users to have a project that uses a different render pipeline than Unity's original one. Unity's built-in render pipeline is their default pipeline and the one that we have been using for the entirety of the book thus far. It is a general-purpose render pipeline that still works fairly well. However, because it is so general it can't offer the best possible graphics features and can't be optimized for a project's particular needs. In order to prepare for the future, Unity has created several other options that can be used by building an entirely new rendering system, the **Scriptable Render Pipeline** (**SRP**). The SRP is Unity's new modular rendering system, where it is possible to choose exactly what type of graphics fit our game. It is possible to customize the render loop via C# scripts, but Unity has built two render pipelines that will pretty much cover whatever needs you have for most titles, focusing on two types of graphical fidelity: the HDRP and the URP. We will discuss the **HDRP** (**High Definition Render Pipeline**) in the next chapter; in this chapter, we will be focusing on the URP.

The **Universal Render Pipeline** (**URP**, previously known as the **Lightweight Render Pipeline** (**LWRP**)) is another way that we can create shaders while keeping performance in mind, is meant for lower-end hardware, and is focused on drawing with a single-pass and decreasing the draw count wherever possible. In this first recipe, you will ensure that your project is set up correctly by using the settings that Shader Graph needs.

How to do it...

To get started, we first need to create our new project:

1. From the Unity Hub, when creating a new project, set **Template** to **Universal Render Pipeline**:

Figure 13.1 – Universal Render Pipeline

As of the time of writing, Unity Hub 3.0 is currently in beta. If you are using it, you will select the **3D Sample Scene (URP)** option.

Figure 13.2 – 3D Sample Scene (URP) option

Shader Graph is currently only compatible with projects not using the built-in render pipeline, so you will need to select **URP** or **HDRP** to ensure that the graph will work correctly.

> **Note**
> Shader Graph is only available with Unity 2018.1 and above. If you are using a prior version, make sure to upgrade before continuing with this chapter.

2. Once selected, click the **Create** button. As you can see in the following figure, this project already includes a number of assets inside it:

Figure 13.3 – Freshly created URP project

3. When the Unity Editor opens, the Shader Graph should be installed and you should be able to check this by right-clicking in the **Project** window and seeing the Shader Graph options under **Create | Shader | Universal Render Pipeline** (for example, `Sprite Lit Shader Graph`). If you see the options there, go ahead and skip the following steps and go to the *How it works…* section. If not, continue.

4. If it is not included, we can install it ourselves by using the Unity **Package Manager**. From the top menu, go to **Window | Package Manager**.

Figure 13.4 – Package Manager

5. **Package Manager** will allow you to install or uninstall different aspects of Unity. You'll notice a dropdown at the top left of the window that currently says **Packages: In Project**. From there, click on the dropdown and select the **Packages: Unity Registry** option.

In the **Package Manager** window, scroll down until you see the **Shader Graph** button, and click it. From there, click on the **Install** button, and wait for it to complete the download and import the content:

Figure 13.5 – Installing Shader Graph

6. Once everything has been downloaded, go to the **Project** tab, select **Create | Shader | Universal Render Pipeline**, and see if you can find the following new options:

- **Lit Shader Graph**
- **Sprite Lit Shader Graph**
- **Sprite Unlit Shader Graph**
- **Unlit Shader Graph**

How it works...

As we mentioned before, Shader Graph is currently only compatible with one of the SRPs. The easiest way to ensure that a project is using that pipeline is by selecting it as the template when creating the project.

If everything's included, Shader Graph has been installed successfully, and you should be able to work on the rest of the recipes in this chapter!

If Shader Graph is not included by default, it is possible to add to our project by using **Package Manager**, which allows you to install or uninstall different aspects of Unity. In this case, you have added the Shader Graph functionality.

Implementing a simple Shader Graph

To get acquainted with the interface of Shader Graph, let's create something similar to what we have seen before by sampling a texture to create a simple shader.

Getting ready

Ensure that you have created a project using the URP, as described in the *Creating a URP-based Shader Graph project* recipe. Afterward, complete the following steps:

1. Create a new scene, if you haven't done so already, by going to **File | New Scene**.
2. Afterward, we need to have something to show our shader, so let's create a new sphere by going to **GameObject | 3D Object | Sphere**:

Figure 13.6 – The setup for this recipe

How to do it...

We will start off by creating a simple shader graph:

1. From the **Project** window, create a new shader by going to **Create | Shader | Universal Render Pipeline | Lit Shader Graph**, and name it `SimpleGraph`. For organization, I placed the graph within a new folder (`Chapter 13/Shaders`):

Figure 13.7 – Lit Shader Graph

2. Afterward, create a new material by going to **Create | Material** (I named mine `SimpleGraphMat`). Next, assign the shader to the material by selecting the material, then from the **Inspector** tab, you should select the **Shader** dropdown at the top and select **Shader Graphs/Simple Graph**.

> **Note**
> As always, you can also drag and drop the shader on top of the material as well.

3. Next, drag and drop the material onto our spherical object in the scene so we can see our shader in action:

Implementing a simple Shader Graph   395

Figure 13.8 – The shader assigned to the sphere

4. Now that the setup is done, we can start creating the graph. If you select the shader, you should notice on the **Inspector** tab that there is a button that says **Open Shader Editor**. Click on the button and the Shader Graph editor will open automatically:

Figure 13.9 – The Shader Graph editor

5. If you do not see all of the parts of the menu such as **Main Preview**, you can click and drag the panels and move them to wherever works best for you.

> **Note**
> To move within the Shader Graph editor, you can use the mouse wheel to zoom in and out, and you can hold the middle mouse button and drag to pan the graph. Alternatively, you can also use *Alt* + left mouse button.

6. To get started, let's add a texture. Right-click to the left of the **Fragment** section and select **Create Node**. From there, you'll see a menu that allows you to either type in the name of a node or select from the menus. To go through the menus, select **Input | Texture | Sample Texture 2D**. Alternatively, you can type in `tex`, then select the **Sample Texture 2D** option using the arrow keys, and then press *Enter*:

> **Note**
> You can also create a new node by moving your mouse over where you want to create one and pressing the spacebar.

Figure 13.10 – The newly created Sample Texture 2D node

> **Note**
>
> Feel free to click and drag any of the nodes on the Shader Graph to make it easier to see.

7. On the left-hand side of the **Sample Texture 2D** node, click on the circle with the dot in it. This will open up a window that will allow us to assign the texture without creating a new variable (I used the **Ground_Albedo** property included with the project):

Figure 13.11 – Selecting the texture to use

Afterward, you should see the data from the texture given in an image under the node.

398   Shader Graph – 2D

8. Click and drag the pink circle on the right-hand side of the **RGBA(4)** output of the **Sample Texture 2D** node to the **Base Color(3)** input on the **Fragment** node:

Figure 13.12 – Connecting the two nodes together

Just like we've learned in previous chapters, we can give a `fixed4` to a `fixed3` and it will just disregard the fourth parameter. Once connected, you should see the **Main Preview** window update to include the new changes:

Figure 13.13 – The updated preview window

If you do not see the changes, you can also right-click on the shape drawn and select the **Sphere** option to trigger a redraw, which should update with the current node connections.

> **Note**
>
> If you are ever interested in what a particular node does or what the properties stand for, feel free to right-click on it and select **Open Documentation**. It will open a window that will give you a description of what the node does.

9. Click on the **Save Asset** button in the top menu and then return to the Unity Editor:

Figure 13.14 – Result of the shader

As you can see, the shader has now been updated to contain the information from the Shader Graph editor!

How it works...

We have been introduced to the first nodes we have encountered. Of note are the **Fragment** and **Vertex** sections on the screen. This is where all of the information about the shader will go. You may notice that the properties are very similar to the regular Standard Shader we've used in the past, and we can modify the properties in a similar manner now, but we can also create additional nodes and connect them together to create unique effects. In fact, this process that we are going through is essentially the same as plugging in properties in a Unity Surface Shader but in a more graphical interface.

The **Sample Texture 2D** node allows us to give the **Texture** property as an input and then give the data from it as an **RGBA** output on the right-hand side (things on the right side of a node are outputs while things on the left side are inputs, such as the **Base Color(3)** property on the **Fragment** node).

Note that the color of the circle from the **Texture(T2)** input is red (the T stands for texture), the output of **RGBA** is pink (the 4 stands for `fixed4`), and the input for the **Base Color** input of the **Fragment** node is yellow (the 3 stands for `fixed3`).

Exposing properties to the Inspector via Shader Graph

It is great to be able to create graphs and set up their properties using the Graph editor, but sometimes it is nice to use the same shader with a simple tweak in the same manner that we've used with the previous shaders we've created. To do this, we can make use of the Blackboard.

Getting ready

Ensure that you have created the **SimpleGraph** shader in the previous recipe. Afterward, complete the following steps:

1. From the **Project** tab, select the **SimpleGraph** shader and duplicate it by pressing *Ctrl + D*. Once duplicated, name the newly created shader `ExposePropertyGraph`.

2. Next, create a new material (`ExposePropertyMat`) and set the shader it uses to the **Shader Graphs/ExposePropertyGraph** selection.

3. Assign the material to the sphere in our scene:

Figure 13.15 – Setup for this recipe

The project should look the same as what we had in the previous recipe since we are using a duplicate of the previous shader.

How to do it...

If you look at our shader from the **Shader Graph** tab, you may notice the **Texture** property with the **Ground_Albedo** image we assigned in the last recipe. A property like this could be something we want to modify from the **Inspector** window, but, by default, it is grayed out so that we cannot change it without going into the Shader Graph. To adjust this, we can expose the property using the Blackboard aspect of the Shader Graph editor:

1. Double-click on the **ExposePropertyGraph** shader to open up the Shader Graph:

Figure 13.16 – The opened shader graph

Notice, at the bottom left, the **ExposePropertyGraph** Blackboard menu. This will contain a list of all the parameters we are able to modify via the **Inspector** window.

> **Note**
> If you do not see the blackboard menu you can go to the top right of the Shader Graph window and click on the **Blackboard** button.

2. From the Blackboard, click on the + icon and select **Texture 2D**:

Figure 13.17 – Texture 2D

3. From there, you can give the property a name (I used `TextureProperty`). Note that, in the **Graph Inspector** window under the **Default** property, you can assign a texture in the same way as was done previously.

Figure 13.18 – Creating the TextureProperty property and assigning a default value

> **Note**
>
> Just in case it's needed, you can rename a property by double-clicking on its name or changing the **Name** property from **Graph Inspector**.

4. From there, to hook the property to our current shader, drag and drop the button with the property name on Shader Graph. Alternatively, you can right-click and select **Create Node**. Once at the menu, you can select **Properties | Property: TextureProperty**. Afterward, connect the **TextureProperty** output of the **Property** node to the **Texture** input of the **Sample Texture 2D** node:

Figure 13.19 – Adding the texture property to the node

5. Afterward, hit the **Save Asset** button and dive back into the Unity Editor:

Figure 13.20 – The changed shader

Now, you should be able to assign **TextureProperty** to whatever you want, through the **Inspector**, and you won't have to dive back into the graph to make those changes!

How it works...

The **Blackboard** menu allows you to create variables that are accessible from the **Inspector**. This works in a similar manner to the `Properties` block in previous chapters. Currently, it supports the following types:

- Float
- Vector2/3/4
- Color
- Boolean
- Gradient
- Texture 2D/2D Array/3D
- Cubemap
- Virtual Texture
- Matrix 2/3/4
- Sampler State
- Keywords (Boolean, Enum, Material Quality)

Properties added to the Blackboard can be reordered by dragging them around, and each property can be renamed by double-clicking on the name.

> **Tip**
> For more information on the Blackboard, check out the following link: `https://docs.unity3d.com/Packages/com.unity.shadergraph@11.0/manual/Blackboard.html`.

Creating a Sprite Outline Shader

Now that we have some background information on how to build shaders, let's look at a real-world example of a shader we could potentially use. For this first project, we will be creating a shader for a 2D game by drawing an outline around a sprite shape. This is something that we can easily do in Shader Graph, which will also allow us to see a non-trivial example of Shader Graph being used.

Getting ready

Ensure that you have created a project using the LRP, as described in the *Creating a URP-based Shader Graph project* recipe. Afterward, complete the following steps:

1. Create a new scene, if you haven't done so already, by going to **File | New Scene**.
2. Since we are going to be creating a 2D example, go to the **Hierarchy** window and select the **Main Camera** object. From the **Inspector** window open the **Camera** component and change the **Projection** dropdown to the **Orthographic** option.

Figure 13.21 – Changing the Camera component to be Orthographic

3. Then we will bring in the sprites that we wish to apply to this shader. I have provided some sprites within the example code for this book, but any sprites should work as long as they have a transparent border around them. Since the project we created is based in 3D after bringing in the files, ensure that in the **Inspector** window **Texture Type** is set to **Sprite (2D and UI)** and **Mesh Type** is set to **Full Rect**. Scroll down all the way to the bottom of the **Inspector** window and select the **Apply** button:

Figure 13.22 – Adjusting settings for the sprites

You'll know if the setting is set correctly if the sprites no longer have a black background in the **Project** window.

The reason we use **Full Rect** is that Unity by default will attempt to shrink the size of the sprite's mesh in order to optimize the project. In our case, we want that extra space as it's where our outline will be drawn.

4. To see the shader in action, let's add the sprites to our scene with an animation. Select all of the sprites at once and drag them into the **Hierarchy** window. A dialog window will pop up asking for a name for the new animation; I used `Walking`. Afterward, press the **Save** button.

Figure 13.23 – Creating a new animation

5. This is optional, but to make it easier to see the 2D effect within the **Scene** view, you can click on the **2D** button in the top bar:

Figure 13.24 – The sprite animating on the screen

Shader Graph – 2D

If you play the game, you should notice that the sprite is animating! This should make it easier to see the outline in action once we've added it.

> **Note**
> I have also created a scene at this point if you'd like to follow along with just the shader portion (`13.4 Creating a Sprite Outline Shader - Start`).

How to do it...

We will start off by creating a simple shader graph:

1. From the **Project** window, create a new shader by going to **Create | Shader | Universal Render Pipeline | Sprite Lit Shader Graph**, and name it `SpriteOutlineGraph`.

Figure 13.25 – Creating a Sprite Lit Shader Graph

2. The following recipe works exactly the same using a Sprite Unlit Shader Graph as well; it just won't receive lighting effects from lights within the scene.

3. Afterward, create a new material by going to **Create | Material** (I named mine `SpriteOutlineMat`). Next, assign the shader to the material by selecting the material, and then, from the **Inspector** tab, you should select the **Shader** dropdown at the top and select **Shader Graphs/SpriteOutlineGraph**.

4. Then, drag and drop the material onto our sprite object in the scene, so we can see our shader being used in action. Right now, the sprite will show up gray, but we will be fixing that shortly.

Figure 13.26 – The gray sprite

5. Now that the setup is done, we can start creating the graph. If you select the shader, you should see that, from the **Inspector** tab, there will be a button that says **Open Shader Graph**. Click on the button and the Shader Graph editor will open automatically. To make it easier to see, I right-clicked on the **SpriteOutlineGraph** tab and selected **Maximize**.

Figure 13.27 – The sprite graph open

6. Firstly, we will add our texture back to the sprite. To do so, we will sample the main texture. From the Blackboard, click on the + button and select **Texture 2D** giving it a name of Main Texture. From there, open **Graph Inspector** and change **Reference Value** to _MainTex. This will create a connection to Unity's SpriteRenderer to give the correct sprite here. To make it easier to tell what is going on, you can go to the **Default** value and change it to one of the sprites used in the animation. You can also right-click on the **Main Preview** window and select **Quad** to make it easier to see how the shader will work on a sprite.

7. Drag and drop the **Main Texture** property onto the graph. Right-click to the right of the **Main Texture** node and select **Create Node** and select **Input | Texture | Sample Texture 2D**. Connect the **Main Texture (T2)** output to the **Texture (T2)** input of the **Sample Texture 2D** node.

Figure 13.28 – The Sample Texture 2D node

412   Shader Graph – 2D

At this point, we could connect **RGBA** to **Base Color** and **A** to the **Alpha** channels on the **Fragment** node and we'd have a sprite shader that works exactly like the normal one.

Figure 13.29 – Creating the default sprite shader

However, we want to have an outline, so we will need to take some additional steps:

1. We want our original texture to stay as normal, so we will create a copy of the **Main Texture** and **Sample Texture 2D** nodes and paste them. To do this, we can do marquee selection by clicking and dragging the mouse over both nodes. Once selected, press *Ctrl + C* and then press *Ctrl + V*. Move the copied nodes below the already created one.

2. To the right of the newly created **Sample Texture 2D** node, click and drag from the **UV (2)** input to the left and create a **Tiling and Offset** node.

> Note
> Clicking and dragging from the inputs/outputs is an easy way to create nodes that are relevant to the properties being used.

3. To the right of the two **Sample Texture 2D** nodes, create a **Subtract** node connecting the **A** of the shifted **Sample Texture 2D** to the **A** input of the **Subtract** node and the **A** of the original to the **B** input:

Figure 13.30 – Creating a drop-shadow effect

As you can see, the result of the subtract node gives us a drop-shadow effect in the left direction.

4. To the right of the **Offset** input of the **Tiling and Offset** node, create a **Vector 2** node. We will be setting the **X** and **Y** properties to the offset we would like to use.

5. From the **Vector 2** node, in both of the **X** and the **Y** inputs, create a **Divide** node:

Figure 13.31 – Adding two divide nodes

With a value of ½ in both divide nodes, you can see how it shifted the sprite 50% in the **X** and **Y** directions.

6. Add a **Texel Size** node to the left of the **Divide** nodes and connect the **Main Texture** variable to the **Texture** input of the **Texel Size** node. Put the **Texel Size** node's **Width** output into the **B** input of the X offset **Divide** node and the **Texel Size** node's **Height** into the **B** input of the **Y Offset** node.

Figure 13.32 – Adjusting by pixel size

Notice that with both divide nodes using a value of 1 for **X**, the **Subtract** node gives us a result with both the **X** and **Y** axes moved over by 1 pixel:

Figure 13.33 – The result of the calculation

7. Click and drag the **Out** output of the **Subtract** node and create a **Multiply** node. To the left of the **Multiply** node, create a color by pressing the spacebar and then selecting **Input | Basic | Color**. Change the color to something bright and easy to see; I used red. One thing that's important is to make sure **Alpha** is set to 255.

Figure 13.34 – Setting a color

8. Connect the **Out** output of the **Color** node to the **B** input of the **Multiply** node.

Figure 13.35 – Multiplying a color

418　Shader Graph – 2D

To complete the effect, we will want to have this happen in each of the four directions so we will need to repeat this effect again. To make this easier, we can use a concept called a subgraph:

1. To create the subgraph, select all the nodes that have been created so far at once and right-click and select **Convert To | Sub-graph**.

Figure 13.36 – Creating a subgraph

2. This will have a dialog window pop up to name the subgraph. Give it a name of `GetEdgeGraph` and click on the **Save** button.

3. Once created you'll see an error stating there is no output. We will fix that next. Double-click on the **GetEdgeGraph** node.

4. To the far right, you'll see a node called **Output**. Select it and then in **Graph Inspector**, under the **Inputs** section, click on the + icon and rename the new parameter to **Edge** and set the type of **Vector4**. Connect **Out** of the **Multiply** node to the **Edge** input that was just created.

5. The **Blackboard** window already has the **Main Texture** property, but it doesn't have a default. If you reassign it, you should be able to see the effect within each of the nodes:

Figure 13.37 – GetEdgeGraph node

You can also see that our output to **Main Preview** is correct:

Figure 13.38 – The output of our new subgraph

Now that we have this working for one direction, we can now use parameters to adjust the direction and how thick our outline will be:

1. To do this, open the Blackboard and click on the + button and create a **Vector2** instance called **Direction** and a **Float** instance called **Thickness**. From the **Graph Inspector** window, give **Direction** a **Default** value of (1, 0) and set the **Default** value of **Thickness** of 5.

2. To the left of the **Divide** nodes, drag the **Direction** node into the graph. To the right of it, create a **Multiply** node and then connect the **Direction** and **Thickness** nodes to it. In **Out** of the **Multiply** node, create a **Split** node. From there, connect **R** to the **A** of the **X** division and **G** to the **A** of the **Y** division.

Figure 13.39 – Connecting the Blackboard properties to the graph

This takes care of all the setup we need to create the other directions!

3. Lastly, we will likely want to customize the color within the material, so right-click on the **Color** node and select **Convert To | Property**. Rename the property Outline Color.

4. Click on the **Save Asset** button and then return to the original graph.

Figure 13.40 – The completed subgraph

As you can see, the subgraph now works just like any other node and we can call it multiple times easily by just copying and pasting it. Before calling the subgraph multiple times, let's add a few more properties in the Blackboard so we can customize it via the material:

1. Go to the **Blackboard** window and click the + button and create a **Float** instance called **Outline Thickness** and a **Color** instance called **Outline Color**. Set the **Default** value of **Outline Thickness** to 5 and **Outline Color** to a fully opaque red like before.

2. Drag both properties into the graph and then attach them to the appropriate inputs to the subgraph.

Figure 13.41 – The subgraph with the properties given to it

3. We are currently not seeing an outline because **Direction** is set to **0,0** but we can now duplicate this three more times and set it to (1,0), (-1, 0), (0, -1), and (0, 1) respectively. Then, create an **Add** node to connect the first two edges together and then an **Add** node for the third and fourth ones.

Figure 13.42 – Adding the edges together

424   Shader Graph – 2D

4. Then add an **Add** node to connect both **Add** nodes together.
5. To the end of the combined **Add** node, create a **Saturate** node and connect **Out** of the **Add** node to **In** of the **Saturate** node:

Figure 13.43 – Connecting the Add node to the Saturate node

6. Now we have the four edges, but we need to add the effect to the original sprite. To do this, create another **Sample Texture 2D** node with **Main Texture** in the **Texture** property.
7. Connect **Out** of the **Saturate** node to **B** of a new **Add** node, which will connect to the original **Main Texture** sprite.
8. We can now connect the **Out** result to the **Base Color** property, but the alpha will not carry over. To do this, to the right of **Out** of the **Add** node, create a **Split** node. Connect the **A** of the **Split** node to **Alpha** on the **Fragment** node.

Figure 13.44 – The final connections of the shader

9. Click on the **Save Asset** button and play your game!

Figure 13.45 – The final result

As you can see the sprite is now animating correctly with our shader applied to it!

How it works...

In this recipe, we utilize a parameter called `_MainTex` within the Blackboard window. This is a built-in property that Unity has that when used will create a connection to Unity's SpriteRenderer to give the correct sprite here.

When we bring in the **Main Texture** property in the graph, its type (**Texture 2D**) cannot be used directly with the **Base Color** property, so we will need to convert it into a type that can be used with the **Sample Texture 2D** node that was used previously.

In order to create our outline, we utilize the **Tiling and Offset** node. Changing the **Offset** setting of the property will shift the image from its initial position. Try using values such as `0.1` and notice how it shifts the sprite in the **Sample Texture 2D** node that it's connected to.

Rather than using tiny decimal numbers, which can be a pain to deal with, we can instead do some math to provide how many pixels we want to shift the sprite.

Instead of using magic numbers, we are going to use the actual pixel amounts for how far the outline should go. To utilize pixels for our outline, we are using the **Texel Size** property, which will give us the width and height of our sprite in pixels. Given that the numbers in the property are a percentage of the sprite, to move the offset one pixel to the left, we can use a value of **1/Texel Width**.

By default, we are stuck with a white outline. To change the color, we can simply multiply the result of the subtraction by a color.

After creating one of the edges, with that idea in mind, we will shift the image in each of the four cardinal directions to create an outline. We will first do this in one direction and then see how we can easily use this for however many directions we would like.

After adding the four edges together, if we tried to add it directly to the original sprite, we would notice something funny:

Figure 13.46 – Adding the edge and the original texture

10. You may notice that there is a gap between the outline and the sprite. This is because some of the values are over 1 due to being added twice. To fix this, we can use the **Saturate** node, which will clamp the values for us.

14
Shader Graph – 3D

In the previous chapter, we were introduced to Shader Graph and some of its possible use cases within 2D games. In this chapter, we will be exploring additional uses of Shader Graph with 3D projects and utilizing the **High-Definition Render Pipeline**, or **HDRP** for short.

HDRP targets only high-end hardware such as PCs and consoles such as the Xbox One/S, and PlayStation 4/5. It's meant for high-fidelity games, graphics demos, architectural renderers, and anything else that requires the best possible graphics.

This isn't to say that HDRP is performant. It's much faster than the standard render pipeline when doing complex graphical things; but if you're going for a simpler type of game, it may be overkill. The other thing to keep in mind is that generally, HDRP requires much more work to fully utilize all the power that it gives us. This is because you'll have to create several additional texture maps in addition to what would traditionally be used for each material. This means that HDRP generally requires a bigger team and a bigger budget. It's recommended to only use HDRP if you are a graphics engineer or have a team with over five people to accommodate the additional workload.

It is important to note that graphics and aesthetics are two separate things and that what makes a game "look good" is often about the aesthetics rather than the graphics hardware used.

The main benefit that HDRP offers concerns its lighting system as it offers things such as real-time global illumination, which simulates the way that lighting bounces, and volumetric lighting, which simulates light passing through particles in the air. It also provides raytracing, which is an advanced way of rendering light, reflections, and shadows in a manner more like how light travels in real life. This feature is computationally expensive but is used quite often by movie studios to create pre-rendered images.

In this chapter, you will cover the following recipes:

- Implementing a glowing highlight system
- Portal Shaders in Unity
- Creating custom Shader Graph functions

Technical requirements

This chapter was created with Unity 2021.1.9f1 but should work in future versions of Unity with minimal revisions.

You can find the files on GitHub at `https://github.com/PacktPublishing/Unity-2021-Shaders-and-Effects-Cookbook-Fourth-Edition/tree/main/ShaderGraph-HDRP`.

Implementing a glowing highlight system

To start off, let's look at a real-world example of a shader we could potentially use. When playing certain kinds of games, you may notice that, when the player faces an object they can interact with, the object may glow, such as in Dontnod Entertainment's *Life is Strange*, The Fullbright Company's *Gone Home*, and even in recent mobile games such as Jam City's *Harry Potter: Hogwarts Mystery*. This is something that we can easily do in Shader Graph, which will also allow us to see a non-trivial example of Shader Graph being used.

Getting ready

Ensure that you have created a project using one of the scriptable render pipelines mentioned in the *Creating a URP-based Shader Graph project* recipe in *Chapter 13, Shader Graph – 2D*. For the purposes of this chapter, we will be using the HDRP, so you can select **High Definition RP/3D Sample Scene (HDRP)** instead of the URP options when creating the new project.

> **Note**
> In the newer versions of Unity, the choice is split up into indoor and outdoor scenes.

Afterward, complete the following steps:

1. Create a new scene, if you haven't done so already, by going to **File | New Scene**.
2. Afterward, we need to have something to show our shader, so let's create a new sphere by going to **GameObject | 3D Object | Sphere**.

Figure 14.1 – Recipe setup

How to do it...

We will start off by creating a simple Shader Graph:

1. From the **Project** window, create a new shader by going to **Create | Shader | HD Render Pipeline | Lit Shader Graph**, and name it `GlowGraph`.

   > **Note**
   > In newer versions of Unity, you may see the menu option as **Create | Shader Graph | HDRP | Lit Shader Graph** instead.

   Figure 14.2 – Creating the Lit Shader Graph

2. Afterward, create a new material by going to **Create | Material** (I named mine `GlowGraphMat`). Next, assign the shader to the material by selecting the material, and then, from the **Inspector** tab, you should select the **Shader** dropdown at the top and then select **Shader Graphs/GlowGraph**.

3. Then, drag and drop the material onto our sphere object in the scene so we can see our shader being used in action.

Implementing a glowing highlight system   433

4. Now that the setup is done, we can start creating the graph. If you select the shader, you should see that, in the **Inspector** tab, there will be a button that says **Open Shader Editor**. Click on the button and the Shader Graph Editor will open automatically.

5. Firstly, we will add a new node called a Fresnel (pronounced *fer-nel*) Effect. To add it, go to the left-hand side of the **Fragment** node, right-click, and select **Create Node**. From there, type in `Fresnel`, and once it has been selected, press the *Enter* key.

> **Note**
> The Fresnel Effect is often used to provide rim-lighting for objects. For more information on it, check out `https://docs.unity3d.com/Packages/com.unity.shadergraph@12.0/manual/Fresnel-Effect-Node.html`.

6. Once created, connect **Out** of the **Fresnel Effect** node to the **Emission** property of the **PBR Master** node.

7. To make it easier to tell what each node does, click on the gray color to the left of the **Albedo** property and change it to a different color, such as bright pink.

Figure 14.3 – Assigning the Fresnel Effect

Notice how the Fresnel Effect is applied on top of the Albedo color due to it using that value for the **Emission** property.

8. We just want the edges of our object to glow, so change the **Power** property of the **Fresnel Effect** node to 4. Currently, the light around our object is white, but we can make it a different color instead by multiplying it by a color.

9. To do this, go to the Blackboard and create a new color by clicking on the + icon and then selecting **Color**. Once created, give it a name (HoverColor) and then go to the Graph Inspector and change **Mode** to HDR. Then, set the **Default** color to something else; I used a light blue color. Make sure to set **A** to 255.

Figure 14.4 – Changing the default hover color

Remember to note the name HoverColor as we will be using it in code later; if it's not exactly the same, the code will not work correctly.

10. Once created, drag and drop the property beneath the **Fresnel Effect** node in the same way we learned in the previous recipe

Implementing a glowing highlight system 435

Figure 14.5 – Fresnel Effect node

11. Now, we need to multiply these together. Create a new node between them by selecting **Math | Basic | Multiply** from the node creation menu. Connect **Out** of the **Fresnel Effect** node to **A** of the **Multiply** node. Then, connect the **HoverColor** property to **B** of the **Multiply** node. Afterward, connect **Out** of the **Multiply** node to the **Emission** property.

Figure 14.6 – Multiplying the Fresnel Effect with a color

12. Save the graph and dive back into the Unity Editor. At this point, you may notice if you return to the scene that the hover effect is not showing up. HDRP scene lights are physically based, which means the lights are much stronger than the default emissive weight. With that in mind, we will need to increase the effect in order to see it.

Figure 14.7 – Scene view not showing the same as the Graph Editor

13. Head back to the Shader Graph Editor. Create a **Power** node. Put in 10 for the **A** input and 4 for the **B** input. Then, create a **Multiply** node. Connect **Out** of the **Power** node to **A** of the **Multiply** node. Then, connect **Out** of the previous **Multiply** node to **B** of the newly created one. Lastly, connect this new **Out** to the **Emission** channel.

Figure 14.8 – Increasing the intensity of the effect

14. Save the graph and return to the Scene view. You should notice that the effect is indeed working as intended.

15. From the **Project** tab, select the `GlowGraph` shader we've created. Notice that the **Inspector** tab includes information on the properties used in the shader.

Figure 14.9 – The HoverColor property

16. Create a new C# script called `HighlightOnHover`. Double-click on it to enter your IDE, and use the following code:

```
using UnityEngine;
using UnityEngine.EventSystems;

public class HighlightOnHover : MonoBehaviour,
                                IPointerEnterHandler,
                                IPointerExitHandler
{
    public Color highlightColor = Color.red;

    private Material material;

    // Use this for initialization
    void Start()
```

```
        {
            material =
                GetComponent<MeshRenderer>().material;

            // Turn off glow
            OnPointerExit(null);
        }

        public void OnPointerEnter(PointerEventData 
                                    eventData)
        {
            material.SetColor("HoverColor", 
                                highlightColor);
        }

        public void OnPointerExit(PointerEventData 
                                    eventData)
        {
            material.SetColor("HoverColor", Color.black);
        }
    }
```

17. Save your script and return to the Unity Editor. From there, attach the component to your sphere.
18. Next, click on the **MainCamera** component. From the **Inspector** window, click **Add Component** and select the **Physics Raycaster** option.

19. Afterward, click on **GameObject | UI | Event System**. Once created, select it and from the **Inspector** window, click on **Replace with InputSystemUIInputModule**.

Figure 14.10 – The original Event System has this component of the old Input System

20. Save your scene and start the game.

Figure 14.11 – The hover effect

Now, when we highlight the object with the mouse, we will see the hover effect, but otherwise, it will turn itself off!

How it works...

The **Emission** property is reflective of the light that an object receives. If **Emission** is white, it will be fully lit with that color. If black, it will act as if it doesn't exist. We make use of that by using black by default.

By default, the HDRP template project uses Unity's new input system, which no longer allows the `OnMouseOver` and `OnMouseUp` functions to be called. Because of this, we are adding a **PhysicsRaycaster** to perform a Raycast at every frame against 3D objects in the scene. This allows messages to be sent to 3D physics objects that implement event interfaces, which we do when we add `IPointerEnterHandler` and `IPointerExitHandler` after the `MonoBehaviour` class that we are inheriting from.

However, for events to actually trigger, we also need an Event System in the scene, which also needs to be converted to use Unity's new Input System.

With these changes added, if we do put our mouse over the object, the `OnPointerEnter` function will trigger, causing it to use the color mentioned.

Portal Shaders in Unity

Portals are something that is used quite often in games in order to allow users to travel to different locations quickly. They also give us an opportunity to see how we can utilize time to adjust our shaders and utilize both the Twist and Voronoi nodes to great effect.

Getting ready

Ensure that you have created a project using one of the scriptable render pipelines mentioned in the *Creating a URP-based Shader Graph project* recipe in *Chapter 13, Shader Graph – 2D*. For the purposes of this chapter, we will be using the HDRP, so you can select **High Definition RP/3D Sample Scene (HDRP)** instead of the URP options when creating the new project. Afterward, complete the following steps:

1. Create a new scene, if you haven't done so already, by going to **File | New Scene**.

2. Afterward, we need to have something to show our shader, so let's create a new plane by going to **GameObject | 3D Object | Plane**. Then, rotate the plane to face the camera.

Figure 14.12 – Recipe setup

How to do it...

We will start off by creating a simple Shader Graph:

1. From the **Project** window, create a new shader by going to **Create | Shader | HD Render Pipeline** (or **HDRP**) **| Lit Shader Graph**, and name it `PortalGraph`.

2. Afterward, create a new material by going to **Create | Material** (I named mine `PortalGraphMat`). With the material selected, in the **Inspector** window, under **Surface Options**, check the **Double-Sided** option and set **Surface Type** to **Transparent**. Next, assign the shader to the material by selecting the material, and then, from the **Inspector** tab, you should select the **Shader** dropdown at the top and select **Shader Graphs/PortalGraph**. Then, drag and drop the material onto our sphere object in the scene so we can see our shader being used in action.

Portal Shaders in Unity 443

Figure 14.13 – Plane placed in the scene

3. Now that the setup is done, we can start creating the graph. If you select the shader, you should see that, from the **Inspector** tab, there will be a button that says **Open Shader Editor**. Click on the button and the **Shader Graph Editor** will open automatically.

4. First, add a **Twirl** node to the graph. Afterward, add a **Voronoi** node. Connect **Out** of the **Twirl** node to the **UV** input of the **Voronoi** node.

Figure 14.14 – Basic portal texture

5. This provides a good static portal, but we want the portal to move. Open the Blackboard and add a **Float** variable called `PortalSpeed`, and from the **Graph Inspector**, set its **Default** value to `0.25`.

6. To the left of the **Twirl** node, add the **PortalSpeed** variable and a **Time** node. To the right of those two newly created nodes, add a **Multiply** node. Connect the **PortalSpeed** value to **A** of the **Multiply** node and connect the **Time** output to the **B** input.

7. Connect **Out** of the **Multiply** node to **Offset** of the **Twirl** node. If all goes well, you should notice that the **Voronoi** node's preview is twisting in a portal-like manner.

Figure 14.15 – Moving portal texture

8. To hide the edges and mask the effect, add a **Texture Sample 2D** (or **Sample Texture2D**) node. Change the **Texture** property to the **Default Particle** texture. Then, add a **Multiply** node and connect the **RGBA** value of the **Texture Sample 2D** node to the **A** input of the **Multiply** node and connect **Out** of the **Voronoi** node to the **B** input.

Figure 14.16 – Masking the portal effect

446   Shader Graph – 3D

9. Now, we want the portal to have color. Open the Blackboard and add a **Color** variable called `PortalColor`, and from the **Graph Inspector**, set its **Default** value to a green color and **Mode** to **HDR**.

10. Bring the **PortalColor** variable into the graph. Then, create another **Multiply** node to multiply the result of the masking to the new color.

Figure 14.17 – Adding color to the portal

11. Much like the previous recipe, we will need to scale the effect to work well on HDRP projects. To do this, create a **Power** node and then set the values to `10` and `2`. Then, create a **Multiply** node and combine **Out** of the **Power** node and **Out** of the last **Multiply** node. Take this final **Out** and connect it to the **Base Color**, **Emission**, and **Alpha** channels of **Fragment**.

Figure 14.18 – Scaling the effect

12. Save the graph and return to the scene. You should notice faint transparency on the plane. To remove that, select the material and, from the **Inspector** window, uncheck the **Preserve specular lighting** option. Save the scene and return to the Unity Editor. It may take a bit of time to compile so it may appear in solid light blue at first but once it finishes, go ahead and play the game.

Figure 14.19 – Final result of the Shader

How it works...

Marking the shader as **Double-Sided** means that it will show up on both sides of the plane; this is very useful in regard to how portals typically work in games.

The Twirl node applies a warping effect similar to being affected by a black hole.

Voronoi, or Worley, noise is generated by calculating distances between a pixel and a lattice of points. By offsetting these points by a pseudo-random number, controlled by input Angle Offset, a cluster of cells can be generated that, for our purpose, allows us to have a procedural texture to work with.

> **Note**
>
> For more information, check out `https://docs.unity3d.com/Packages/com.unity.shadergraph@12.0/manual/Voronoi-Node.html`.

Creating custom Shader Graph functions

While utilizing the built-in Shader Graph nodes is useful, it is also possible to create nodes of our very own utilizing our own custom script files. This can be especially useful when certain actions need to be done several times, such as when you need to use a `for` loop. In this recipe, we will see how we can use the Custom Function node to generate an output.

Getting ready

Ensure that you have created a project using one of the scriptable render pipelines mentioned in the *Creating a URP-based Shader Graph project* recipe in *Chapter 13, Shader Graph – 2D*. For the purpose of this chapter, we will be using the HDRP, so you can select **High Definition RP/3D Sample Scene (HDRP)** instead of the URP options when creating the new project. Afterward, complete the following steps:

1. Create a new scene, if you haven't done so already, by going to **File | New Scene**.
2. Afterward, we need to have something to show our shader, so let's create a new sphere by going to **GameObject | 3D Object | Cube**.

Figure 14.20 – Recipe setup

How to do it...

We will start off by creating a simple Shader Graph:

1. From the **Project** window, create a new shader by going to **Create | Shader | HD Render Pipeline | Lit Shader Graph**, and name it BoxBlurGraph.

2. Afterward, create a new material by going to **Create | Material** (I named mine BoxBlurGraphMat). Next, assign the shader to the material by selecting the material, and then, from the **Inspector** tab, you should select the **Shader** dropdown at the top and select **Shader Graphs/BoxBlurGraph**. Then, drag and drop the material onto our sphere object in the scene so we can see our shader being used in action.

3. Now that the setup is done, we can start creating the graph. If you select the shader, you should see that, from the **Inspector** tab, there will be a button that says **Open Shader Graph**. Click on the button and the **Shader Graph Editor** will open automatically.

4. From the graph, create a **Custom Function** node. Select the node and then open up the **Graph Inspector**. From there, set **Type** to **String**.

5. Under **Name**, put Box Blur. Then, in **Body**, insert the following code:

```
const uint iterations = 3;

float4 sum = 0;

for (uint y = 0; y < iterations; y++)
```

```
        {
            for (uint x = 0; x < iterations; x++)
            {
                float2 displacement = float2(x, y) -
                    (iterations - 1) / 2.0;
                sum += Source.Sample(State, UV + displacement
                                        * Offset / iterations);
            }
        }

        Output = sum / (iterations * iterations);
```

6. Next, in the **Input** section, create the following variables with the following types:

    - **Source / Texture 2D**
    - **State / Sampler State**
    - **UV / Vector 2**
    - **Offset / Float**

7. Then, in the **Output** section, create a **Vector 4** called **Output**.

8. Change the **Source** texture to a value you'll recognize. I used the `HDIcon` included with the project template.

9. Create a **UV** node. Connect **Out** of the **UV** node to the **UV** input of the **BoxBlur** custom function.

10. Create a **Time** node. Connect **Time** to the **Offset** property.

11. Finally, connect the output of the **BoxBlur** node to **Base Color** of the **Fragment**.

Figure 14.21 – Connecting the BoxBlur Custom Function node to Fragment

12. Save the graph and return to the scene to play the game.

Figure 14.22 – The final result of the recipe

How it works...

This recipe is an implementation of a BoxBlur filter, similar to, but simpler than, a Gaussian blur filter.

For more information on the BoxBlur algorithm, check out `https://en.wikipedia.org/wiki/Box_blur`.

By utilizing the **Custom Function** node, we are able to run HLSL code within our graphs. The inputs act as parameters that can be used within the function and the outputs act as return values.

We utilized the String method, which allowed us to have our code all within the Unity Editor, but it is also possible to create them within text files and load them. For more information on that, check out `https://kylewbanks.com/blog/unity-custom-hlsl-functions-with-shader-graph`.

It is also possible to take this concept one step further and actually make a custom node with this functionality. For more information on that, check out `https://blog.unity.com/technology/shader-graph-custom-node-api-using-the-code-function-node`.

> **Tip**
> I could write much more on the subject of Shader Graph, but, unfortunately, there isn't enough space in the book. If you would like to explore Shader Graph in even more detail, Andy Touch has put together a lovely group of examples of Shader Graph being used that could be great research material. Check it out at `https://github.com/UnityTechnologies/ShaderGraph_ExampleLibrary`.

Packt>

Packt.com

Subscribe to our online digital library for full access to over 7,000 books and videos, as well as industry leading tools to help you plan your personal development and advance your career. For more information, please visit our website.

Why subscribe?

- Spend less time learning and more time coding with practical eBooks and Videos from over 4,000 industry professionals
- Improve your learning with Skill Plans built especially for you
- Get a free eBook or video every month
- Fully searchable for easy access to vital information
- Copy and paste, print, and bookmark content

Did you know that Packt offers eBook versions of every book published, with PDF and ePub files available? You can upgrade to the eBook version at packt.com and as a print book customer, you are entitled to a discount on the eBook copy. Get in touch with us at customercare@packtpub.com for more details.

At www.packt.com, you can also read a collection of free technical articles, sign up for a range of free newsletters, and receive exclusive discounts and offers on Packt books and eBooks.

Other Books You May Enjoy

If you enjoyed this book, you may be interested in these other books by Packt:

Unity 2021 Cookbook - Fourth Edition
Matt Smith, Shaun Ferns
ISBN: 978-1-83921-761-6

- Discover how to add core game features to your projects with C# scripting
- Create powerful and stylish UI with Unity's UI system, including power bars, radars, and button-driven scene changes
- Work with essential audio features, including background music and sound effects
- Discover Cinemachine in Unity to intelligently control camera movements
- Add visual effects such as smoke and explosions by creating and customizing particle systems
- Understand how to build your own Shaders with the Shader Graph tool

Augmented Reality with Unity AR Foundation

Jonathan Linowes

ISBN: 978-1-83898-259-1

- Discover Unity engine features for building AR applications and games
- Get up to speed with Unity AR Foundation components and the Unity API
- Build a variety of AR projects using best practices and important AR user experiences
- Understand the core concepts of augmented reality technology and development for real-world projects
- Set up your system for AR development and learn to improve your development workflow
- Create an AR user framework with interaction modes and UI, saved as a template for new projects

Packt is searching for authors like you

If you're interested in becoming an author for Packt, please visit `authors.packtpub.com` and apply today. We have worked with thousands of developers and tech professionals, just like you, to help them share their insight with the global tech community. You can make a general application, apply for a specific hot topic that we are recruiting an author for, or submit your own idea.

Share Your Thoughts

Now you've finished *Unity 2021 Shaders and Effects Cookbook*, we'd love to hear your thoughts! Scan the QR code below to go straight to the Amazon review page for this book and share your feedback or leave a review on the site that you purchased it from.

https://packt.link/r/<1839218622>

Your review is important to us and the tech community and will help us make sure we're delivering excellent quality content.

Index

Symbols

2D games
  Water Shader, implementing for 248-255
2D texture 90

A

advanced reflection probe features
  reference link 189
Albedo Color and Transparency
  reference link 183
Anisotropic Specular type
  about 160
  creating 160-170
anti-aliasing effect
  used, for mimicking imaging effects of real-world cameras 23-26
arrays
  heatmaps, implementing with 375-386
AUTODESK
  reference link 74

B

binding semantic
  about 237
  reference link 239
Blinn-Phong Specular type
  about 155
  creating 155-159
bloom optical effect
  used, for mimicking imaging effects of real-world cameras 23-26
BoxBlur algorithm
  reference link 452
brightness, with screen effects
  using 298-305
built-in CgInclude files
  reference link 352
  using 352-357

C

calibration chart
  reference link 177
celluloid (CEL) 138

Index

C for Graphics (Cg)
　about 289
　reference link 58
circle
　creating, around terrain 119-126
　steps, for following character 126, 127
color grading
　used, for setting mood of scene 27-31
color spaces
　reference link 358
　using 357, 358
components 38
contrast, with screen effects
　using 298-305
CrazyBump
　reference link 74
cube maps 187, 188
culling 104
custom CgInclude files
　creating 359-361
　using, within Surface Shaders 361-365
custom diffuse lighting model
　creating 130-138
custom lighting models, in Surface Shaders
　reference link 152
custom Shader Graph functions
　creating 448-452

D

debugging 61
depth of field
　used, for obtaining filmic look 14-22
diffuse shader
　implementing 65-70
dot product 136, 219
dust and scratches 324

E

energy conservation 172
ErrorShader
　example 60
extrusion maps
　adding 212-214

F

fading object
　transparencies, adding to PBR 181, 182
filmic look
　obtaining, with depth of field 14-22
　obtaining, with grain 14-22
　obtaining, with vignetting 14-22
Filter Mode
　location, setting to Bilinear 96-98
fixed-point values
　reference link 49
fixed variable 265
float variable 265
fog
　used, for creating horror
　　game look 31-36
Fresnel reflectance 172
Fur Shader
　additional examples 375
　implementing 366-370
　properties, adjusting 372
　real fur, versus shell fur 372-374

G

Glass Shader
　implementing 244-248
global illumination (GI) 172

glowing highlight system
    implementing 430-441
GNU Image Manipulation
        Program (GIMP) 221
grab passes
    using, to draw behind objects 240-243
grain
    used, for obtaining filmic look 14-22
Graphics.Blit
    reference link 293
graphics processing unit
        (GPU) 45, 211, 284

H

half variable 265
heatmaps
    example values, for heatmap drawer 384
    implementing, with arrays 375-386
    intensities, of heatmap drawer 384
    radiuses, of heatmap drawer 384
    textures, setting 381
High Definition Render
        Pipeline (HDRP) 388
Holographic Shader
    creating 83-88
horror game look
    creating, with fog 31-36

I

input semantics 238
inspector GUI name 52
Inspector, via Shader Graph
    properties, exposing to 400-404
insulators 177
Integrated Development Environment
        (IDE) 156, 302

International Commission on
        Illumination (CIE) 305
inward extrusion 214

L

Lambert 115
Lambertian lighting model 131
Lambertian reflectance 130
Lengyel's concentric fur shell
        technique 372
lerp() function 118
light baking
    about 189
    into scene 189, 194-196
    light probes, configuring 190-192
    static geometry, configuring 190
    steps 193
lighting models 160
lightmap 194
light probes
    configuring 190-192
    reference link 196
light probing 196
light transport 189
Lightweight Render Pipeline (LWRP) 388

M

macro
    reference link 202
masking 71
material chart
    reference link 177
material properties
    reference link 53
metallic setup 173-177

metallic, versus specular workflow
  reference link 174
microsurface scattering 172
mirror-like surfaces
  creating 183-189
mobile device
  shaders, modifying for 277-282
mobile platforms
  profiling 277
models
  extruding 209-211
model-view-projection matrix 237
mood of scene
  setting, with color grading 27-31

N

National Television System Committee (NTSC) 336
night-vision screen effect
  creating 337-348
  noise 339
  scan lines 338
  tinted green 338
  vignette 339, 340
non-playable characters (NPCs) 190
normal extrusion 209, 227
normal mapping
  used, for creating shader 72-82

O

OnRenderImage
  reference link 293
Oren-Nayar Reflectance Model
  reference link 160

output semantics 239
Overlay Blend mode
  using, with screen effects 316-319

P

packed arrays
  accessing 70-72
  modifying 70-72
  reference link 72
PBR Texture Conversion
  reference link 177
Phong Specular type
  creating 147-154
Photoshop-like blend modes
  using, with screen effects 306-311
physically based rendering (PBR)
  about 43
  transparency, adding to 178, 179
Pixel Shaders 236
polygons 90
Portal Shaders
  in Unity 441-448
Post Processing Stack
  installing 2-13
Profiler
  using, in shaders 268-277
properties
  adding, to shader 48-53
  using, in Surface Shader 54-59
Pyro Technix
  reference link 229

Q

Quixel MEGASCANS
  reference link 177

R

ramp map 139
real-time strategy (RTS) 119
Red-Green-Blue (RGB) 214, 319
reflection probe 188
reflection unity manual
  reference link 189
reflective surfaces
  creating 183-189
renderer component 192
render queues 109

S

saturation, with screen effects
  using 298-305
screen effects
  blend modes, adding 312-314
  creating 322-337
  dust and scratches 324
  Overlay Blend mode, using
    with 316-319
  Photoshop-like blend modes,
    using with 306-311
  sepia tone 323
  vignette effect 324
screen effects script system
  setting up 284-297
Scriptable Render Pipeline (SRP) 388
semi-transparent materials
  transparencies, adding to PBR 179-181
sepia effect 322
sepia tone 323
shader
  about 349
  creating, with normal mapping 72-82
  properties, adding to 48-53
  texture, adding to 90-96
Shader Compilation Target Levels
  reference link 114
shader data types and precision
  reference link 262
shader errors 61
ShaderLab 99
ShaderLab commands
  reference link 110
ShaderLab material properties
  reference link 99
ShaderLab tags
  reference link 107
shader replacement 110
shaders
  modifying, for mobile device 277-282
  optimization techniques 258-267
  profiling 268-277
shader variables
  reference link 103
shell technique 373
Show in Explorer option 47
simple Shader Graph
  implementing 393-400
skinned mesh renderers 196
skyboxes 188
smearing 71
snap 145, 146
snow shader
  implementing 215-218
snow shader, steps
  geometry, modifying 219, 220
  surface, coloring 219
solid geometries
  with holes 182, 183
Sprite Outline Shader
  creating 405-427

462 Index

Standard Shader
  about 91
  creating 38-46
Standard Surface Shader 91
static geometry
  configuring 190
Substance Designer
  reference link 177
surface function 64
surface occlusion 172
Surface Shader
  custom CgInclude files, using 361-365
  properties, using 54-59
  reference link 70
  vertex color, accessing 198-202
  vertices, animating 203-209
Surface Shader property types 52

T

terrain
  circle, creating around 119-126
texture
  about 48
  adding, to shader 90-96
  applying, to material 355
  blending 110-118
  desaturating 356
  packing 110-118
  scrolling, by modify UV values 98-104
texture import settings
  reference link 98
texture mapping 90
Theory of Physically-Based Rendering
  reference link 177
thermal visor 349

toon shader
  creating 138-145
toon shading 138
Transform component 38
transparency
  adding, to PBR 178, 179
transparent material
  creating 104-110

U

Unity
  about 91
  Portal Shaders 441-448
Unity Asset Store, snow effects and props
  reference link 220
UnityCG.cginc file
  built-in helper functions, using 352-356
Unity download archive 47
Universal Render Pipeline (URP) 388
URP-based Shader Graph project
  creating 388-393
UV data 90

V

variable name 52
variable types
  fixed 265
  float 265
  half 265
Vertex and Fragment Shaders 232-238
vertex color
  accessing, in Surface Shader 198-202
vertices
  animating, in Surface Shader 203-209

view-dependent effects 147
view direction 152
vignette effect 324
vignetting
　used, for obtaining filmic look 14-22
volume ray casting 229
volumetric explosion
　implementing 220-228

W

Water Shader
　implementing, for 2D games 248-255

Z

Zbrush 4R7
　reference link 74
ZBuffering 110
Z ordering 104

Made in the USA
Middletown, DE
16 September 2022

10639298R00269